Heartbeats

The Story of My Recovery from Addiction

Wes Hollis

Kindle Direct Publishing
A Division of Amazon

This book was printed and shipped by Kindle Direct Publishing, a wholly owned division of Amazon

First Amazon paperback edition: April 2019
First Amazon eBook edition scheduled for Spring, 2019

For information about special discounts for bulk hardcover purchases by institutions, including educational, treatment and therapeutic communities, please contact the author at:
heartbeats2019@yahoo.com

Amazon trade paperback ISBN: 978-1-09-294868-5

Cover Designs by Jason Barton

Printed in the United States of America

Disclaimer

This is a work of nonfiction.

The contents herein represent this recovering alcoholic's personal thoughts and opinions, and are an expression of my unique experience, strength and hope. I do not speak on behalf of the Alcoholics Anonymous organization, nor the employees and volunteers of its Central Service and intergroup offices, subsidiaries, or related entities and facilities, nor its literature and media operations, nor any recovering person who participates in the program of Alcoholics Anonymous.

Names and circumstances have been modified in a number of instances in order to protect the anonymity of recovering individuals.

Please rely upon the guidance of your sponsor, or recovery professionals, in all matters pertaining to your personal program of recovery.

Dedication

This book is dedicated with love and gratitude to Bill Wilson, Bob Smith, and to the millions of courageous recovering men and women in the halls of Alcoholics Anonymous who have done what I couldn't do – you loved me unconditionally, and you taught me how to love myself.

"A Full and Thankful Heart"

"I try hard to hold to the truth that a full and thankful heart cannot entertain great conceits. When brimming with gratitude, one's heartbeat must surely result in outgoing love, the finest emotion that we can ever know."

Bill Wilson, Co-founder of Alcoholics Anonymous
"As Bill Sees It," page 37

dead man blues

drained that glass, caught that high,
and blew some smoke to help me fly
need my snow, it's makin' me numb
dropped a tab, here comes the sun
thanks, man, it's just for the pain
other than that I got nothin' to gain
been there before, and I'll be there again,
it's just another night in the city of sin

caught up with the Man, and he sold me an eighth
that did it for me, so screw gettin' straight
I promise it's only just for one time,
I lied as I hit that first sweet white line
out all night, and gone the next day,
damn, this game's making me pay
but I've been there before, and I'll be there again,
so it's just another night in the city of sin

this life's getting' hard, it's breakin' my will,
gotta slow down, and take that red pill
Alice found truth in the looking glass,
how far down the hole must a dying man pass?
I'll know when I'm done, I'm almost there,
but please baby just one more, just to get square?
this shit's gonna' kill me, but it won't tell me when,
can't wait to hook up with all those dead friends
been there before, and I'll be there again,
for just one more night in the city of sin

Part One: The End

Damn, I hate the night!

I woke up screaming a little while ago, my heart pounding in my chest. It had been a long time since the demons came to visit, so I guess they were overdue. Things have been going pretty well for me lately, but I know their pattern – they just like to remind me once in a while that they haven't forgotten about me, so they send the nightmares which always arrive in the darkest hours, creeping silently like the fog to steal my dreams.

There's a saying that you hear around the halls of Alcoholics Anonymous that it's always 3:00 a.m. in the heart of an alcoholic, and I suppose to some extent that's true. But the bad guys don't come as frequently anymore, and I know how to handle them now, so perhaps it's just God's way of reminding me that I'm only one bad decision away from returning to that terrible place of loneliness and despair that had ruled my life for twenty-five years.

So I whisper a prayer in the darkness, requesting only that He strike me dead before I take that next drink.

≈≈≈

One day God rang me up, and said, "Write your book, Wes, and I'll take care of the rest."

And I said, "Okay, sounds good to me, God, so here goes - I hope they like it!"

And God said, "As long as you like it, that's all that matters, so just write your book, Wes."

So I did, and then God called again and said, "Cool, now that will be a five hundred dollar consulting fee, and I don't accept checks or credit cards, just cash or precious metals, and you can drop it off in the collection box down at St. Margaret Mary's."

"Such a bargain," I said, then inquired, as was my habit when negotiating matters such as this, "Hmmm, so I don't suppose there's any chance you'd take bitcoins instead?"

And God just muttered something under his breath, then said with more than a little exasperation, "You're pushing it, my son, right to the edge. Why must you always be different from the rest of the flock, why must you always push it?"

I felt no compulsion to answer Him, because we both knew why - that's just how it rolls in WesWorld.

≈≈≈

My name is Wes. I'm a recovering alcoholic and drug addict, and an onion, and I'm a whole bunch of other types of addict as well. I am powerless, but not helpless, sober, but never cured, confident, but not arrogant, recovering, but never recovered, grateful, but never entitled, and when I'm at my best I'm just another nameless face in the crowd.

I'm your brother, your aunt, your student and your childhood friend, your boss and your employee, your neighbor walking his dog and the name on the grave of the can't-miss kid who died before he won the prize, the elderly woman who sits silently knitting in the corner, the twenty-year old junkie shaking it out in his fourth detox and the old man hoisting one back as he sheds a tear over the grave of his Vietnam buddy, the precious little newborn opioid baby, stunted, gasping for breath, whose first day is her last, the nurse who cooled your feverish brow, the policeman walking his talk as he walks his beat, the salesman who sold his soul for a line of coke, the teacher who knew everything except how to say no, the rock icon, broken and burned, who learned too late that death was the loneliest gig of all, and the cabbie who sits quietly smoking at the train station as the evening snows swirl through the lights from the hospital across the road.

And I am the blind man who sees not with his eyes, but with his heart.

I am you and you are me, and I pray, and I pray and I pray that I never consider my battle against addiction to be won, for that will surely be the day that I shall die.

So after all is said and done, and the last call has been made, I'm just a chaos junkie, and what I'm addicted to is anything that has the potential to allow me to avoid reality, and which will put up a great big wall between myself and the rest of the human race.

But for the purposes of this book I'll stick to the alcohol and the drugs, because they're what finally brought me to my knees, nearly killed me and, by the grace of God, gave me a life today that is second to none.

It is a life that I never imagined could have existed, a life of hope, promise, companionship, and integrity, a life that was handed to me in my darkest hours.

I suppose that a head doc would diagnose my condition as a cancer of the soul that if left untreated will devour my humanity, my dignity, and my morality, and it will kill me just as surely as any physical cancer of my body could. I know through painful experience that my only salvation lies in abstinence, and in the maintenance of a physical, mental and spiritual condition that is based upon love and acceptance for my fellow alcoholics and addicts.

So I guess that when we get right down to it what I'm really addicted to is "more," and anything that will fill that great big hole in my soul that's been haunting me ever since I was a little kid. Alcohol and drugs did a swell job of satisfying it for quite a while, until they didn't, and then there was Hell to pay, because when the walls come down they come crashing down if you're an alcoholic at the end of your last run.

It's never pretty, never easy, never fun, but if you've been there you already know that, so you just kept right on drinking and drugging to delay the inevitable reckoning.

If we're lucky, we survive. If not, I suppose it wouldn't matter all that much, except perhaps to the people who loved us once upon a time.

For the rest, well, they stopped caring a long time ago, but in our arrogance and hubris we just never noticed, nor gave a damn.

I ought to know, because I was you once upon a time, lost, broken and forgotten, just as you are me, and either of us can find ourselves back out there in the wastelands with just the snap of our fingers at the end of a bad day.

My name is Wes, and I'm an alcoholic, a drug addict, and an onion, one of the fortunate ones, and these are my heartbeats.

≈≈≈

I was a techie in the late 1990's, and as part of the continuing education process I took a network engineering course in order to acquire some important job certs.

For the most part the course was dry, boring and highly technical, but one evening the instructor gave the class perhaps the most important lesson that I have ever received for not only solving complex computer riddles, but more importantly for solving most of life's challenges.

As is usually the case, its beauty lay in its simplicity, and in its universality.

Dave, the instructor, told us to ask ourselves a short, simple question when the system was crashing down all around us:

"Look back, and ask yourself, 'what changed since the last time everything was working perfectly?'"

Think about that, because if you can track back and locate the nexus, that nearly inaudible click of the key in the lock which arrived just before everything hit the fan, then you'll have a head start for solving just about any challenge that the Universe will ever throw at you.

I learned that lesson in 1998, in a computer seminar, and that one simple little concept has stuck with me ever since, and I have solved some nifty conundrums with it.

It would have been swell if somebody had mentioned it to me in 1966, however, because my life might have turned out very differently.

But nobody ever did, so c'est la vie, because like Jagger sang, "You can't always get what you want, but sometimes you get what you need."

Well, perhaps, but in my case that turned out to be a twenty-five year vacation in Hell, so I probably would have skipped it if had the choice, thank you very much.

≈≈≈

In retrospect, ground zero was clear as a bell from day one, but I was just too young and stupid and arrogant to recognize it for what it was.

I mean, it wasn't like I just woke up one sunny morning when I was sixteen and said to myself, "Gee, Wes, what to do on this beautiful summer day? Oh, cool, I know, I'll start drinking and drugging, and then I'll become a screaming, raging, piss-drunk alcoholic and addict for the next twenty-five years, and I'll see whether I can ruin every opportunity I have for a good life, and just drink and drug myself to the brink of death, or beyond! I mean, why not, I've got nothing better to do today!"

No, the evil twin stepbrothers, Alcoholism and Addiction, don't play that way. As the 12 Steps remind us they're cunning, baffling and insidious, so they prefer to give you a little tease, just enough to con you into thinking that you're the boss, that you can stop anytime you want, and then they'll steal away everybody and everything that ever meant anything to you, and they'll set your dreams on fire and they'll tear out your heart and stomp on it.

They let me get away with it the first time I drank. It was 1966, the Vietnam War was raging, and the Beatles and the Stones were fighting for first place on the charts. I was a "war baby," I had just turned sixteen, and one night my best friend Greg picked me up at my house in his parents' Mustang convertible. I took the co-pilot's seat, and we picked up our friend Steve, and we headed out to the back roads of Westwood, Massachusetts, which was a middle-class suburb of Boston.

Westwood was also a "dry" town, which meant that alcohol couldn't be sold in it, and I have often wondered over the years whether that contributed to my inevitable downfall. After all, what's better than the mystery of the forbidden fruit for lighting a budding alcoholic's fire?

It was a warm, sultry, late summer evening, and we had each raided our parents' liquor cabinets. I had been elected bartender, so I was responsible for mixing up some gin, whiskey, vodka, bourbon, a little of this, a little of that, and for good measure I tossed in a half inch of Creme de Menthe, then stirred everything up in a quart-sized Coca-Cola bottle, and finally I shook it a half dozen times for good measure.

James Bond would have been proud of me.

For each of us it might just as well have been the nectar of the Gods, rather than a noxious, foul tasting 80 proof bottle of swill, but that jungle juice got the job done. This was my initiation to alcohol, it popped my cherry, and it took me to a world I could never have imagined.

That first hit burned a path to my gut, and I choked, coughed and gagged, but it stayed down, and then it hit me like a ton of bricks, and suddenly it was ohhh, sooooo cooool!

And that was that — Lucifer had turned the key in the lock and snagged another sucker.

Two hours later Greg swerved to a stop in front of my house, whereupon I fell out of his car, then staggered over to the bushes near the side entrance, where I puked, and puked, and then I puked some more.

There, I thought, that should've cleaned out just about all of the poison from my system, so I stumbled inside and bounced off the walls to my bedroom, where I promptly passed out, fully clothed, on top of the sheets, reeking of alcohol and vomit.

Less than an hour later I found myself holding onto the toilet bowl for dear life, hurling my guts out, and then I looked around and saw my father glaring at me, disgusted by what he was witnessing. He didn't utter a word, just scowled and stormed back to his bedroom.

It was then that I heard my mother crying in the background.

Attaboy, Westie, you the Man!

The next day wasn't a particularly fun one for me, but I was young and stupid and a jock, so I quickly recovered from the physical effects of my hangover. The shame and embarrassment lasted a little while longer, as did my loss of driving privileges, but a week later I was back in high school, playing sports, my privileges restored, and with the exuberance, or ignorance, of youth, all memory of that night had been erased from my mind like it never existed.

And that would prove to be rather unfortunate, because that was my last chance to receive a free hall pass from spending the next twenty-five years of my life in Hell.

Ah, but such is youth, the pain so sharp yet fleeting like a summer storm, and soon forgotten, while behind my back my two new best friends, Alcoholism and Addiction, winked slyly at each other, for they knew that they had hooked another rube, and they didn't intend to ever let me go — not alive, anyway.

≈≈≈

So that was my first drunk, but I don't remember my last one.

They tell you in the halls of Alcoholics Anonymous that you should always remember that final drink, and think about it long and hard before you take another one, because it just might keep you sober, and alive.

But I don't recall one single moment of it.

I do know, however, that I was out there for five or six days, but that's the extent of it, because I've never been able to piece together an instant of it, from the minute that first slug of bourbon hit my lips until the moment I finally crawled out of my blackout.

It's all just a blank, gone, like it never existed - poof!

So the way I figure it, the very fact that I can't recall it, and that I lost a rather considerable chunk of my life to that binge, probably means that I earned my seat in AA after all, because if that didn't do it, I'd sure as hell hate to see what would.

But I do know this – it must have been a doozy of a last call.

≈≈≈

It was early June, 1992, and I had been sober for almost two months, since my last thirty day stint at a now shuttered alcohol treatment facility called Beech Hill, which was nestled in the scenic Monadnock Range near Dublin, New Hampshire.

With somewhat jaded detox humor we "guests" had renamed the place 'The Irish Alps,' due to its location in Dublin.

It was quite the rehab in its day.

When I returned home I played the sobriety game pretty well for a while, but that was my customary scam after every one of my amusing little trips to the detoxes, because all I had ever considered them to be were one long series of cons that I ran on the world, and on myself.

Bottom line? These time-outs were great for cleaning the alcohol out of my system, but they were nothing more than a tune-up and an oil change, and I had never remained sober for longer than a day, or a week, or a month after any of them.

And this most recent little vacation turned out to have been no exception to the rule.

Denial's a swell way for an addict to avoid reality, but I always knew deep down that I was just biding my time until the next handy excuse came along to let me do what I did best – drink myself to the brink of death.

Hitting the detoxes and treatment centers, and pretending that "this time" would be different, and that I really intended to remain sober, was my modus operandi. But that was all just noise, a lowlife drunk's stereotypical line of bullshit intended to keep my family, friends and employers off my ass while I set myself up for my next big jackpot.

Naturally, there'd been a woman involved this time – aren't there always? She was the only woman I had ever loved, a woman with funky blonde hair, a lithe, slender body, and the most beautiful, shy, ice blue eyes that I have ever gotten lost in.

But I had screwed things up royally the last time I had been with her, so I decided to punish myself as only I could do, and after trashing myself unmercifully for a few days I reverted back to form and did what I did best - I said the hell with it all, and I picked up a bottle, and I hid in it.

And so, right on schedule, and for reasons that would only be important to a drunk full of denial and self-hate, I drove to the closest packey, bought a couple of half-gallon jugs of Jim Beam, and a carton of Marlboro reds, then proceeded to cross over to the Dark Side one final time.

≈≈≈

This latest shitstorm had started out pretty much the same way they always did. As I left for the liquor store, my lifelong pal (the con artist who rented space in my head) had convinced me that we (we?) were only planning to pick up a half-pint of bourbon, and a couple packs of smokes. Our goals were modest, so we figured that we'd just nurse one tiny little drink while we did some deep thinking about our future.

But that brilliant plan lasted about four fucking minutes, so when we arrived at the package store and stared at all of those beautiful bottles of liquid magic gesturing seductively to us, my good old pal suggested that I (oh, so now it was "I" again?) might as well pick up a decent supply.

You know, just so we'd have something on hand in case company dropped by during the next year or two, or I stubbed my toe, or somebody's dog died.

But we both knew that was all a crock, because visitors rarely came by anymore, at least not since I had gone off the deep end in a rather large way, and that had been years ago.

And as to the remainder of my litany of pathetic excuses, who was I shitting?

Not that it would have mattered, however, because I was one of those paranoid drunks who hid all of my booze. That way, on the remote chance that anyone was naive enough to stop by expecting to share a nice stiff convivial adult beverage, and some stimulating intellectual conversation, I could always claim that the cupboard was bare, and my stash would remain safe.

And that was Wes's first law of addiction - keep the stash safe at all costs, because running out of alcohol and drugs at 4:00 a.m. was not to be tolerated.

Now, on the other hand, if you happened to show up with a couple of grams of coke, then accommodations could always be readily made, and my bourbon would magically appear, because there are always exceptions to every rule when it comes around to maximizing one's high.

But the bottom line is that after I got done with all of my self-serving bullshit and rationalizations, everything evolved into one basic fact of life - simply put, as my AA pal Tony used to say, "I took a drink, then the drink took me, and then I was off to the races."

It was all so linear and logical the way my little forays into insanity played out exactly the same way every time. They always started out with my good little buddy whispering sweet nothings in my ear about how it was perfectly okay to take that one simple little fucking drink. Just one, but then I'd be gone, back out there for one more death-defying thrill ride.

"Go ahead, Wes, you can have a drink, it'll calm your nerves, help you to think better. Things are gonna turn out great, you'll see, this time's gonna be different - I promise!"

Because, like, yeah, "this time" will always be different when you're jonesing for your fix.

You'd think I'd have learned.

Well, actually I had learned, of course. It wasn't like I was fooling anyone, particularly myself, because that's the point of it all, isn't it, to have plenty of booze around when you're making a decent attempt at drinking yourself to death? And wasn't that the endgame all along, to wind up dead? My life wasn't exactly hitting on all cylinders, but even after a lifetime of screw-ups and failures I still didn't have the balls to pull a trigger.

So, enter alcohol - the painless, mindless .45 caliber solution for all of a drunk's problems.

≈≈≈

I had already subconsciously worked the numbers, so I knew that the bourbon would last me perhaps four or five days, and that was just the right amount of time to tie on a proper bender, and take one more trip to the 'Land of Blessed Oblivion.'

So as soon as I returned to the apartment I poured a nice big fat one on the rocks, lit a smoke, stretched out in the recliner, and commenced to nurse that one tiny little fucking drink.

And with that first sip I entered into what I pray was my final waltz with Death by alcohol.

≈≈≈

It was so close, so damned frustratingly close, but I couldn't quite reach it. It was right there in front of me, just beyond my grasp, shimmering in the afternoon sunlight, just inches above the surface of the water, slipping in and out of focus, tantalizing, mocking, calling out its siren song to me, but I just couldn't quite reach it.

It seemed like I'd been trying for several hours, but I had no real point of reference to judge the passage of time in this cold, dark void I was floating through, and it didn't really matter much because the result was always the same. And so I'd take another deep breath, and dive deep, always deeper than the last time, and I'd coil, waiting for that one perfect moment when my heart rate had slowed almost to nothing, and my breathing was strong and steady, my muscles taut, contracting, and then I'd exhale sharply, blasting the air out of my lungs, uncoiling in a powerful, fluid release of all the kinetic energy I had stored in my body, and I'd explode toward the surface, my legs pumping, chest and arms on fire from the exertion, reaching, flailing, straining to get up and out of the water, my hands clawing for that one strong branch that would be my salvation.

And always it was so close, so damned frustratingly close, but I just couldn't quite reach it, and then my momentum would fail me again and I'd falter, and in my nightmare I'd sink once more into the cold and the darkness and the terror.

Man, coming out of a blackout was always a ballbuster!

≈≈≈

That drunk dream was the last thing I could remember until I crawled back into consciousness in my apartment in Norwood, Massachusetts, sometime around noon on a sunny Sunday in early June, 1992.

I didn't realize it at the time, but that would mark the day that I finally surrendered to the diseases of alcoholism and addiction, without any reservations whatsoever.

I need to repeat that last phrase, if only for myself, "without any reservations whatsoever," because as Chapter 5 of the 'Big Book' of Alcoholics Anonymous reminds us, "half measures availed us nothing," and I'm living proof of that. The chain of events that occurred during the remainder of that day took away any last doubts and denial that I may have been desperately clinging to, and it is my belief that by finally letting go of those reservations I was saved by a Power greater than myself, who I chose to call God.

There's just no other way to explain it.

≈≈≈

When I finally came around my head felt like it was stuffed full of cotton, and I was shaking and numb all over, but I sucked down that last half-inch of warm bourbon in the glass in one long, magnificent gulp.

Ahh, the breakfast of champions!

I waited several moments for the alcohol to spread its warm, fuzzy glow throughout my body, took a deep breath, and then somehow I managed to climb out of the recliner and stagger into the bathroom.

Even I, as jaded as they come, was shocked by what I saw, because staring back at me from the mirror was a vision from Hell. I hadn't shaved, showered, brushed my teeth, changed my clothes, or eaten during the entire binge. My eyes had that dead thousand-yard stare, blood red, lifeless and sunk way back into their sockets. I had a week's growth of beard, I was shaking and wobbly, and my clothes were hanging off me like a scarecrow's.

I looked like somebody in a scene from '*Dead Man Walking.*'

Just then a wave of nausea hit me, and I went down on my knees in front of the crapper and emptied my guts. I studied the mess as it filled the bowl, watching particularly for any evidence of blood. I had a buddy who drank like me, and he had survived two esophageal hemorrhages caused by his binge drinking, but the third one finished him off. His last moments were spent lying on a hospital gurney in an emergency room, puking up blood and fighting intubation. The staff couldn't control him, so they finally backed off and he bled out, and that was that. He was forty-seven years old, and he'd been a full blown alcoholic for thirty years.

Lesson learned, I always checked for blood in my vomit also.

This time I got lucky. It was all clear, hot fluid, nothing solid, no chunks of semi-digested food, no sign of blood, just good old American eighty proof bourbon and stomach acid burning my esophagus raw on the way back up.

It soon turned into the dry heaves, and it was another five minutes before I could stop gagging.

Blood, or no blood, my first thought was, "Shit, it's finally happening. I'm dying."

My second thought was "Shit, it's Sunday, it's Massachusetts, and the freakin' liquor stores are closed. How much booze do I have left before the DT's hit, and how the hell do I get my hands on more?"

I'd had the delirium tremens damned near a hundred times over the past dozen years, and they were ungodly, so I'd do practically anything to avoid them, but hitting one of the local Walpole bars was out of the question. No bartenders in their right minds would serve me in the shape I was in, or if they did I'd be face-down on the railing after two drinks.

And, besides, how could I risk driving and a possible DUI stop, because the thought of going cold turkey in a drunk tank was beyond anything imaginable. I'd been "PC'd" a half dozen times over the years for drunk driving, and I will guarantee that the last place you ever want to wake up from a blackout in is a jail cell that you never remembered getting locked up in to begin with.

That, my dear friends, is the stuff from which nightmares are made, and you can damned well take that to the bank.

Now, on the other hand, it would take forever to get a cab, and then what was I going to do, have him drive me fifty miles each way to the New Hampshire border, just so I could buy more alcohol? Or over to South Boston to find a backdoor bar operation where I could grab a couple of bottles of overpriced rotgut? Or just keep him on the clock while he chauffeured me around the booze dumps down in the Norwood flats, all of which I'd get tossed out of twenty minutes later?

Decisions, decisions, what's a poor lost alkie to do when he's dying for his fix?

. ≈≈≈

I had one remaining option that I'd been hoping to avoid, but my time was running out, so I would need to come up with a plan, and fast, before the withdrawal sickness really hit hard.

First, however, I had to check whether there was any liquor left to steady my nerves.

I managed to stumble out to the kitchen, then said a silent prayer of thanks to the 'Gods of the Lost Drunks' when I saw that my last bottle of bourbon had three inches of precious lifeblood left in it. I also noticed that there were now three empty half-gallon bottles lined up neatly on the counter, brave little dead soldiers, plus this one lonely survivor that I was polishing off, and a couple of packs from a second carton of Marlboros.

Based on simple math it was clear even to me that I had ventured out at least once for supplies, and God only knows what else. I shuddered with relief that I had made it back in one piece, although now I had to check to see whether my car was out in the parking lot.

How many times over the years had I gone out searching for a missing vehicle after a rough night or weekend? It got so bad at one point that I ended up organizing search parties with my friends. That had worked out swell, at least until they stopped returning my calls.

And then one day I stopped having friends, which pretty much made all of that pain in the ass social stuff a moot point.

But, like they say, God looks after fools and drunks, and I was both, so on this day my car sat shimmering in the sunlight.

I performed some rapid calculations then, and quickly came to the conclusion that it was time to consider that final option I had been procrastinating about. And, thank you God, there was sufficient bourbon remaining to implement it.

I called it my "Backup Plan DT," which was to attempt to be admitted into a detox or treatment facility - that's if I could find one that would take me again, and that might present a problem based on my recent track record.

At this point I wasn't seriously considering another futile effort to stop drinking forever, but I knew that I'd beaten the stuffing out of myself, and that I'd soon be in a beaucoup nasty withdrawal. I also recalled that all of my most recent self-detox attempts had been bona fide nightmares, so I simply didn't have it in me to go it alone this time - I was just too exhausted.

I was already becoming nauseous again, dizzy, twitching and aching all over, and I knew that it would get a whole lot worse as the alcohol leached out of my system.

I could also tell from the pressure behind my eyeballs, and the banging sound in my ears, that all of my vitals were spiking through the roof. It felt like my eyes were about to pop out of my head. My personal best blood pressure reading of all time was 220 over 140 after a week of around-the-clock binging on cocaine and bourbon several years previously, and I feared that I was challenging my record this time around.

The elevated vitals led me to wonder momentarily whether I had scored some blow during my binge – coke was the cruelest game of all, and it had owned my ass from day one. I had chased it hard for a dozen years, but I didn't really have any connections these days, and there was none of the usual drug paraphernalia lying around.

No, bottom line, this must have been just another monster alcohol hangover, one of hundreds that I had experienced over the years.

I'd never had seizures while detoxing myself - that I knew of, anyway - but a guy standing next to me on the night before I left the Alps two months previously had gone down like a sack of bricks with a grand mal seizure. It was terrifying to watch, and no doubt it was a lot more terrifying to experience firsthand.

I realized that I was susceptible this time around, and I was in no mood to do any field research on the subject. You die from seizures, all alone, convulsing, swallowing your tongue, choking to death. But, as miserable as I was at that moment, I was still full of enough self-hate to want to remain alive, if only so that I could to go on hating myself for just a little while longer.

So the die was cast, and I decided that some R & R was in order, because the more I thought about it, the more I looked forward to taking a nice escape from the World for a few weeks.

There would be decent food, no irritating little phone calls from concerned family, friends, and another soon-to-be-former-employer, and a steady supply of nifty downers to ease my heebie-jeebies.

Naïve, but arrogant to the end, I actually believed that I was still running the show, and that I could dictate the terms of my own surrender.

What a crock, because truth be told I was nothing more than a conniving, clueless drunk on another in a long line of losing streaks.

Talk about pathetic!

≈≈≈

I might have been chock full of the arrogance and false pride that's only found in an alcoholic in denial, but nevertheless I still considered myself to be a rather sophisticated rehab veteran. I had learned through trial and error over the past five or six years which detoxes and treatment facilities would meet my rather discriminating standards, so I began to explore my options while I nursed my bourbon.

First out of the gate were the State of Massachusetts detoxes. For the most part they were roach motels, but they were cheap, and they served a purpose, namely to get you dried out and off the streets for a week.

As an added bonus they were also a great place to hide out from any number of angry, vindictive individuals who might be seeking out the pleasure of my company. I had used one for a week the prior winter, in order to straighten out and disappear from a pissed-off former employer who wanted their company car back for some strange reason that I just couldn't seem to comprehend at the time.

So I'd spent a week at the Framingham, Massachusetts detox back in January. I wore the same ratty bathrobe, pajamas and smiley slippers for the entire stay, slept on a cot in a crowded room that stunk of urine, sweat, vomit and shit, ate two day old donuts, Chef Boyardee spaghetti and meatballs, and Gorton's fucking fish sticks three times a day, then got topped off with 400 mg of Librium daily.

At one point during my fun-filled holiday I leaned over to switch the channel on the 1970's era television in the dayroom, but thanks to the Librium I lost my balance and started falling.

It seemed like it took me ten minutes to hit the floor, but ohhh, cooool... it... sure... was... fun... until it wasn't.

It's a strange fact of Nature, but if you're a low-life stinking drunk the ground always seems to rise up and smack you in the kisser sooner or later. Please feel free to call it one of "Wes's Laws of Fucked-up Gravity."

Other iterations of said law relate to major decreases in bank accounts, self-respect, sex appeal, employment opportunities, quality of residential address, and quantity of, and social status of, friends.

But no, I didn't think that I had a problem, even though I looked like Jack Nicholson at the end of 'One Flew Over the Cuckoo's Nest' when I finally booked my ass out of there a week later.

Because the state detoxes had confidentiality regulations they also attracted their fair share of individuals like myself, who were hiding out, on the lam from pissed-off friends, relatives, spouses, bill collectors, drug dealers, various law enforcement agencies, or employers.

So until you caught the rhythm of these places it never hurt to keep your mouth shut, and to be careful about who you hung out with in there.

But, on the other hand, if you kept your eyes and ears open you might just pick up a few nifty new tricks, if that was your bag. Spend an hour listening to the string of lies and broken promises that flow out of a junkie's mouth like mother's milk when he's two days off the needle and you'll know what I mean.

Talk about effortless, if somewhat pathological.

On a positive note, however, the staffers were all in recovery, real professionals, dedicated to helping any and all sick, suffering alcoholics and addicts who walked through the door, and they brought in local AA groups to put on meetings a couple of times a week.

If nothing else, those meetings broke up the monotony, and in some cases they offered hope to individuals like myself, who had none of our own.

But the bottom line was that these facilities were usually nothing more than crash pads to stop the shakes before you went back out into the world to play your games all over again.

The Framingham Detox wasn't exactly a garden spot, even though it was the best of the State facilities, so I checked it off as last on my list of places to take another fun-filled vacation from Planet Earth.

Well, unless things got *really* bad that is, which after all was the reason I had ended up there in the first place.

I'll tell you, though, God must have been making some long term plans for me during that prior stay, or was just having a chuckle while he screwed with my head, because Pat R., the Clinical Coordinator of the facility, would become my recovery counselor several years later.

Pat conducted my out-take interview at Framingham, and gee whiz, believe it or not, for some strange reason he figured out that I hadn't quite hit my wall yet.

Nonetheless, he was instrumental in my eventual recovery, and I ended up dumping all of my garbage on that poor bastard every two weeks for five years.

I'm honored to call him my friend to this day.

And there were some bonus points there as well. Pat was a scratch golfer, and he built golf clubs for a hobby, so by the end of my counseling years I had a nice new set of handmade clubs, had knocked five strokes off my game, had discovered a new addiction, and was beginning to look for a Golfers' Anonymous meeting.

So who says '*The Great Handicapper in the Sky*' doesn't have a plan for each of us, or at least a sense of humor?

I only wish that He could have given me a hand with my putting, however, because I've still got the fuckin' yips on the three footers.

$$\approx\approx\approx$$

Next up on my dance card was the middle echelon of detoxes and treatment centers, where I had been in-patient three or four times over the years.

My facility of choice here was *NORCAP*, which operated a seven day detox program in Norfolk, Massachusetts, as well as a longer term treatment facility in Foxboro.

I had matriculated to both of them at various times during my career, played the sober game for a while after I returned home, but always ended up drunk on my tits within a couple of months after every one of my stays there.

It wasn't all their fault, however, because at least they tried, whereas I didn't. Meh!

These mid-range outfits were newer, better equipped, the food was good, and they held plenty of in-house meetings, in addition to inviting local AA groups in.

Some of them even had barebones exercise facilities, so there were at least a few creature comforts.

Many were also affiliated with hospitals, as was the case with *NORCAP*, and they had on-staff counselors to work with the patients on developing a recovery plan for when we went back out into the 'World.'

I guess I didn't pay enough attention to the counseling part of the program, considering my .000 batting average every time I departed said premises.

I was also somewhat concerned that health insurance might become an issue here, and certain that it would for the upscale treatment centers if I decided to fly first class.

I actually had health insurance at the time, compliments of a company plan that I had been covered under. I'd been given a six month grace period on it after I was fired by that former employer back in January for, among other things, "a history of inconsistent results, which culminated in disappearing with a company car for two weeks after he was given his last verbal warning."

For my part I had fired back with an indignant letter of my own that challenged their unfriendly comments as "nuance and innuendo, wrapped up in wild supposition."

There, take THAT you miserable turds!

But I did get the insurance, and it financed a much needed thirty-day trip to Beech Hill for treatment of alcoholism just six weeks after my January stint at Framingham Detox.

So, as circumstance would have it, I suppose that my former employer's accusations weren't all that "nuanced" or "wild" after all.

Well, whatever. I still considered them to be egregious slugs, just on general principles, and besides, they hurt my poor little feelings!

The problem now was that I didn't know whether the insurer would be willing to kick in again, just two short months after they blew $19,000 on my thirty day respite at the Alps.

That wasn't exactly a stellar return on investment, at least not if you're an insurance auditor. But I had a swell time, anyway, and believe it or not it helped build a base that would ultimately save my life.

I was also somewhat wary about applying to NORCAP for another reason, however, because I was a three-time loser there, and it occurred to me that my odds weren't all that great for improving the outcome this time around.

I ascribed that concern to the likelihood that I had developed a mental block about their program that would be difficult to overcome.

Please, a fucking mental block? Seriously?

That rationale was pure nonsense, of course, like most of my best thinking in those days, but I was as apathetic about the place as I was about Brussel sprouts and bean curds, so I just couldn't get a hard-on about going back there. It left me with the total blahs, so I decided to take a pass on *NORCAP* for the time being, and would instead concentrate on the upper tier facilities.

And, besides, I considered the high-end joints to be more in keeping with my life style and breeding, so why not go first class this time around?

I had four prospects in mind, last of which was the Alps, so I took a deep breath, pounded down another slug of bourbon, lit a smoke, then commenced to smile and dial.

≈≈≈

God mentioned later that He'd been getting a big kick out of my desperate maneuvers and machinations that day. He referred to them as, "a pathetic attempt by the Captain of the Titanic to negotiate with the iceberg."

Happy to hear that, God, I'm thrilled to know that somebody was getting some chuckles out of my misery, because after all I'm here merely to serve at your pleasure!

≈≈≈

Thirty minutes later the shakes were coming on harder, and I was down to my last inch of bourbon, and one final treatment center – the good old Alps.

The other three facilities had refused to consider me because it was Sunday, so they wouldn't be able to receive a confirmation that my insurance was valid until the next business day.

What, they wouldn't take my word for it?

I'd been afraid of this. It wasn't that I didn't want to go back to the Hill, because it was a perfectly good facility, and I had received some beneficial counseling during my prior visit.

I had even made some good friends up there, which was a rare occurrence for me, because I don't trust. Period.

And I had met Blue Eyes there, and we just seemed to hit it off, which was an even rarer occurrence for me because I had always been a "love 'em and leave 'em" type, and because I don't trust. Period.

The big problem, after the uncertainty of insurance coverage, however, was that I felt like I'd be returning to the Hill with my tail between my legs, a failure for all to see. "Pride goeth before the fall," perhaps, but nonetheless it had only been two months since I graduated, and here I was drunk on my ass again, about to go begging for a bed.

But, really, that's pretty much just another steaming pile of cheap rationalization and bullshit, just more crap spewing from the mouth of an out of control, arrogant alcoholic in denial. I had become an expert at conning myself and the rest of the world - well, conning myself anyway, because in retrospect I'm not so sure that 'the World' was still buying anything that Wes was pitching, or even cared whether Wes was dead or alive.

And could I blame them?

The plain truth of the matter was that I'd done a damned good job of destroying my life over the past twenty-five years through a near-fatal addiction to alcohol and drugs, and half the world knew it. But I never gave a good goddamn about them in the first place, and come to think of it I never gave a rat's ass about the other half either.

Because I didn't trust. Period.

Well, at least not until Blue Eyes came along, because she saw through all of my childish nonsense in about two minutes flat, and left me howling at the moon.

The bottom line, however, was that I'd experienced loss after loss after loss, the likes of which I could never have imagined possible once upon a time. Yet here I was coming back to an alcohol rehab for the nth time, and all I could worry about was my damned image? Or how I'd come across to a bunch of suffering people who were still drooling on themselves after a couple days off the sauce? Seriously? Most of those poor souls probably had plenty of worries of their own, so I'm sure that the last thing on anybody's mind that day was having to fret about how another down and out drunk from Boston was making out with his DT's.

Ahh, the indefatigable ego of the alcoholic in full bloom, filled to the brim with lies, arrogance, denial and excuses.

Curiously, I rather liked Beech Hill, although I will admit that some of my rationale was a little bit fuzzy. In fact, make that very fuzzy – unless you're an addict, that is.

A case in point, one big kicker for me was that they handed out the blue 10 milligram Valiums to bring you down, rather than Librium. A minor detail you say?

Not to me!

I freakin' hated Librium, because it turned me into a zombie, but I'd always had a thing for Valiums, because they let me float along in my own safe little cocoon, oblivious to the world.

They were also a great hangover cure, and sometimes I mixed ground-up 5 mg. yellows with my cocaine to take the edge off when I was getting a little too jacked up toward the end of a forty-eight hour binge weekend. I nicknamed the concoction 'Yellow Snow,' after the Frank Zappa song.

That was one of a dozen nifty little drug combinations I had perfected over the years, that were capable of killing every single emotion I had ever felt, and I suppose it's one of the reasons why my first alcohol counselor had mentioned that I should have been a chemistry major in college.

But really, when you came right down to it, I was merely a pathetic coward who thoroughly disliked the pain of coming down off a bad drunk. So, thanks to the blue 10's that they pumped into me, re-entering Earth atmosphere had been a fairly easy ride when I arrived at the Hill in full blackout mode back in March.

And that was a very good thing, and certainly an experience I endeavored to repeat this time around.

So my thinking was that if it ain't broke, don't fix it - just keep feeding me my blues, please and thank you, and let me go into a corner to suck my thumb and sulk until I'm ready to rejoin the world.

But just how does one argue that case to the admittance director of an alcohol and drug rehabilitation facility? I mean, aren't I supposed to sound like I'm just a little bit repentant?

"Well, sir or madam, I'm applying to your fine institution so that I can get my hands on an almost unlimited supply of my favorite pharmaceutical, in order to bring me down slow and easy off my latest jackpot. Oh, and yeah, to cop a free high just for shits and giggles. So please, may I have a few fistfuls of your blues, just to keep me level until the pain goes away? I really do want to get clean and sober, but I can't concentrate on sobriety when I've still got the screaming horrors. I promise that this time will be different, really!"

Yeah, right!

Like I said, fuzzy logic at its best, another addict needing to get high to get straight. But that was me, always trying for an angle that would keep me floating along, immune to the pains of reality, without any of the downside.

And always failing miserably.

To round things out, however, the staff and counselors at the Alps were compassionate and caring professionals, and I had benefitted from some of their suggestions – that is, when I wasn't checking out Blue Eyes' perfectly formed derriere.

And, adding to the attraction, the food and the rooms were well above average, the views of the Monadnock Range were spectacular, and for the physically fit drunks there were some scenic walking trails that wound throughout the surrounding forest.

One other strong point was that they had some great AA meetings at the Hill, including a Saturday night barnburner that brought in recovering alcoholics from throughout the region. There were always some strong, entertaining speakers in those crews, which made for a nice change of pace - not that their inspiration had done me any good, of course.

And, no shit, they even had an outdoor swimming pool, and it was June so most of the ice would probably be out by now!

And last, but certainly not least, to top it all off with a great big juicy red cherry, the piece de resistance was that they had a great phlebotomist who always hit your vein just right when he was doing blood draws to check your liver enzymes. That may seem a bit trivial, but you'll know what I mean if you've ever had a nervous, shaky phleb poking around your veins with a sharp needle for ten minutes, trying unsuccessfully to get a good stick while you're coming down hard off a screaming, raging, binge drunk.

Trust me on that one.

So to sum it all up, what more could a low-life stinkin' drunk with delusions of grandeur ask for than a nice vacay in the Alps?

Aye, laddie, the Hill was the next best thing to a month in the Caribbean!

I stared at the bottle. There was one nice big fat warm fuzzy drink left, so what the hell - I picked up the bottle and I picked up the phone and I drank and I dialed.

Little did I know, I had just saved my life.

≈≈≈

It was a foregone conclusion how things would turn out, but we had to play the game, so we performed our traditional dance. It was a farce, but as always everything worked out in the end.

Practice makes perfect when you're negotiating the terms of your own surrender. I had learned that lesson the hard way a couple of years previously when I was applying to *NORCAP*. I had been blowing about a dot three four on the breathalyzer, drunk out of my mind and speaking in tongues. The only way I could get admitted was to hand the phone over to a slightly less drunk friend of mine, now deceased, thank you Demon Rum, and he had successfully conducted the interview on my behalf.

But even then things had almost bombed out at the very last minute, when they requested my credit card information as a deposit, because I gave them the numbers off an expired Texaco gas card.

Oh, in case you're wondering, my deceased friend's name was Doc. He was a great drinking buddy. He was a PhD psychologist with one of the highest IQ's I have ever known, and he had a long and distinguished drinking career, but in the end the booze beat the IQ hands-down like it always does. So Doc drank his multi-million dollar clinic into the ground, and eventually wound up sleeping on a wooden cot in a filthy old basement, next to an ancient washing machine.

The last time I saw him alive he weighed somewhere around one hundred pounds, down from two hundred, and he was lying on the cot shooting cheap vodka into his gut through a feeding tube. He had lost most of his mouth and jaw and throat to cancer from the drinking and the cigarettes, so the tube was his only viable delivery system.

What can I say, you do what you need to do when that cold-hearted monster owns your ass, and I ought to know, because I would have done the same damned thing if I was in his shoes.

So now I was conducting my own negotiations. I had a high degree of confidence, because I'd practiced the lines I planned to use so many times, on so many admittance directors, that I could have recited them in my sleep, or even blind drunk like I was now.

Or so I hoped, anyway.

For Beech Hill's part I was certain that the staff would soon be turning down the covers on my bed, and leaving a mint on the pillow, while they waited breathlessly for the six hundred dollar per day insurance authorization to arrive.

But the bottom line was that none of this polite, formal bullshit that we were about to engage in really mattered much, anyway, because at the end of the day it was always just about the Benjamins.

So I conned them, and they conned the insurance company, and everyone was happy, even that poor fuckin' auditor who had taken it up the ass for nineteen large on my previous Alpine adventure.

And, besides, now that the auditor had been burned once he would no doubt lay off his bets to a half-dozen reinsurers this time around, so what was the big deal? Life goes on, the wheels turn, the rivers still flow to the seas, everyone grabs a piece of the action, and this game wasn't any different from the way the Vegas bookies arbitraged their own risk.

Hell, the way I figured it I was just boosting the economy and spreading the wealth around a little, so I should receive a medal for that, comrade!

≈≈≈

After five minutes of shuffling papers, and keeping me on hold, Dave finally picked up. That was just 'The Man,' letting me know who was in charge. Fine, Dave, I'm sure yours is bigger than mine, so can we get down to effin business now?

"So, Wes, why now? You just left here two months ago, and obviously things didn't go too well. What's different this time? Why do you want to get sober now? What do you hope to accomplish?" *This oughta be good for a chuckle!*

Jesus H. Christ, what's this, a freakin job interview? "Well, Dave, I, ahh, I worked really hard last time, *uurrrppp*. It's just that I caught a couple of bad breaks when I got home an I screwed up an I didn't hit enough meetins… oh, yeah, an I never got a sponsor or went to counseling. But I want sobriety more than anything else in the world right now, an I ahh, ahhhh, an I know what I did wrong, an I just need one more chance, so please help me, please." *Blah blah blah.*

"Are you willing to do everything we suggest to remain sober this time? I mean it – everything?" *You've gotta be shittin' me - better get the Fishbowl ready again, we've got a live one here - he's as ripped as the last time around!*

"Absolutely, Dave! I know that I don't have a lot of chances left. I just need to get away from the, ahh, noise fer a while, so I can get centered an work on a strong recovery plan. Beech Hill has all the tools an I know I can learn how to use them this time, you'll see… yer my last, ahh… hope. I've surrendert." *Blahdee blahdee blahdee.*

What the hell is this guy on, he sounds like he's on a nod. "You have to understand, Wes, you'll be admitted provisionally until we can get your insurance straightened out. We should be able to pick you up in a couple of hours, and we should get an approval from them by tomorrow. But if they decline you, for any reason, you'll need to take a bus home on your own dime. Agreed?" *I'm sure as hell glad I'm not the poor sucker who has to drive this whackjob up here.*

Yippee, the rube's buying my shit again! "Yes, of course, Dave, I understand, and that would be fine. Thank you so very much for givin' me this chance again... ahh, I'll, ahhh, work really hard an you won't regret it. Thank you thank you thank you!" *Blahdee fuckin' blah.*

"It's two o'clock, so the driver should be able to get down to your place sometime around four, four-thirty." *And they call this a freakin' career?*

"That's great, perfect! Ahhm, ahhm, thank you, so much... I'll be ready! See you soon!" *Now how the hell am I gonna get the driver to stop once we get over the New Hampshire border so I can snag a bottle of vino for the ride?*

"Ok, Wes, we'll see you in a few hours, and please try to get some food in you," Dave said, about to hang up.

Time to go for the gold! "Oh, by the way, Dave, I was wonderin', my Doc has specified that I should only be given Valiums. I believe they're the blue ten milligram ones, to assist in my, uh, ahh, my detossification. He says Librium is not an appropriate drug in his perfessional opinion, too many dangerous side effects. Do you, ahh, see any, uh, any problems with that?" *Please, God, help me, just this once! I promise never to lie again!*

Jesus H. Christ Allfreakingmighty, do you want us to wipe your ass too, you arrogant shit? "Sighhh, no problem, Wes, I'm sure the doc can accommodate your needs." Click.

Oh yeah, Baby! I'll snag the vino as soon as we hit New Hampshire. I can nurse a quart for an hour, keep a nice buzz on, and I should have my first blues an hour after I'm through the door. Yesss! It'll be a nice smooth glide slope, comfortably numb for the rest of the day! I wonder how long I can drag out the scrip for the blues? At least a week, I should think.

Victorious, I took a long, slow, loving swallow, and polished off the last of my bourbon.

"Rest in peace, Mister Beam," I said, "it's been a pleasure to know you, but hopefully we'll soon meet again."

I still had a full package on as I stumbled into the bathroom for a shave and a quick shower - after all, I wanted to look presentable for my new fun adventures in 'Rehab Land.'

First, however, I had to take care of another case of the dry heaves, which meant that I'd probably lose all the therapeutic benefits of that last mouthful of Beam, and perhaps a small piece of my esophagus as well.

Shit!

≈≈≈≈

The bathroom break cleared me up, somewhat, but I was becoming more squirrelly as my buzz began to ease off. This was the dangerous part, because the scary stuff would be hitting me soon, and it would be close to three hours before I could scam a jug of wine, and probably four before I could pop my first valiums.

And those damned shakes had no intention of waiting that long.

I hated them, and all the rest of the crap that came along with alcohol withdrawal – the puking that morphed into the dry heaves, the dizzies, the insomnia, the blinding headaches, the blood pressure spikes, the cigarette burns all over my body and clothes, the paranoia, the sweats, the shits, the stomach full of razor blades, the mysterious cuts and bruises, the freakin' Brahms rhapsodies playing over and over and over again in my head even when there was no music on, and worst of all the pure hating myself for having to go through this nightmare all over again.

This had the makings of a very long day shaping up, and I couldn't wait to get my hands on that bottle of wine that was already calling out to me from just over the New Hampshire border.

I had just forced myself to start packing my duffel bag when the phone rang.

Uh oh, a snag this soon with Beech Hill? Did that freaking insurance company decline me already? Who the hell else could be calling?

I was in for a surprise, and it broke my heart, but it changed my life.

≈≈≈

The call was from Blue Eyes, my drop-dead gorgeous friend from my previous stay at the Hill. She was the last person I expected to hear from that day, but dear God, she was the only person I wanted to hear from.

She had rolled into the Alps back in March, a week before me, and we ended up in the same counseling group once I was judged competent to join the rest of the population.

There was just something about her that grabbed my attention like nobody ever had, and we hit it off pretty much from day one.

I don't know which one of us had more pent-up anger when we first met, but we were good for each other. Pretty soon I was looking forward to seeing those killer blue eyes brightening up when we met at the meal tables, and I began trying to provoke one of her shy, sexy smiles with some of my patented wisecracks.

We opened up to each other about our stuff, and pretty soon I was telling her things about myself that I had never told anyone. And she did the same with me, and my heart went out to her when I heard her story.

For a guy who had shut himself off from the world a very long time ago, a guy filled with nothing but self-loathing and anger, this was something really special.

Fight it as I may, I knew that I was falling in love with her, and I knew that she was falling for me.

But that was the worst thing that could happen at a treatment facility, because detox romances hardly ever work, and usually they end up in a trail of tears, with one or both of the parties using again.

We took a long walk through the forest to the *'Money Tree'* on the morning that she left for home. That ancient oak was a good luck omen – you took a quarter and you banged it into the trunk with a stone, and as long as it remained in place it was supposed to guarantee that you'd remain sober after you left 'the Hill.'

For her it worked.

For me, not so much.

It had been a sunny, warm, perfect mid-April day in the mountains. There was a large boulder lying next to the tree, so we climbed up on it and lay there for a couple of hours, soaking up the sun, talking about life, and making our promises to get together after we returned home.

At some point during that magical morning I fell into her eyes, and I never came back. Blue Eyes set my soul on fire that day, and I was changed forever.

We lived about thirty miles apart, so we began seeing each other almost immediately after I returned home, and I had some great times hanging out with her and her precious little girl.

Suddenly an enjoyable evening wasn't drinking myself into a stupor, but rather it had become pizza, a good movie and a game of Jenga. Her daughter always won, and I didn't even let her.

But one night when I was up at her place the voices of the demons from my past started whispering to me again. They were haunting me, eating away at my happiness for no reason I have ever been able to fathom, and I began to shut down.

It was nothing that she had said or done – quite the contrary, we were having a wonderful time, and I felt a deeper bond with her that night than with any other human being I had ever known.

But out of nowhere all of my shields began to go up, and I became tense and non-communicative. I went stone cold silent, and just shut her out.

I was dying inside, but I couldn't tell her any of the things that were in my heart, those thoughts and dreams she wanted and needed to hear from me. I couldn't tell her that I was falling in love with her, that I couldn't imagine spending my life without her, or that she was the most wondrous, perfect woman I had ever known.

Perhaps it was the depression that had plagued me all of my life, or the self-hate and urge to self-destruct that had hounded me since before I could remember, or maybe it was the lifetime of scars I had worn ever since I was a little kid that still prevented me from showing my soul to her.

Maybe the wounds were still too deep, or I was just too broken, or too new in sobriety to open myself up all the way to anyone, even Blue Eyes.

Or maybe I just couldn't believe that I deserved something so good and so beautiful to happen in my life.

Or maybe I just wanted to drink more than I wanted to remain sober, so by hurting her I could hurt myself enough to drink again, and God, I wanted to eat a round for even imagining that.

I'll never know why, and that's the hell of it, but to this day it's what I think about whenever I wake up alone in a cold sweat from a drunk dream in the darkest hours of the night, and the demons that slip out of the shadows at 3:00 a.m. always make sure I remember that evening from so long ago.

Whatever the reason, I went into my cocoon, and I know that I hurt her feelings very badly that night. She had begun to open herself up to me, trusting me, making herself vulnerable, and it took a world of courage for her to do that because I knew where she had come from, and it was the same half-acre of Hell as I had.

And yet I couldn't say a word. I couldn't even hold her in my arms and tell her that we were going to be alright. I just went cold and dead inside, pouted, shut her out and shut down every emotion I had in my body.

She let out the biggest sigh of disappointment that I've ever experienced when we hugged good-bye the next morning.

I couldn't speak - I just left.

The ride home was terrible.

They tell us in the Program that we should never hold on to regrets. Well, maybe so, but I'll go to my grave not forgiving myself for that night. You see, I grew a conscience at some point over the years, and the knowledge that I let her down and turned my back on her when she needed someone to tell her that she was going to be alright has been one of the most heartbreaking weights I have ever carried.

Blue Eyes deserved more from me, much more, but I shut down and disappeared.

And thus I had my excuse. The self-hate and self-destructive urges had won out again, as they had a hundred times before, so I trashed myself good and proper the next day, and the next, and then finally I went out and bought those two bottles of bourbon, and did what I had always done best.

I guess we know how that turned out.

≈≈≈

I was shocked but elated to hear from her now, although I couldn't help but wonder at the timing of it all.

"Hi Wes, I haven't heard from you for a while, are you doing alright?" *Tentative, nervous, cautious.*

"Hey, pretty lady, this is a nice surprise, but nah, not so hot. I screwed up. I picked up. I'm a mess, and I'm heading back to the Hill today, just waiting on my ride."

There was a moment's silence, then, "Oh, Wes, somehow I had that feeling. I'm coming down, I'll wait with you." *Softly, quivering, hurt.*

"No, you don't want to do that. I'm toxic. It's bad. It's not cool to be around me - it could be dangerous for you, too."

"I don't care. I'm coming down, no arguments. I'll be there in an hour." *Click.*

Well, as I knew from day one, this woman had spirit and a strong will, and there was nothing on Earth that could stop her once she had made her mind up to do something.

≈≈≈

Blue Eyes arrived forty-five minutes later, while I was still attempting to pack my duffel bag. The shakes were getting worse and I was having second thoughts about going back to the Hill just as she walked through the door.

I was never so happy to see anyone in all my life, or so bitter, for knowing the reason that she was there.

By the way, there's something else you need to know about Blue Eyes - she's far and away the best hugger I've ever met, and I've been hugged by hundreds of women over the years. It's an AA thing - we hug a lot. I used to cringe about it when I first began hitting meetings, but I got over it. In fact, I like it now, a whole lot. Blue Eyes taught me well.

And this time was no different - she pulled me in deep and never let me come up for air. All I could do was hold on tight, try to catch my breath, and enjoy the experience.

≈≈≈

I suppose that it's pretty easy to take charge when you're the mother of a six year old girl, and you're dealing with a six year old adult. She went into overdrive as soon as we unwrapped, and my packing was finished a couple of minutes later. That's just the way she's always been, and it was one of the many reasons that I had fallen in love with her.

We didn't talk very much. After all, there really wasn't too much to say, so we sat on the sofa for almost an hour, virtually silent, and she held my hand the entire time. But just her physical presence, like some beautiful Angel of Mercy, was all I needed.

She had a calming influence on me. I was still wired, on edge, fighting off the shakes, but just the physical and emotional connection to her was enough to make a difference, if only for a few moments.

Blue Eyes didn't know it, but she helped save my life that day, and I'll love her and be grateful to her for that until the day I die.

And I don't wonder about the timing of her call anymore - I know who had set it all up. There's no doubt in my mind that she was a gift from a Power greater than myself, telling me that Wes was finally going to be okay.

It was June 7, 1992, and it was the day I ran up the white flag of surrender to my disease.

It was the last day I ever took a drink - one day at a time, one hour at a time, one moment at a time, one heartbeat at a time, or whatever the hell it takes.

≈≈≈

I still had a long way to go before this day would come to an end, and sooner than I would have wished I heard a car pull up outside the apartment's backyard gate.

It was followed seconds later by the honk of a horn.

My ride from the Alps had arrived.

Blue Eyes' hand tightened around mine, and she was biting her lip, brushing back a tear.

I was close to tears myself, as I searched for something to say that was even a little bit encouraging.

"Hey, everything's gonna work out fine," I whispered gently, not believing it for a second.

"I know," she said, her voice wavering, "I'll come up to visit once you're settled in."

"That would be nice."

With that I grabbed my duffel bag, and we went out through the sliders to the waiting car.

≈≈≈

The driver was exiting his vehicle as we approached, and he greeted me, "Hi, Wes, you probably don't remember me, I'm Bill, I drove you up to the Hill back in March. Sorry to be seeing you again under these circumstances. Here, let me take your bag."

Bill might have remembered me from the pick-up back in March, but I didn't know him from Adam. I had no recollection of him, or of any aspect of my trip up to the Hill. I had spent the entire two hours passed out on the back seat, except for one short break when I woke up long enough to have him pull to the side of the road so that I could vomit. We arrived around midnight, and it had taken him and an orderly to drag me out of the car, whereupon I collapsed in a heap at the front door. They carried me inside to the admitting desk, and from there straight into a glass-sided triage unit located right behind it. This was the infamous "Fishbowl," where they kept an eye on the really sick ones until we were stable enough to be assigned a bed.

"Hi, Bill. Can't say it's nice to see you again, but the fact is, I don't remember you, no offense."

I handed him the bag, he chuckled, then said "None taken," as he tossed it into the trunk. He snapped the lid shut, looked at Blue Eyes and me, and said, "Take your time," as he climbed into the driver's seat.

"Thank you," was all I could manage as she pulled me in one more time. I knew that she was fighting back the tears again, and so was I.

I briefly wondered what was up with all this crying nonsense that I was suddenly susceptible to, because I didn't cry, period!

I'll be up to see you soon," she whispered, "so please take care of yourself and do what they tell you, Wes, please! I'll be up soon."

I finally let go of her, slid into the passenger's seat, and Bill slowly pulled away. I couldn't look back - I couldn't bear to see her standing there, all alone.

Bill had the good sense to remain quiet for the next fifteen miles, while I silently raged at myself.

≈≈≈

We made decent time as we headed north on Route 128 toward Route 3 and New Hampshire. Bill was keeping to himself out of courtesy to me, and I had no desire to talk anyway - I was too absorbed in working off another case of the shakes, while I wallowed in self-pity.

The good news, if you could call it that, was that my withdrawal from the alcohol was going a little better than I had anticipated. I don't know whether it was because I still had too much booze in my system, or if it was from all the vomiting, or from becoming more active, or if Blue Eyes had cast a spell on me with her magic touch, but for now things were somewhat manageable.

Well, somewhat anyway, but I was numb all over, sweating profusely, fighting a blinding headache, my hands were shaking to beat the band, and my thought processes were far less than lucid, bordering on the hallucinogenic at times.

But that was all garden variety detox stuff, certainly nothing life-threatening, nothing that I hadn't shaken out hundreds of times before.

More than anything I wanted to vomit again, even if I had to force it, because I knew that I'd feel better once I was able to rid myself of most of the poison that was still seeping into my system. But there was hardly any fluid left to bring up, even though my gas-filled stomach felt stuffed, and was churning violently.

And, of course, I was pissed off at the world, and more so at myself.

"What the hell," I raged silently, "what the hell have you done now? You had it all, you dumb shit, and you threw it away for nothing, just to get freakin high again! When the hell are you finally gonna learn, when you're fuckin' dead?"

I must have been vibrating from my little diatribe, because Bill picked up on it almost immediately.

"You know, trashing yourself really won't get you anywhere, Wes, because it just makes things worse. I oughta know, been there myself once or twice," he said, his voice measured, calm, reserved.

"Oh, swell," I thought, "just what I need, another missionary who has made it his life's duty to be the savior of my soul! Evidently this guy, who doesn't even know me, has taken it upon himself to assume the role of designated mind reader, as well as chauffeur, so am I going to have to listen to his song and dance for the entire ride?"

"Yeah, well I already have that tee-shirt, Bill, so you're telling me this because…?" I asked, scowling.

"Because… I was sitting in your seat eight years ago. I'd lost it all - everything! Wife, kids, house, job, friends, the car, the dog, the golf clubs, you name it. You think you're the only one who screwed up your life because of booze and drugs?"

Then he laughed under his breath, and I couldn't tell whether he was laughing at me, or at himself. Not that it mattered by now, because he had just qualified for top spot on my shit list.

"Yah, well that sucks for you, but I really don't give a damn about the rest of the world right now," I replied.

He just chuckled and continued on in that same subdued tone, "Keep coming, Wes, just keep coming, you'll be okay."

Then, sensing that discretion was in order, he lapsed back into silence as we headed north on Route 3 toward Nashua.

I turned my thoughts back to more important matters then, namely trying to figure out how to snag that jug of wine that now lay a mere fifteen minutes up the road, so screw him!

≈≈≈

Bill broke the silence again as we approached Nashua and the New Hampshire border.

"Wes, listen, I've been where you're at, and I know what you're thinking, that it's hopeless, that it's never going to get better, so why bother? Just say screw it and drink and put up the barricades, and the hell with the world. I was in that same place for a long time."

I could see that he was taking the conciliatory approach this time, so he evidently considered himself to be some kind of hostage negotiator who was fighting for my mortal soul.

I wasn't buying any of it.

"Yeah, well excuse me, but who asked you? You seem to think that you know me for some reason, but you don't know squat. I screw up - that's what I do. Drunk or sober I screw up, so it's a hell of a lot easier staying high, because I don't have to listen to preachers telling me how to save my soul. I lost that a long time ago, and it ain't coming back anytime soon, trust me on that."

"Yeah? You screw up everything? So why did that beautiful lady who thinks the world of you show up today just to keep you company until your ride came? I saw the way she looks at you, and you're breaking her heart! So yeah, keep it up and you will for sure screw that up too, Ace, guaranteed."

Damn! Now I was really pissed off and on the verge of boiling over, even if he did have a point. Damn him, I didn't want to play his game, and I was still dying for a drink, anything just to sedate my shattered nerves. But as much as I needed to keep him as a temporary ally, at least until I got my fix, I was still too stubborn to back off and get humble. We had just crossed into New Hampshire and the beer and wine stores were open, so I was looking for my spot.

"What the hell do you think you know about her? You don't know jackshit! I already ruined any chance I might have had with her, so I have no idea why she came down to see me. Maybe she just wanted to make sure that I was gone for good, and that I was out of her life."

But that was a crock, and we both knew it.

"You are so full of beans," Bill taunted, "are you listening to yourself? Get off the pity pot! Poor me, poor me, pour me another drink. Where do you want me to stop? You think I don't know you want a bottle right now? That's what this bullshit is all about, isn't it, just staying high? Who are you kidding, I told you I've already been there, and I played that same con long before you ever thought of it!"

"Yeah, and what do you have to show for it? You're sitting here in a beat up old piece of shit on a beautiful day, driving a freakin drunk to a detox, like you're on some kind of secret mission from God. Is that all you have to show for your great sobriety? This is your swell life, chauffeuring drunks around? They oughta make a movie about you, you can be the next freakin Mother Teresa!"

Uh oh, that got him. His face went red and the veins in his neck appeared ready to pop as he began to say something, then stopped.

And then he began again, and again he stopped.

It was then that I realized I had flunked the first rule of hostage negotiation – never talk trash about a guy's car.

But I had to give him credit, because if it had been me taking that childish nonsense I would have been wading in throwing both fists by then.

≈≈≈

We drove along in silence for another five minutes.

When he finally spoke again he was quiet and reserved, but it was clear that he still had an edge on.

"Don't pretend to think you know me, Wes," he said slowly, "I own this beat up piece of shit outright, and I'm proud of it. I own every one of my possessions outright. I lost everything and everybody eight years ago, and I've worked my ass off and struggled and bled just to get my life back. And, anyway, it's not about the toys, but what's inside," he said, slapping his chest, "that's what makes me the person I am today, and I'll take my life over yours any day of the week!"

He paused, then continued before I could interrupt, "I have my family back, and they love me. And I have friends, real ones, not drinking buddies who disappear the moment the booze and the drugs run out. They're there for me no matter what, just like they know I'm there for them. I've got my self-respect back, I like myself today, and I'm grateful for the life I have!"

Another pause, then he quietly delivered the punchline, "Can you say the same?"

I sat there silently, raging at myself as I searched the roadside for the first gas station that had a beer sign in the window.

Naturally, there weren't any on this stretch of the road.

Damn, what are you doing to me, God?

God? Now where did that come from?

≈≈≈

41

Moments later I found my opening. He had lobbed it right out there for me to hit, and I didn't even need to come up with a con. All I had to do was play his humility game, toss in a couple of lines of "I surrender," and I'd have him stopping at the next beer and wine store.

Hell, he'd probably pay for the jug.

I spoke up after a minute or two, trying my best to sound humble, "Okay, Bill, I apologize. I'm not doing so swell, and it's been a mother of a day, so I'm sorry if I took it all out on you. It was wrong of me. That's not who I usually am, and I respect you for what you've accomplished."

I paused for dramatic effect, then continued, "You've just gotta understand that I'm tired of all this crap, and I'm broken, and I've been on a losing streak for longer than I can remember. So yeah, you're right, I do want a drink, bad. I'm hurtin' all over, man."

I hesitated once again, then went for the money shot, "Is there any way we could possibly stop so that I could get a couple cartons of smokes for up there? Oh, yeah, and maybe one last bottle? I'm freakin' bad, and I just need something to get me to the Hill in one piece before I lose it! I'm afraid that I'm gonna go into convulsions, it's happened before," I lied, "please, just one last drink to help chill my nerves?"

It might have been somewhat manipulative, but technically it wasn't a *real* lie.

And, besides, I knew that he wouldn't buy it, but he didn't need to. He'd already given up and wanted this ride over as quickly as possible, and if that meant letting me grab a bottle, then fine and dandy. We were about an hour away from the Hill, and it would be a nice smooth ride if I was pacified the entire way. Maybe I'd do us both a favor and pass out again like the last time, so he's thinking what could possibly go wrong in one hour, and then he'll be rid of me for good.

Damn, I wanted to puke again! That would clear everything out, and make plenty of room for that cheap sweet wine that I could almost taste right now. Hell, maybe I could even bag a jug of Mad Dog 20/20, which would really knock me flat on my ass for my swan song.

Bill broke into my reverie then, "I'm not gonna fight you anymore, Wes. You're an adult, so I won't get in your way if you want to drink yourself to death. There's a place right up ahead. You won't be the first one I've stopped there for, nor the last, but before you step out of this car we're going to make a deal, understood?"

"Sure, whatever you say."

He pulled off the road and rolled up toward the front of a convenience store, then parked the car, but left the engine idling.

"You're under my care, Wes," he said. "You're a mess. I have a responsibility to deliver you to the Hill safe and sound, and alive. I'm not supposed to be stopping for stuff like this. We've still got an hour's ride, so go in, get what you need, and get your ass back out here fast. Get a cup of soda, toss out the soda and drink whatever it is you're drinking out of the cup. I don't want you swilling out of a bottle for the cops to see. Neither of us needs that, and I will ask them to PC you if it comes down to it, and then you can thumb your sorry ass home whenever they let you out."

He hesitated, then continued, "You brought the booze with you, if anyone at the Hill asks. We never stopped for it. I didn't know you had it until we were on the road. I don't need them thinking I enabled you, or got you loaded. I'm doing you a favor and I'm playing it straight with you, so I expect the same in return."

A final pause, then, "No more trouble. No more side trips. No more nonsense. Agreed?"

What more was there to say - he had just handed me the keys to the kingdom.

"Thanks, man, I really appreciate it."

I didn't wait for him to change his mind, so I leaped out of the car like I had been shot out of a cannon.

I could smell that sweet wine calling out to me from the store. It was so close, what could possibly go wrong?

≈≈≈

I only took two steps from the car before I was overcome by a wave of vertigo that sent me careening into a van that was parked next to us. I bounced off it and went down hard on one knee, bruised, shaking, confused. I felt another spasm of nausea pass through me, but there was hardly anything left to bring up, so I just knelt there for a few seconds, retching and trying to stop the spins.

Somehow I managed to struggle to my feet and get my wind back. Out of the corner of my eye I could see Bill climbing across the front seat, reaching out to grab me, but I lurched away from him and stumbled toward the store.

All I succeeded in doing, however, was play bumper cars with his vehicle and the van. Eventually I ran out of both car and van, then tripped on the curb and collapsed onto the sidewalk near the front door of the convenience store.

By then I had accumulated a half dozen bemused spectators, plus the store clerk, who was glaring at me through the glass door, stone-faced.

But I had to hand it to Bill. For an old fart in his mid-50's, and somewhat overweight, he was quick on his feet, and strong. In a matter of seconds he launched himself out the driver's door, took a dozen long strides, and grabbed me by the collar of my sweatshirt. He half dragged and half propelled me back to the car, jerked open the rear door and literally threw me into the back seat.

I tried to rise, but he slammed his hand into my chest, and pushed me back down onto the seat.

"You stay there. You do not move. Do you hear me? I said, do you hear me?" He had a fierce look in his eyes, and I thought for a minute that he wanted to smack me.

"Awright, take it easy, I'm not going anywhere, so just chill, will ya!"

"You bet your ass you aren't going anywhere, except straight to the Hill. No stopping for cocktails, no piss breaks, no snacks, no nothing. Your drinking privileges are officially over. If you don't like it you can walk home from here, because I don't give a rat's ass anymore."

"Aww, c'mon, can't you at least get me a couple of beers now that we're here? I prom…"

His glare cut me off in mid-sentence, and then he slammed the rear door shut and climbed back into the driver's seat.

I felt a momentary flash of panic when I realized that I'd be detoxing without any outside help for the next hour - shit!

Bill started up the car, backed out of the parking space, and melted a little rubber as soon as we were back on Route 101.

We headed west in silence.

≈≈≈

"You remind me a lot of myself, you know, how I used to be when I was out there running the same dumbass games you are," Bill finally said over his shoulder. "That's not a compliment, by the way. I was pigheaded, arrogant and clueless. I disrespected everybody and everything, but the whole time I was scared shitless, acting tough, like everything was all just a great big joke, just like you're doing now."

He paused, then said, "Do you get it yet? This war's over, and you lost. It's just a matter of how you want to go out."

And, for good measure, "You've got a choice, Wes. You can live sober and have a good life, with happiness, self-respect and people who really care about you, or you can go out in a box, alone, dying a drunk's death. It's up to you - we've all got choices in this world, Wes, so all you have to do is choose Door #1 or Door #2. What's it gonna be, tough guy?"

If Bill was attempting to embarrass me, or frighten me, or piss me off, it wasn't working. I had been inviting all manner of indignities upon myself for several decades, and I had changed over the years. I was hardened to it all, and nothing embarrassed me anymore, nothing whatsoever. No matter how low I sank, it was all just the cost of doing business, paying my dues for feeding the beast within.

I looked at myself dispassionately in those days. I understood nothing of morality or ethics or personal honor, nor did I bother to concern myself with such abstractions. I viewed the world clinically, almost pathologically, as if with cold, dead reptile eyes. The world existed merely to pleasure me, to cater to my basest instincts, to feed the perpetual drinking and drugging machine that I had become.

Nothing else mattered except staying high, numb, and dead inside – nothing!

And through it all I wore my cynicism proudly, like a crown of thorns.

But somewhere deep inside me something was stirring now. I was just plain beaten, so very exhausted. I bore a weariness in my body, and a soul sickness the likes of which I had never known before. It was as if every one of my cells was crying out for rest, and for an end to the struggle.

Yet still I fought it tooth and nail. Drinking and drugging were all I knew, and I couldn't imagine life without them. They were the armor that kept a hostile, terrifying world I had never understood at bay.

But underneath it all I was still just a terrified little kid, hiding from the world, hiding from my feelings, hiding from all that was good and pure and beautiful, just like I had been in the bad times so long ago.

Bill's comment had hit home on that one.

Dear God, where had that innocent child's dreams gone?

≈≈≈

Almost as if on cue Bill spoke up again, "It gets better, Wes, it really does. You don't need to fight this war anymore, so let it go, just let it all go. You can't beat it, it's bigger than you, it's bigger than any of us."

"Let IT go? Let WHAT go? What the hell do you want me to let go of? Why the freakin riddles? That's all I ever hear from you people – riddles and fairy tales and let it go, let it go, let it freakin' go!"

"Just stay away from a drink and the drugs for one day, Wes, that's it, that's all you have to do. Let go of the booze, let go of the drugs, let go of this damned stranglehold you seem to have on life. You'll find your answers, you'll figure out the rest when you're ready for it."

He paused, then continued, "Look at yourself. You're going to die, and sooner, not later. Is that what you really want? Is that how you want to be remembered? Is that what you want to do to that beautiful lady back home?"

"Don't you dare bring her into this! I'm warning you - she's off limits, period! You want to give me a batch of bullshit, that's fine, but leave her the hell out of it! I don't need any more fucking guilt trips today!"

"Okay, sorry, I didn't mean to get your knickers in a twist, but you're walking a thin line, son, and you're running out of time."

I was too beat to argue with him anymore, and my stomach still felt like it was full of battery acid, so I changed the subject.

"You're in okay shape, for an old guy," I stated grudgingly.

"Not really, you're just a wuss. I was a bouncer back in the day, so I took care of wise guys like you every night. It's all just about getting the leverage."

"I'll be sure to remember that for the next time."

"I wouldn't worry about it, you keep doing what you're doing and there probably won't be a next time."

"Whatever you say, Mr. Happy!"

"You can't keep doing this to yourself, Wes, your body can't take it like it did when you were young. It won't bounce back like it used to, there's just too much damage done over time to all the major organs and systems. That poison you're pouring into yourself eats away everything, like its acid."

"Yeah, well I'm not worried," I snorted, which was only half true. I had given up caring about myself in any type of physical or emotional way a long time ago, but somewhere deep inside me there had always burned a faint spark, not of hope, but of curiosity. It was hardly ever in my conscious mind, but every once in a while it popped up, unbidden, and asked one simple question:

"What if?" What if I could change? What if I could stop the drinking and drugging? What if I were free to live my life on my own terms, rather than on a bottle's? What if I were free of the "bondage of self" that they were always talking about in that AA literature? What if?"

It had popped up during my detox in the Alps two months previously, when I first met Blue Eyes.

And now here it was back again, like that damned TV battery bunny clanging away on the cymbals, playing games with my head, turning me into a dreamer.

Damn, it must be the last remnants of the alcohol draining out of me, I'm hallucinating again!

Idle supposition was a nice hobby, I suppose, but one thing the fatalist in me knew was that nothing would ever change, not in my world, anyway.

≈≈≈

We rode along in silence for a while, through the peaceful late afternoon New Hampshire countryside. I was exhausted, my pulse was still pounding, my temples were throbbing, I still had bouts of dizziness, and I had a burning ache from the pit of my stomach all the way to my throat. My hands were still trembling out of control, and those freaky Brahms rhapsodies were playing in my head again.

I hated to admit it, but this jackpot had kicked the ever-loving snot out of me. Maybe Bill was half right after all, maybe it was time to call it a game.

"You don't have to do this alone, Wes," Bill broke into my thoughts, "you never have to be alone again."

"Yeah, well I kinda like going it solo. I take my own counsel. One of my insurance clients used to call me the 'Lone Wolf,' and that's me, out there doing things my own way, so I don't have to depend on anybody's bullshit and back stabbing, I learned that real early in life."

Bill shot a quick, appraising glance my way, and then his eyes bored straight through me. "Yeah, that rugged individualist shit's really swell, Wes," he smirked, "so how's it working out for you these days?"

"I'm crapping Twinkies, Bill, can't you tell?"

"Attaboy," he chuckled, and once again I couldn't decide whether he was laughing at me, or at himself for being stuck in this never-ending car ride to Hell.

Damn, I wanted a drink.

≈≈≈

It had been bugging me since we first hit New Hampshire, and finally I had to ask, "So, why'd you quit?"

I was waiting for some cutesy smarmy little patented line of nonsense like, "I got sick and tired of being sick and tired," but his answer was more forthright.

"I told you - I lost it all. One day I woke up in the hospital after another in a long line of binges, and I was in restraints. I had gotten ripped, and had been in a bar fight, and for a change I got the shit beat out of me. I guess I went a little nuts and they put me away in a psych ward for a couple of days. I'd already been kicked out of the house and had lost my day job by then, so I was pretty much out on the streets."

A pained, faraway expression had settled into his features while he spoke – taking a trip back to the scene of the crime sucks, and I knew that better than most.

But then he continued, "I had a record, mostly juvie stuff, a few bar fights and one DUI, but the judge was a straight shooter, a real hard-ass, so he sentenced me to sixty days in the House of Corrections. He told me that he'd suspend it if I agreed to enter an alcohol treatment program for thirty days, then spend a year in a halfway house and do four AA meetings a week. The final condition was that I would need to get my sheet signed by the secretary at each meeting, and then turn it in to the Court every two weeks."

"You're shittin me, you did all that stuff voluntarily?" I asked, incredulous.

"You're kidding me, right, make a choice between jail and a halfway house? I jumped at the chance, and went in for a thirty day stint at Beech Hill that night. The judge had also revoked my license for a year, so I was pretty much grounded anyway. At first I fought the strict rules in the halfway house, and the AA stuff, but somewhere along the line something changed in me, and I finally surrendered."

Again that faraway look, but his features had softened, and he went on, "It was the strangest thing, like nothing I've ever experienced. One day I just stopped fighting the world, and to this moment I consider it to have been the grace of God coming into my life. I just let it all go, everything, the stress, the worry, the fear, the anger, the shame, the self–hate, and in their place this feeling of peace and calm came over me. I finally felt like I knew where I was supposed to be, like I was home, that I belonged, and everything's been on the up and up ever since. It was like I had lost the battle, but won the war."

He remained silent for a moment, almost like he was back there at the epiphany, and then he changed the subject, "So how about you, any good war stories?"

"Yeah, a few," I replied, "nothing big though. I got PC'd and spent the night in jail a half dozen times for driving under, had a few drunk driving accidents, and I had to plead nolo once to drunk driving. They fined me $200, and sentenced me to attend a Whiskey 101 class at the county courthouse one night a week for two months. It was a joke, half the people who attended showed up hammered every night, slept through it and went back to the bars as soon as the class was over. I had a sales job on the road, and needed my license, so I played their game, stayed free of trouble for a year, and then they cleared my record."

I hesitated for a moment, then added, "I've also lost about five or six good professional jobs to the booze, and disappointed a lot of good people along the way."

"That's par for the course. Any drugs, or other troubles?"

"Yeah, plenty of drugs, I've done just about everything except heroin and the needle. The way I went over the top with everything else I always knew that the smack would kill me for sure, so I never even snorted it. Coke's the big one, my second love right behind the alcohol. When I coke I can drink more, and when I drink more I need to coke more."

"That's quite the vicious circle," Bill observed, "it must be great for the nervous system! Did you ever stop to think that there are a hell of a lot of ways to die from alcohol and other drugs besides shooting dope? There's a saying in the Program that goes, 'it doesn't matter whether you smoke it, snort it, swallow it, shoot it or shove it up your ass, it all goes to the same place.'"

"I'll be sure to remember that, maybe I'll tack it on the wall by my bed, but I'm not worried," I said, then added, "in fact, my first alcohol counselor suggested that I should have been a chemist, what with the way I mixed all of my drugs and alcohol."

Bill just shook his head in exasperation.

After a moment I continued, "I had a couple of bar fights, but they were no big deal, although I got stomped really good at a roadhouse bar over in Maine by three guys about ten years ago, and I almost lost my right eye and my right nut. One of them didn't like me dancing with his girlfriend. The assholes lifted a grand in coke money off me for my trouble, which really pissed off my friends when I showed up empty-handed the next day."

Then I added, "And wouldn't you know, my buddies didn't seem to care all that much whether I was half dead, they just wanted to know where the freakin money and the coke were, neither of which I had answers for."

"Tough luck, but as they say, shit happens, you oughta know that by now, Wes."

"Yeah, whatever... so you've been sober ever since you left that halfway house?"

"Oh yeah, sober and grateful for having survived all of that crap, and I even got back together with my wife. The kids have pretty much accepted me also, except for my oldest, but he's having his own problems with substance abuse. It's a family disease, after all," he said, then added proudly, "and they even gave the day job back to me."

"Do you still hit meetings?"

"Hell yeah, I hit meetings, because I wouldn't be sober or alive otherwise! I still attend four meetings a week, sponsor a couple of guys, and volunteer at the Hill. I love sober life, and hanging out with recovering people. They're the best medicine you could ever imagine, they taught me how to laugh and cry again, and how to live life on life's terms."

He paused, then cracked a big shit-eating grin and said, "And this is the fun part, getting my "remember-when's" by driving guys like you up here. It keeps everything green and fresh in my mind, and makes me really, really grateful that I'm not you anymore," and then he broke out into a hearty roar of laughter.

"You're a real bundle of laughs, Bill, so maybe someday you could win a comedy hour and make enough money to buy a new freakin car," I said, scowling.

"And maybe someday you'll be fortunate enough to look back at all of this and laugh also, Wes. I'm praying for that, because today could end up being the best day of your life, if you just allow it to be."

We were approaching a rest area, and I said, "Yeah, you're absolutely right, Bill, things are hitting on all cylinders today. But meanwhile, could you pull into that rest area so I can puke again? I wouldn't wanna ruin your fine Corinthian leather upholstery."

"Sure, whatever you say, Mr. Lone Wolf, you're running the show," he said, and then he broke out into another spasm of uncontrolled laughter that was really beginning to get on my nerves.

"Screw you," I muttered, and then I leaped out of the car and collapsed onto my knees behind a nearby stand of bushes.

≈≈≈

"We're almost there," Bill announced, as we made a right turn off the main road and began climbing a bumpy dirt track that wound through a steep, wooded incline.

I knew that we were beginning the long ascent to the Alps, which was situated at the very top of the hill.

We had driven along mostly in silence for the past twenty minutes, and I was finally feeling a little better. That last bout of vomiting had done its job, and much of the remaining poison had been expelled from my system.

Now I was just weak, exhausted, washed out, uncaring, and I remained silent as we proceeded up the slope. I just wanted to swallow two or three blues and go to sleep for about a week, and I surely wasn't looking forward to the check-in process, and the endless questions and poking and prodding.

And I was praying that they still had that same steady-handed phlebotomist who had found my vein on the first stick the last time I was up there.

We exited the tree line and arrived at Beech Hill, rolling to a stop at the main entrance to the building. I recalled with dismay that I had walked out this very same door, sober and full of short-lived hope and optimism, just two short months ago.

Yet now here I was, back again, just another broken down drunk crawling into rehab in defeat. What was this, five times, or six in the past five years? I couldn't remember, and I no longer cared.

But my new best pal wasn't finished with me quite yet.

"Wes, do me a favor," he began, as he shut down the engine, "just give it a try. Play the game whether you believe in it or not. What have you got to lose? You're a good man, and it's clear that you've got a good head on your shoulders when you want to use it. But sometimes it's the smart ones who have the biggest problem getting sober, because they think they can outwit their disease. You can't beat it, nobody can, and you'll die trying if you keep fighting it. You deserve better than that."

He let that sink in and then continued, his eyes boring into me, "One day, just keep it to one day, or one hour, or one heartbeat if that's what it takes. I'm telling you straight, anybody can stay sober for that long - anybody! I'm a living example of that, and you can be too!"

"Yah, well, I'll see. I just want to go to sleep now, for a really long time. I'm beat, more tired than I've ever been in my life."

"Well, maybe that's the fight going out of you - maybe you're finally ready to surrender and get on with your life. You deserve it."

"I don't know about that. Maybe it's just the booze going out of me, but like I said, I'm beat, and I don't want to talk about it anymore."

"One day, Wes, just one day at a time."

Finally I bit, "One question, Bill. Was it worth it? In the end, no bullshit, was it really worth it?"

"Oh yeah, it was worth every second, Wes," he said, as a slow, easy smile spread across his face.

We exited the car then, and Bill went around to the trunk to retrieve my duffel bag. It was a serene late afternoon in the Monadnocks, and the spring foliage had acquired that vibrant green hue that is so characteristic of June in the northern mountains of New England.

I suppose that to many people the scenic beauty would have represented an affirmation of the eternal renewal of Nature, and of the human spirit, but I couldn't have cared less at that moment. I was wrapped tight, sick, vibrating, and all my shields were up. I just wanted a fistful of my blues, and a quiet bunk to crash in.

Bill handed me my duffel bag, then stared hard into my eyes once again. He stuck out his hand, and I shook it as he reminded me, "Just one day at a time Wes, that's all, one day, one hour, one moment, or one heartbeat, whatever it takes."

He paused, and then he said something that I have never forgotten, "And remember this, Wes, God deals with forever, but you just need to take care of twenty-four hours."

I was beaten and broken, hoping for a really quick goodbye with no last minute AA sermons, and just then a staffer walked up, took my bag, and indicated that I should follow him, so I turned and started toward the door.

Bill wasn't giving up without one final comment, however, as he called after me, "Oh, yeah, and that judge who sentenced me to all of those AA meetings and the halfway house? He's my sponsor now," he yelled, "I learned from a master," and with that he roared with laughter as he climbed back into his car.

I turned, just as he began to pull away, and shouted, "Yeah, well I'll be calling you pretty soon to ask you to be my sponsor, Chief, so we'll see how long your swell serenity lasts."

He must have heard me, because that old shit bucket of his began to accelerate, its tires chirping, and then he went fishtailing down the drive throwing up a wall of gravel in his tracks.

I could have sworn that I heard his fiendish laughter even after his car had disappeared into the tree line.

I turned once more toward the entrance, fought off a dizzy spell, then walked cautiously toward the front door, mindful again of the bitter irony that was tearing me apart. It had been almost two months since I walked out this door full of hope and optimism, looking forward like a naive sixteen year old to a new life, and to getting together with Blue Eyes back in the World.

But now, again, for God only knew how many times, all I felt was hopelessness, self-loathing and an emptiness of the spirit that I feared would never know peace for as long as I walked the earth.

All that was left was to repeat to myself a line from a book that I had read a long time ago, about a grunt going off to do battle in a faraway land, as he muttered his sad existential lament to the Gods of the Darkness, "Fuck it, don't mean nothing, so just drive on."

And that summed it up for me in spades, so I took a deep breath, squared my shoulders, pushed open the door, and then stepped through the looking glass one final time.

"Yeah, drive on, soldier, and never let 'em see you sweat, no matter what!"

No big deal, because it was just another day in the life of a down and out drunk.

≈≈≈

A blast of cool, refreshing air hit me as I entered the main lobby of the building. The weather had turned much warmer since my last trip up here, so the building's air conditioning made a welcome contrast to the stuffy atmosphere in Bill's beaten up old junker.

I took a couple of moments to study my surroundings, and to regain my bearings. I was still light-headed, feeling shaky and apprehensive, and I hadn't quite gotten my equilibrium back yet.

Nothing had changed much since my last visit, although I had been expecting to see more residents, so I figured that most of the population was out on the back observation deck that doubled as a smoking facility, taking in the views and getting a last hit of nicotine before dinner was served.

Then I remembered, however, that Bill had mentioned that the population was about half of what it had been back in March. He told me that the Canadian province of Ontario, which had been a major supplier of residents to the Hill, had recently ceased the financing of treatment programs in the United States for its citizens.

That was a damned shame, I thought, because I rather liked those Canadian drunks and addicts. It turns out that we're all pretty much the same wherever we live, and I thought that I would have enjoyed going on a respectable weekend binge with most of them.

Alcohol and drugs, the great equalizers, they hold no respect for international boundaries, they merely seek out the lowest common denominator.

Well, c'est la vie, that explained why the Canadian flag was flying at half-mast on the pole in front of the building. I had to hand it to the prankster on that one - it was a nice touch.

≈≈≈

I couldn't stall any longer, so I began to walk slowly across the spacious, circular common room. It held a couple of group meeting areas, several counseling cubicles and, at the far side of the room, the nurses' station that doubled as an admitting desk.

Even from this distance I could make out the *Fishbowl*, which was situated right behind the station. It was a makeshift mini-ER, and it was there that I had been placed under constant observation during my first night at the Hill back in March.

Hallways split off from the sides of the room, one each heading for the men's and women's residential wings, while others led to the cafeteria, private counseling and administration areas.

I had made it almost halfway across the room, and was about to congratulate myself for not falling flat on my face, or going into convulsions, when a young, slim woman in nurse's scrubs came striding toward me from a corner office.

She was clearly intent on intercepting me, and she looked vaguely familiar as a warm smile of recognition came to her face.

"Hi Wes, I don't know if you remember me - I'm Donna. We talked a few times when you were up here back in the spring," she said, still smiling as she held out her hand.

Then it all came flooding back to me in a rush - of course I remembered her! Donna had been my Nightingale when I first arrived in March, and had been on the floor when I was carried in by Bill and the orderly. She was a kind and gentle soul who found great satisfaction and fulfillment in administering to the perpetual conga line of sick and suffering alcoholics and addicts who arrived daily at the Alps, and she had always taken the time to be supportive whenever we ran into each other on the floor.

You just knew that there was something very special about this woman - it was in her soft-spoken words, her eyes, and in the natural grace with which she flowed around the floor administering to "her" clients.

I shook her hand tentatively, somewhat embarrassed by my forgetfulness.

"Hi Donna, I'm kinda scattered right now, but yeah, I surely do remember you, because you had some good advice for me, and I wish I'd taken it. This latest jackpot was a killer, I never knew what hit me."

She nodded in understanding, then said, "How about we go out back and talk for a while before you check in? Would that be OK?"

She caught me by surprise with that one, and true to form my alkie paranoia kicked into overdrive. Shit, what's she trying to tell me, that they're booting me before I even get checked in? Did that damned insurance company bail on me? Am I gonna have to head back home tonight with Bill? Are the beer and wine stores still open? Damn, good luck with that, Chief, because if they're kicking me loose then you will most surely earn your hazardous duty pay on that run!

Yet all she had asked was, "How about we go out back and talk for a while before you check in? Would that be OK?"

The anxiety must have been written all over my face, because Donna smiled again, then quickly reassured me:

"Relax, everything's fine. I already got it cleared with the Doc. I just want to talk to you about some things. You're a good man, Wes, and you deserve to have a good life. A few of us on staff today were saddened to hear that you'd be coming back up here, so I just want to give you a hand."

"Well, I'll be honest with you, Donna, I made every effort to find another detox before I called here. No offense, it's just that..." and my words trailed off.

"I understand, Wes. I know that it must have been difficult to make that call, but there's nothing to be self-conscious about. The main thing is that you're here now, and we all want to help, so follow me."

With that she led me toward a door that was situated off to the right of the nurses' station. It opened up onto a small, shaded patio and garden that overlooked the surrounding hills, and it was obviously a quiet oasis for staffers to escape the stress on the floor, have a snack, or grab a quick smoke.

At this time of day the patio appeared to be enveloped within an unworldly aura, softly lit by the late afternoon sun that filtered through the oaks and maples protecting the rear of the building.

The view across to the Monadnock Range was magnificent, the sun splashing the vibrant green mountains with a subdued yellow glow that mesmerized me.

≈≈≈

We settled into garden chairs, and then I pulled out my cigarettes and looked inquiringly at her. She nodded an okay for me to light up, and we sat in silence for a few minutes taking in the views.

"So, do you want to talk about it?"

"I don't know, there's really nothing much to say. I just don't seem to get it, so I get frustrated and wonder why I bother, and then the next thing I know I'm coming out of another jackpot. I tried, Donna, I really did, but every time I start to think that I can make it I end up self-destructing. Things were going pretty well, really well actually, but it's like I figured out that I don't deserve good stuff to happen to me, so I intentionally fu... excuse me, sabotage myself."

"You certainly aren't alone there, Wes, that's part of your disease, but you can change that thought process. It isn't wired into your DNA, so you just need to think it through and cut yourself some slack. You CAN change! You're a good person, and whether you realize it or not people like you, they respect you, they want to be around you."

I gave her a sideways glance of skepticism at that, then snorted sarcastically, "Yeah, that's me, Donna, I'm a real people magnet - they come from miles around to sit at my knee and learn about life according to Wes, hell, I even have a fan club!"

She chuckled momentarily, but then her eyes clouded and a serious expression came over her face. "There you go, bringing yourself down again. That's your disease talking! It lies to you, because it wants you drunk and high and out of control, and it wants you dead! Do you understand that, Wes? It wants you hating yourself, shunning the world, fighting life, because it wants you dead!"

I started to say, "Well, maybe it's got the right idea," but then thought better of it.

She paused, then continued in a softer tone, "But you can stop it. You just need to be willing to change. That's all you have to do is be willing - willingness is the key that opens the door to change."

"You make it sound so easy - just make a wish, snap my fingers, click my heels and everything will be swell again. It doesn't work that way for me, Donna! It's like I have a built-in self-destruct mechanism that kicks in as soon as I think I have a chance to make it this time. It's been like that since I was five years old! I screw up everything, before it screws me!"

A frown crossed her face briefly after my last words, as if she recognized something, but then she continued, "Do you hear yourself? You're still negative, talking yourself down! You don't need anybody else to sabotage you when you think like that, you do it to yourself! But you can change - you must change if you're going to survive. Please, Wes, give yourself a chance, because you're running out of time!"

I hated to admit it, but she had a point. Living the life that I had put myself through over the past twenty-five years had taken me to places I could never have imagined I would experience in my worst nightmares.

Then I recalled a saying that I'd heard at one of the handful of AA meetings I had forced myself to attend over the years, "If somebody else did to me what I've done to myself, I'd beat the snot out of them."

Now that, I understood.

And yet I continued to sabotage myself, time after time after time, but now the clock was inexorably ticking out the last minute or two before midnight.

Somehow, somewhere, and without ever noticing it, I had crossed that invisible line which I had once upon a time in an innocent child's fairy tale promised myself I would never violate.

I had become accustomed to the decadence and moral equivocation with which I lived my life. I fed into the distrust, the fear, self-hatred, lies, betrayal, and the total alienation from all that was good and fair and beautiful in the world. I maintained a negative, almost pathological view of life, for if I didn't believe that anything good could ever happen, then it stood to reason that I could never be disappointed.

It was as if my addictions had altered my DNA to the point that I was a mutant, an exile from humanity.

Donna was correct. I hadn't lived, I had survived, at least so far, and I had crossed a lot of boundaries that in another time I had considered inviolable, in order to do just that

But now the denial was coming to an end, and I was broken, dead inside, feeling a hopelessness and a soul sickness that made the very act of breathing almost too difficult to attempt.

Continue to survive like this? Why bother, I had stopped caring.

Somehow change my thinking, somehow believe that there was hope for my recovery, for a better life? Inconceivable.

And yet what was the alternative? It was change, or die - there was no middle ground left for me to hide in anymore.

But now here was Donna, picking up right where Bill had left off, challenging me to do the most terrifying thing that I could conceive of – to change, to become vulnerable, to admit defeat.

To surrender.

My skin crawled at the very thought of it.

Donna broke into my thoughts then, "Have you ever heard of 'HOW?'" she asked.

"How, what?" I replied, curious.

"It's an acronym, H, O, W. The letters stand for honesty, open-mindedness and willingness," she said, pausing to let the words sink in.

Then she continued, "The 'h' means becoming rigorously honest with ourselves, and with other people, the 'o' is for remaining open-minded to the possibility that we can change who we are, and how we look at life, and then, finally, the 'w' means having the willingness, and courage, to actually change, and to do the work we need to do to get better."

Three little letters, but to me they stood taller and more intimidating than the mountains that surrounded the building.

"That sounds like quite a lot of work, Donna."

"Yes, it is, Wes, but you don't have to take it on all at once. All you need to do is keep an open mind, and try to change, a little bit at a time. Just take it little by slow, like they say in the program. It's all about progress, not perfection, just trying to get a little bit better every day."

"I wouldn't know where to begin."

"Wes, don't you see, you've already begun - you started down the path five years ago when you went to your first treatment center. That was the beginning! And now you're here, again, still trying. There's something inside of you that keeps plugging away, always trying to come back, always trying to recover from this disease."

"Yeah, well if I was a doc I'd probably tell them to pull the plug right about now, because this guy's toast."

"You know you don't mean that, you can't even fool yourself anymore, you're here, and that says it all!"

"Yeah, but this is about the sixth rodeo I've been to."

"Don't look back, Wes, that's over and done with, and you can't change it, so just look inside yourself at the 'here and now.' Today can be the start of a brand new life for you!"

I remained silent, and then she changed her tack, "What are you looking for, Wes? What's the one thing you want more than anything else in the world right now?"

Damn, that hit a nerve, and I didn't even need to think about it, because it had been renting space in my head for years. I had been a tortured soul for longer than I could remember, always negative, always afraid to open myself up to opportunity, always seeking to kill the pain and fear and shame and doubt and disgust that ruled my life in the only way I knew, by drinking and drugging myself to the brink of death.

Yet all along I had been seeking just one simple little thing.

"All I ever wanted was to find some peace of mind, and to stop hating myself," was all I could say.

She reached over and took my hand, then whispered softly, "You're here. You're doing that right now. You're being honest with me, and with yourself. And you're not alone, you never have to be alone again, Wes, never!"

"It's too hard, too overwhelming. I took things way too far, there's no going back!"

"No, that's not true! It's like I said, just take it easy, and take it one day at a time, one hour at a time, one moment at a time, or one heartbeat at a time, whatever it takes! That's all you need to be concerned with, Wes, because a journey of a thousand miles starts with a single step. So just don't pick up a drink for one day, or one damned second! You can do this! Please, Wes, you need to do this, so let it all go!"

"It still seems impossible."

"Try it, Wes, just for one day – today! What do you have to lose? It's like we say, if AA and recovery isn't for you then you can always go back out there, and your misery will be happily refunded."

"Just today, huh?"

"Just today, just for this one moment! There's nothing left for you out there, Wes, you've run out of options - it's over! This terrible war that you've been fighting your entire life is over, but don't you see, you've won, you're alive, you're here, you're being honest with me and with yourself! You've been given the keys to the Kingdom, now use them!"

I'll never fully understand why, but it was as if the weight of the world slipped off my shoulders at that moment. Perhaps it was this woman's gentle grace and unconditional love for a broken man, or maybe it was just my time, or this quiet garden, or perhaps the sequence of events that had played out over the past six hours as if by divine intervention.

Whatever the reason, I felt a sense of peace and belonging that I had never experienced before settle into my body. It was as if all of my muscles went slack at the same moment, and then my mind stopped its tortured racing for the first time in memory.

≈≈≈

I surrendered then, in that serene little garden on a mountain in New Hampshire. I let it all go, let it all drain out of me and, unabashedly, I wept. The tears began streaming down my cheeks as I cried like a baby. They might have begun as grief, but soon I was overcome by feelings of joy and release, and I knew then the serenity that Bill had spoken about just an hour before when he told me about his own surrender.

"That's it, just let it all out, Wes, let it go, you're going to be okay, I promise, you're going to be okay," Donna whispered softly, reaching out to hold my hand again.

For the first time in my life I felt like I had come home, and I knew no shame as the tears continued to flow.

≈≈≈

Donna and I talked for another twenty minutes, and toward the end I laughed. It was deep, genuine, from the gut. I found myself liking it, and I couldn't remember the last time I had laughed like that.

She took me by the hand, then led me back into the building, and over to the admitting desk.

I was shivering, but not from the air conditioning.

Her final words of advice on that tranquil afternoon were, "Don't look back Wes, look around you, right here, in the present moment. Live for today, and just don't drink for one single day."

And then she hugged me, and that was that.

≈≈≈

I filled out some papers at the front desk, then signed them.

The staffer informed me that the insurance company hadn't made an official decision about my status, but the representative had indicated that it was just a formality due to it being Sunday. He had called his decision-maker and had run my case by him, and his boss had given it a preliminary approval, and would confirm it in the morning if everything checked out okay.

Ordinarily I would have fallen prey to my normal paranoia, fearful that he'd change his mind overnight, but I decided to go with the flow and look at it optimistically.

After all, what choice did I really have?

Them the admitting nurse hit me with a bunch of the usual questions, and took my vitals. No surprise, they were still way up there in the red zone, but heading in the right direction at least.

She then called over my favorite phlebotomist and he slipped that needle into my vein so easily I hardly knew he had done it, and that was all there was to admittance.

But then something peculiar occurred. The nurse informed me that the dayshift Doc had scripted me for the valiums, so she suggested that I take one, just to bring me down a little. But I declined her offer, and rather than experiencing apprehension or fear, I felt relaxed, strong, at peace with myself and with my decision.

To this day I believe that my refusal to take that one little pill to solve a so-called problem marked the first real validation that I had surrendered to my disease.

A staffer then showed me the way to my room. There were three beds, but there didn't appear to be any other luggage, nor evidence that there were other residents occupying the room. That was just as well, because I didn't feel like company that night, and I really wanted to avoid getting trapped in a long drunkalogue session with curious new roommates.

The staffer informed me that the dining hall was still open, and that they had saved some of the nightly specials for me. The last thing I wanted was a big meal at that point, but I was still edgy and wired, so I figured it would be a good excuse to get away from the room for a while.

The dining room was located on the way to the smoking deck, which was my primary destination, so I decided to grab some tried and true remedies for the acid stomach that always came along after one of my binges.

Ten minutes later I had politely refused all of the specials that the cook had been saving for me, and was picking away at a pile of french fries that I hoped would line my stomach. I had also polished off one large glass of ginger ale, and was now nursing a second one.

I began belching out of control then, but that was perfectly okay, because experience had taught me that the drink would act as a natural antacid, and would offload a lot of the gas that was making me feel bloated and on the verge of nausea.

Evidently my home remedy was working, a little, anyway, so I picked up my spoon and dug into a large soup bowl that was full to overflowing with chocolate ice cream. It tasted like manna from Heaven.

French fries, ginger ale and ice cream, a feast fit for kings, so what more could a detoxing drunk ask for?

I soon polished off everything, belched a half-dozen times, and then made my way out to the smoking deck.

≈≈≈

There were perhaps a dozen residents who were sitting or standing around in small groups when I arrived on the deck.

I still didn't feel like entering into any big discussions at that moment, so I walked to the far end of the platform and peered out through the gathering darkness to the shadowy outlines of the Monadnocks.

They were shimmering, washed softly by the illumination of the rising full moon.

I let my exhausted mind go blank then, as I absorbed the sights and sounds of that beautiful late spring evening in the mountains. It was cooling off rapidly, so I drew several deep breaths and exhaled slowly, allowing my tortured body to relax and release some of its toxins, as I listened to the gentle chirping of the season's early crickets.

I remained silent and alone, leaning into the railing of the deck, while a sensation of peace and calm unlike anything I had ever experienced slowly descended upon me. I felt relaxed, empowered, and unencumbered by my past.

I wondered, then, "Is this what it feels like to be free of the obsession to drink, to stop fighting life? Is this what Donna and Bill meant by "letting go?""

I had no answer for that, but I held out hope that someday I would.

≈≈≈

A few of the other residents came over several minutes later, so we exchanged introductions. Two of them were members of the diminishing Canadian contingent, so I had a smoke while we talked about that, and then they gave me the lowdown on the current events at the Hill.

I gave them a five minute recap of my own day, then excused myself, almost asleep on my feet, and mentioned that I would catch up with them in the morning.

≈≈≈

My luck held. I had no roommates that night, so I took the bed next to the window that looked out onto the valley and the mountains beyond. I unpacked, stored away the small wardrobe that Blue Eyes had skillfully arranged, and hit the sack by ten o'clock.

I was exhausted, but my mind couldn't stop racing yet, so I thought back to the events of the day, and recited a prayer of thanks that I had survived it. I thought of Blue Eyes, and Bill, and Donna, and wondered anew at how they had appeared as if by heavenly design to save me from myself. I had never been religious, but even somebody as cynical as me had to marvel at the manner by which everything had played out on this day.

And then, in the twilight between waking and slumber, I recalled the words to the First Step of Alcoholics Anonymous: "We admitted we were powerless over alcohol, that our lives had become unmanageable."

Well, that pretty much summed it up for me. I was the poster boy for unmanageability and chaos, and it was beginning to look so simple that I briefly wondered how I could ever have ignored the obvious for so long.

But then I realized that this was what Donna and Bill had meant when they urged me to "let it go," to remain anchored in the present moment, and to just not drink for one day.

I knew that I had a lot of difficult, painful work ahead of me, if I was to survive, but if I could stay away from a drink and the drugs for just one day then I had hope, and a chance at having a good life.

It was at that moment that a quote from one of the few AA meetings I had attended over the years came to me: "The journey of a lifetime starts with the first step," so that was where I would begin.

The darkness closed in upon me then, and my last thought before slipping off into the Sleep of the Dead was, "What if?"

Part Two: The Beginning

"When you ain't got nothing, you got nothing to lose."

From the song, "Like a Rolling Stone"
by Bob Dylan

God reveals Himself to me in many forms today - in the perfect silence of a solo trek through the snowy Vermont woods on a brilliant January morning, in a newborn's contented gurgle as it suckles at its mother's breast, in the luminous pools of a woman's eyes, in the glint of the spring sun reflecting off the dew-lined web of a spider at daybreak, in the sharp, violent death of a meteor that flashes across the August sky, in the solitude of a walk along a beach in the gentle early morning rain, and in the tears of an alcoholic who has surrendered to his disease, and who by losing has won the biggest prize of all.

≈≈≈

I was unceremoniously delivered into the world in a hospital in Boston, Massachusetts, in the summer of 1950, and I believe that the wisest thing my parents could have done that day would have been to wheel me out of the delivery room and straight into a meeting of Alcoholics Anonymous.

But they didn't, of course, even though that simple act might have prevented all manner of nonsense and heartache for me, and for anybody who had the misfortune of loving or depending on me over the next forty years.

Or maybe not. Perhaps I was destined to drink every drink and ingest every drug I could get my hands on, until I was on the brink of death, because only then would I be able to discover something in myself worth living for, something that would turn an angry, lost man into a grateful recovering child of God.

So I guess it's like the song says, "You know you've got to go to Hell before you get to Heaven." Well, I was knocking on the basement door, no doubt about that.

For whatever reason I was a natural born drunk, so I sought out the insanity from an early age, and a little earlier you got to read all about the final pathetic results of that twenty-five year reign of terror that I waged upon myself, and upon the world.

Oh, and by the way, there's another saying that you hear once in a while in the Halls that goes, "I stopped drinking on the day before I was to die," and I believe that is true in my case. I was on my last legs and going down for the count at the ripe old age of forty-one, physically broken, emotionally dead and spiritually bankrupt, with a chip on my shoulder that you could have landed a 747 on.

I wasn't a nice person, nor was I was a reliable friend, brother, son, lover, employee, neighbor, boss, you name it.

In fact, I wasn't even a good drinking or drugging buddy, because I wanted all of yours also.

But please don't take it personally. It's not that I disliked you, it's simply that I despised myself, so you were just a convenient target for me to deflect my self-loathing at while I pretended that everything was just fine and dandy in my dysfunctional little world of denial.

I called it WesWorld, and it was a wretched, sordid, pathetic little insane asylum, a mythical land where the laws of gravity, common sense, free choice and love for my fellow human beings had been warped beyond all recognition, and then ground into dust.

The good news today is that by the grace of God, and the Fellowship of Alcoholics Anonymous, I don't need to live in that neighborhood anymore.

And the better news is that you don't ever have to live like that yourself, if you just take life one day, one hour, one moment and one heartbeat at a time, and you just don't drink or drug, no matter what.

It really is that simple.

But that doesn't mean it's always that easy, because life has a way of keeping things interesting.

≈≈≈

If you came here today seeking solutions for all of your life's problems, well, I regret to inform you that I don't have any quick fixes or magic formulas for you. This book is primarily about recovery from addiction, and I don't have the experience, nor the diplomas, to discuss the extensive laundry list of problems that we all face in this insane, chaotic world we're fighting to survive in today.

That said, many of the issues that people in recovery struggle with are issues that must also be faced by the population at large, so if you can find any source of strength, or healing, or solace, or inspiration here, then I will be very grateful for having had the opportunity to help you along your path.

It's possible, however, that you're reading this book because you're already in a recovery program for a variety of addictions, and are therefore interested in reading about the general topic of recovery, or to find a fresh slant on it, or to top off the tank with a few additional ideas about it.

If that's the case, then I hope that you will find some food for thought here.

But it's also likely that some of you are reading this book because somewhere deep inside you there's a frightened little voice that's been crying out for help, and you fear that something just isn't right in your life. Perhaps you're afraid that everything is spinning out of control, and you suspect that it might have something to do with the alcohol or the drugs that you've been hitting way too hard, and for way too long.

Perhaps you're thinking, "What happened? How did it ever get this crazy? When did my life run so terribly off the rails?"

Or perhaps it's even reached the point where you're asking, "How do I stop this insanity? I'm frightened, ashamed, but I can't ask anybody for help. I feel like such a failure, so perhaps this misery is all that I deserve!"

Please, stop right there, because now you're indulging in the alcoholic's favorite recreational pastime – stinkin thinkin - and your disease is working you hard. I am here to tell you that you do deserve good things in your life, health, happiness, to love and to be loved, to have the opportunity to live up to your human potential, to have the courage to dream, to go for the stars. We all do, and that is why our Creator placed us all on this tiny little mote of dust in a secret little corner of the Universe, where we may experience fulfillment, and love.

So if you're at the crossroads, and you don't know where to go, or how to stop the insanity, and you came here seeking help for your alcohol or drug problems, then my best advice for you is to read this book, then put it away for a year or two and get your fanny to an Alcoholics Anonymous meeting just as fast as you possibly can.

In fact, skip the book for now and just get your fanny to an AA meeting – today - and if you don't like that meeting, fine, then get yourself to another meeting, and then another, and another, as long as it takes until you find that one special meeting that you connect with.

And I guarantee that sooner or later you will find that one magical meeting that fits you like a glove. You will know beyond a doubt, because you will feel like you have finally come in out of the wilderness, and are home – I promise you that!

≈≈≈

Okay, so first things first – we need to find you a meeting, and that's really simple! Just go to your computer or phone, do a Google search for either "AA" or "Alcoholics Anonymous," then add the name of the town or the zip code that you're interested in on the search line, and voila! In seconds you will find plenty of links to AA sites, meeting lists with days and times, even what type of meeting you're interested in: Open, Closed, General, Men-only, Women-only, Youth, Big Book, 12 Steps and 12 Traditions, Discussion, Gay/Rainbow, meetings with handicapped facilities etc. etc. etc.

There is a meeting for every alcoholic, and for every need, so put this book down right now, walk over to your computer, and do that search that may very well save your life!

And, while we're on the topic, there are similar meetings for many different types of addiction, including narcotics, gambling, sex, smoking, co-dependency, overeating, and many more, so if you fit into any one of those categories you can do that search as well.

In fact, start your own meeting if you can't find the one that addresses your addiction. I just did, and I can proudly state that it's been two months since I touched a golf club, just one day at a time!

Perhaps someday you'll thank me for this, or perhaps not. Either way, please don't worry - I can handle it because I get better just by trying to help you get better. That may sound self-centered, but hopefully you'll understand someday when you're "passing it on" to another sick and suffering alcoholic or addict who has asked you for help.

And when you walk through the door into your first AA meeting beg for help from the first person who comes up to you and shakes your hand and says, "Welcome," even if it's the janitor. It might just save your life, because I promise that from the moment you come through that door you will be introduced to a whole new world of kind, good hearted, courageous people who love you even though they have never met you.

And if you're not into being loved, tough beans. None of us were in the beginning, so we fought it tooth and nail and we lost, and by losing we won, because we now have a life today that is second to none, and you can have that life also!

Oh, and one more thing, please be just like me, and be sure to attend your first meeting filled with plenty of anger and brimstone and objections and arguments about why you're not really an alcoholic or addict, but just terribly misunderstood. People at AA meetings get a big kick out of that because it takes each of us back to when we were new and green, and just as lost and scared and lonely as you are, and I was right there at the head of the class when I came crawling into the Halls straight from the last of my many trips to the detoxes and treatment centers.

But, like the saying goes, "I didn't know what I didn't know," so I had to put myself and everyone I came into contact with through absolute hell before I eventually "got it." Hopefully you can avoid that, and the key there is finding the willingness to change, and having the courage to become humble, and to ask for help.

Yes, it's scary at first, but I promise that it works, and it could save your life.

So what was the "it" that I finally found? Sobriety, peace of mind, health, hope and happiness, and a new way of life that is second to none, for which I will be eternally grateful. And gratitude isn't a word that rolled easily off my tongue when I started coming around the Halls, but I will look you straight in the eye today and tell you that I am the most grateful person on Earth just to have my sobriety, and to have my life back.

You see, I have hope today, and choices, and freedom from fear, and so can you, if you just join us.

≈≈≈

Okay, so here's the thing about that love stuff that's probably had your skin crawling ever since I just mentioned it. Fight it all you want, but you really do deserve to be loved. Yes, you really do, so surrender to your addiction, find a new way of life, and open yourself up to being loved.

There, now that's not so difficult, is it?

Certainly not, because if I could do it, then anybody can!

And if nobody told you today that they love you, well I do – really! I. Love. You. It's a drunk thing, so you probably won't understand it yet, but you just might save my life today because I might run into you at a meeting in a couple of hours, and something you say could make the difference that will prevent me from picking up a drink or a drug for one more day.

And if that isn't reason enough to love you, then I don't know what is.

So we folks in recovery spread unconditional love to each other, and by "giving it away" we get more of it back then we could ever have dreamed possible. It is through this love for one another that we begin to trust, to heal, and to love ourselves, many for the first time in our lives, and it is through this spiritual bond that we remain sober and alive for another day.

We call it being happy, joyous and free. Free from alcohol, free from the drugs, free from fear, free from the bondage of self, and free to live our lives on life's terms!

≈≈≈

"Yesterday's history, and tomorrow's a mystery."

Okay, so while I'm trying to destroy your drinking career, and to transform your very existence, here's a new way to look at the calendar – in a word, don't! Please, just throw it out the window, because all any of us really has is "Today," just twenty-four very brief hours, so why try to complicate things?

I believe that if you and I can remain firmly anchored to this one perfect moment in time, then we will have the opportunity to experience happiness and peace of mind beyond our wildest expectations. We will find ourselves living for the moment in a tiny, safe, manageable bubble known as "Today," and that is all anyone should ever need to be concerned with.

So here's a little "thought experiment." Try to imagine that you woke up this morning and found yourself in a time machine, but this machine is special, and very different from the ones that we read about in science fiction novels by H.G. Wells and others, because it doesn't travel into the future, or back into the past.

In fact, our chariot only exists in space and time for exactly twenty-four hours, no more, no less, and then it ceases to exist. In a blink of God's eye it never was, and it never will be again.

Your role in this experiment is very simple. All you need to do is stay away from a drink and a drug for one day, today, and dedicate your entire effort to maintaining a happy, productive life for the duration of your time machine, just one day, twenty-four hours, and you can't look back with regret, and you can't project your hopes, fears and expectations into the future.

So what would you do? What would you change about the way you live your day? Who would you spend your time with? Where would you go? Would you stick to some type of routine, or would you strike out on a bold new path, experimenting, exploring, testing your limits, taking the road less traveled, smelling the flowers, maybe even writing a book like this, or visiting that museum you always wondered about, or taking your child to the zoo, or visiting that friend who you haven't seen for far too long?

Think about the possibilities – your opportunities would be infinite, and limited only by the extent of your imagination and dreams!

And please remember that when you're in your time machine you only have today, so wouldn't you want to make it the very best day you possibly could? And don't you think that's what your Creator has always wanted for you?

I believe that by remaining present, centered and aware, and grounded and mindful, living only in the present moment, we have the opportunity to experience joy and freedom on a scale unlike anything we have ever known.

Wasting half of our day just hoping, hoping, hoping instead of doing, doing, doing will cease. Mourning a past that we regret, but that we cannot change, will cease. Fretting and worrying about an uncertain future that we have absolutely no control over will cease.

All of those chains that destroy our creativity and optimism, that steal so much of our energy and spirit, that keep us running around like rats on a treadmill, will simply cease to exist.

And, miracle of miracles, when we have cast off all of that nonproductive, soul-draining garbage, in the void that is left we will now find new opportunities, peace of mind, self-respect, fulfillment, happiness and love, many of us for the first time in our lives. And isn't that what we all want at the end of the day, to have the opportunity to live up to our God-given potential, to know peace and serenity, to live life to its fullest?

I vote yes to that, so please strap yourself into your time machine and take it for a spin, just for today, and take things one day at a time, one hour at a time, one moment at a time, one heartbeat at a time, or whatever it takes.

And relax, and don't take yourself too seriously, because life does have a way of working out in the end once we stop trying to micromanage every moment of it.

"Let go, and let God," as we say, "and seek out your joy."

≈≈≈

Hmm, did he just bring up the topic of "God?"

Yes, I did, because when life has beaten you to your knees, it probably wouldn't hurt to say a little prayer to the Big Guy while you're crawling around down there.

≈≈≈

If you're a newcomer who has recently begun attending AA meetings then you have no doubt heard us speak about God, and it wouldn't have been out of the ordinary for you to have applied a religious connotation to that word – I know that I did in the beginning, anyway.

However, after several decades of attending AA meetings, and working a committed program of recovery, it is my strong opinion, but only *my* opinion, that there is no such religious connotation either implied or stated by Alcoholics Anonymous.

I ought to know. In my final drinking years, when I had been introduced to AA and was bouncing in and out of treatment centers and meetings, I searched high and low for that little secret, hoping to discover that AA was just a front for organized religion. I wanted desperately to find that connection, because at the end of the day I wanted any excuse I could dredge up to keep drinking, because that was the easy way out, and because I was terrified of change.

In effect I had created a great big wall of denial that I could hide behind, which meant that I stayed away from AA for many years after I was initially introduced to it. And in my blindness and denial I lost, in too many ways to count, because for me that presumed connection between the God, or Higher Power of AA, and that of the Gods of organized religion, simply didn't exist.

I had mistaken religion (a shared group consciousness of a specific Being) for spirituality (an individual's yearning to be close to "the One").

There may be many reasons not to get sober, although I can't think of any legitimate ones, but fear, anger, distrust or cynicism about the God(s) that we individually pray to in Alcoholics Anonymous should never be one of them.

In my case the rationale for rejecting AA was based on my general distrust of all organized religions, and I feared that AA would force me to adhere to the teachings of a strict, rigid, religious God of AA's choosing.

As it turned out, nothing could have been further from the truth.

I humbly admit today that I was wrong, because AA has never once in twenty-six years asked me to make a religious statement, or to support a religious point of view of any kind whatsoever.

What AA has done, however, is help me to get sober so that I can make more informed choices about my ethics, morality and spirituality, and who or what I worship. As a result, my life has been enriched by that freedom of choice in so many ways that I could never have imagined.

My personal concept of God is multifaceted, and it draws upon many experiences and observations over the years that have brought me to this singular place in the world which I inhabit. This is my unique space, and it has been shaped by *my* own personal life experiences, spirituality, and sobriety. It is the realm of the God of *my* understanding, not anybody else's, and *my* Higher Power, who I chose to call God, seems to be perfectly fine with that.

≈≈≈

I've thrown in this brief discussion about God because I believe that those three little letters have kept more people away from recovery than any other word in Webster's Dictionary.

And I ought to know, because I was one of them for many years, and my denial cost me more things than I can count. By staying away from AA I lost friendships, relationships, my health, jobs, finances, self-respect, love, and so much more.

But most of all I lost me.

I shudder to think how many other sick and suffering people, particularly potential newcomers, have also misunderstood, misinterpreted or rejected the concept of "God," as it is used in the Fellowship, just as I had done. As a result, many have stayed away from recovery programs such as Alcoholics Anonymous, and many, including the people they love, have suffered the same terrible consequences that I did.

So when everything finally hit the fan, and I surrendered to my disease, one of the most difficult things I had to come to grips with during my early sobriety was my spirituality, or more to the point, my lack of spirituality.

From what I've heard around the halls of AA over the years I wasn't alone.

I had been brought up in one of the Protestant sects, and had attended church and Sunday school until I reached the age of twelve, at which time organized religion and I went our separate ways. There was no defining gee-whiz moment where I broke away, rather just apathy, hormones, and a growing sense of independence which bordered on rebelliousness.

A few years later I took my first drink, and then my first drugs, and I was off to the races.

I didn't invite God along for that death-defying thrill ride, and for the next twenty-five years I never once considered that God existed, or would ever have cared about Wes as I went hurtling down the road to self-destruction.

Needless to say, it was a lonely, barren world I inhabited.

All my denial ended in that quiet garden on the mountain in New Hampshire, however, where I surrendered to my disease. Without fully realizing it I had established a spiritual relationship with the God of my understanding, because I had turned my will and my life over to the care of a Power greater than myself, who I called God.

What I have discovered over the years is that God is, for me, a kind and loving companion who watches over me, and who offers support and friendship, inspiration, hope and affirmation. My God is not a God of any formal religion, but rather of the spirit – my spirit.

My God also allows me to make informed choices, reach out of myself to engage the world, take chances, chase my dreams and go for the prize in the Cracker Jack box, and my church is a beach, and a mountain and a forest where I celebrate Mass.

My God is also patient, because I certainly seek Him out a lot on any given day, and I have even been known to give Him advice once in a while.

The funny thing is, He seems to get a big chuckle out of that, so I'll relate an anecdote about one of the most fun experiences I've ever had, and leave the discussion about God to that.

≈≈≈

It was a sunny, warm, late summer's afternoon in 2009 as I sped down the narrow Appalachian Gap Road from Camel's Hump toward the picturesque village of Waitsfield, Vermont.

To my delight, while sliding out of a sharp turn just above Mad River Glen, I happened upon a yearling moose which stood just over six foot at the shoulders. He was strolling blissfully down the uphill lane without a care in the world, so I slowed my car to a crawl, threw the transmission into neutral, and coasted along next to that magnificent creature.

I was awestruck.

We couldn't have been more than three or four feet apart, which probably wasn't the brightest thing to do on my part, but so be it. I got sober, but that doesn't necessarily mean that I got sane, and I'm sure that several of my friends would readily attest to that fact.

Ever the glib conversationalist, I decided to be first to make the introductions.

"Yo, Bullwinkle, how ya doon?" I inquired in my best formal Boston accent, craning my neck to look up at him in wonder.

He stared at me rather quizzically, then continued on with his afternoon constitutional.

"Super day, eh? You digging this weather, or what?"

Nothing, no response, not even a shake of the antlers, this was one taciturn moose.

"You meet any cute moosettes out heah?" I queried.

I was greeted with a forlorn stare, and what I interpreted as a grunt of displeasure.

But, ever the optimist, I forged ahead. "So, whaddaya think about this stock market meltdown? You got any commodity ideas that'll work in a recession? Gold, silver? Whaddaya think about Treasuries? You shortin' any currencies?"

He snorted and stared balefully at me, so I thought it prudent to take that opportunity to make sure that my foot was pumping the clutch, ready to pop it and skedaddle out of there if he got testy - you know, just in case he was getting his clock cleaned in the financial markets like me and everybody else.

I coasted along next to Bullwinkle for a couple hundred more yards, happily chattering away. To his credit he never uttered a word, just eventually snorted again, shook his head in what I could only interpret as disdain for the incredibly boring human, and then drifted silently into the forest.

I will believe until my dying day that I spoke to God on that remarkable summer afternoon - there is just no other way to describe the joy I experienced in that serendipitous meeting. That single, perfect moment in time was a personal gift that shaped *my* life experience, *my* beliefs, and was woven into the cloth of *my* sobriety.

And to this day it forms a basis for *my* spirituality, not anyone else's.

I have discovered great beauty, order and serenity in Nature over the years, and I believe that there is a perfect, exquisite wisdom, ageless, that underlies and unites the fabric of the Universe. I interpret it to be a spiritual heartbeat that pulsates throughout all existence, wherein there dwells a Higher Power that is certainly far stronger, far wiser, and far more loving than Wes.

And I don't need to understand *why* that power exists - I just need to believe that it does. My chance encounter with that magnificent creature demonstrated that fact to me once again, and I chose to call that power God, and on that perfect summer day God spoke to me through a moose.

So I'd like to toss this idea out to anyone who is having a problem developing a relationship with their own Higher Power, particularly if it's preventing you from recovering from a terrible and often fatal disease:

You don't need to believe in God in any sense of the word, in fact, you don't need to believe in much of anything. All you really need to do is go to your meetings, surround yourself with the love and support of your friends in AA, keep an open mind, and just stay away from a drink and a drug for one single day, just one twenty-four hour period in your time machine. That's all, but if you do that for enough twenty-four hours then maybe someday you too will find the God of your own understanding.

And if not, you can always borrow mine - you don't even need to ask.

≈≈≈

If seeking out your own personal Bullwinkle doesn't do it for you, however, here's another idea that also worked for me, and it may benefit you as well.

What I found helpful in those early days as a newcomer was a growing belief in a group of courageous people who had reached out and surrounded me with their unconditional love and acceptance, and who inspired me with their personal stories of experience, strength and hope.

Over the days, months and years I began to rely upon them, and to trust them. And, one day, I began to love them, and by so doing I began to love myself.

It was through these people, miraculously, that I was able to remain sober for the first time in my life.

So to this day, whenever I think of God I also think of that "Group Of Drunks" who saved my life, and for me "GOD" is simply an acronym for a bunch of caring, loving, unselfish recovering alcoholics and addicts in the western suburbs of Boston, on a beach in Florida, and in the mountains of Vermont.

Those kind people handed my life back to me, and they did what I couldn't do - they loved me, and they taught me how to love myself.

They were God's gift to me, they were made in God's image, and I thank God every day for bringing them into my life.

And yes, if you're wondering, I think of Bullwinkle every once in a while, and that magical encounter in Vermont. Usually it's when my spirit is in dis-ease mode and I'm seeking shelter from the storms of life, so I laugh a lot, and cry a little, and experience again the joy and wonder that reveals itself so freely when I am most in need.

≈≈≈

So that's basically it for my view from forty-thousand feet. All the rest is just noise, and that's all I am too, just another bozo on the bus, a rather loud one sitting way down back in the cheap seats.

But I'm a bozo who loves you, and there's nothing you can do about that.

Oh, and one final thing - please cut yourself some slack. As my old friend Lois H. was fond of saying, "We all take ourselves too damned seriously!" I know that I did, so if you're like me, please, just lighten up on yourself and take life little by slow, one day at a time, one hour at a time, one moment at a time and one heartbeat at a time. Really, it makes things so much simpler - take it from one who didn't, and who paid the price.

≈≈≈

I surrendered to my disease during that final stay at Beech Hill in early June, 1992, and I have not found it necessary to pick up a drink or a drug ever since.

I didn't accomplish that miracle through any act of willpower, intelligence or strength on my part. In fact, quite the contrary, for it was only after I had run up the white flag and admitted that I was powerless over alcohol, drugs, other people, and life itself that I could begin to recover and be set free from my bondage.

It was a long, slow, painful crawl up and out of the depths of my disease, depravity and depression, as it is for most of us. I certainly didn't do everything right, but I stuck with it and made sobriety my first and only priority on a daily basis.

And to this day I still do that - I call it maintaining my attitude of gratitude.

I began to listen for a change, and to admit that I didn't have all of the answers. In fact, early on during that last stay in the Alps I realized that I didn't have *any* of the answers, because my best thinking for the prior twenty-five years had landed me squarely over a toilet bowl, physically, mentally and spiritually broken, shaking and vomiting my guts out on that fateful Sunday afternoon.

≈≈≈

I could have remained in my room on the morning after my arrival, sleeping late, working off the last of my DT's and downing my valiums. I felt like I had just gone ten rounds with Marvelous Marvin Hagler, and lost badly, but instead I forced myself to get up out of bed, showered and dressed, and headed down to the dining hall for breakfast.

I didn't even consider checking in at the nursing station to receive my little blue pill. I was shaky and wobbly, but I got stronger with every step, and I enjoyed every bite of food I ate that morning - it was the first real meal I could remember having for a very long time.

In fact, I couldn't remember a time when I had been grateful for something so relatively simple as a good meal, or, for that matter, grateful for anything whatsoever.

After I finished my breakfast I returned to my room for a few minutes and reflected upon the events of the prior day. I looked back with gratitude at the love and kindness that Blue Eyes had shown me as we waited for my ride, and at the tough love that Bill had laid on me when I needed it the most.

And finally I thought once more of Donna's patience and compassion, and of her gentle, quiet manner of talking some sense into a stubborn, angry drunk in denial.

These three people had been my Holy Trinity, my saviors, and I will never forget them. They were God's gift to me that day, and I know that I would not be alive today were it not for the love and acceptance that they had shown me.

≈≈≈

I was still restless and edgy as the last remnants of alcohol continued to leach out of my system, so I walked out to the smoking deck to take in the views.

A few minutes later I met up with a couple of the people from the Canadian contingent who I had spoken with on the prior evening, and we continued our discussion about life, the challenges of recovery, and some of the personal stuff that we had each gone through.

I realized once again that we're all pretty much the same when you come right down to it, and I had to acknowledge that I wasn't the "Great I Am," or legend in my own mind that I had always considered myself to be.

I finally concluded that what I needed to be mindful of on a daily basis was that I was an alcoholic and an addict, nothing more, nothing less, but I didn't need to allow my addictions to define the remainder of my life.

Rather, I just needed to stay sober, and to remain grateful for one day at a time. If I could do those two things on a continuing basis then my life, unfettered by addiction, might define itself in ways I could never have imagined.

So instead of hiding out in my room, excused by my free pass from the head Doc, I decided that I would attend the Monday morning "Wake Up" meeting for all residents. It was designed to be equal parts orientation and inspiration, and it served to establish a focus and goals for our recovery work during the upcoming week.

I knew that this would be the perfect venue for me to commence my new life, so what better time was there to start than right now, right here?

≈≈≈

I arrived at the small amphitheater ten minutes before the meeting was scheduled to start, and decided that it would be a wise idea to grab a seat up at the rear of the room, where I could remain a passive, anonymous observer.

Halfway to the back of the hall, however, I changed my mind, turned, and headed back down to take a seat in the front row. I figured that it was about time I stopped hiding from the world, putting up walls around myself, being that damned "Lone Wolf" that had spent most of its life lost in the wilderness.

Jim, the day's staff moderator, entered the room minutes later and asked for a moment of silence for the sick and suffering who were still out there, lost in their addictions, and then he led us in the Serenity Prayer:

"God, grant me the serenity to accept the things I cannot change
Courage to change the things I can
And wisdom to know the difference."

I noticed that Jim kept his eye on me while we recited the prayer, and I realized that he must have remembered me from my previous stay. No doubt the word had circulated around the staffroom pretty quickly that another member of the flock had crashed and burned, and had come crawling back for one more shot at the brass ring.

It was then that I began to question the wisdom of sitting down front, because I really didn't want to draw a lot of attention to myself, to be viewed as the failure, the rehab veteran who couldn't straighten out his act for more than a couple of months, the five-time loser who couldn't survive where it mattered most – out in the World.

But then I realized that all I had to worry about was "today." The past was the past, and I couldn't change a moment of it, but I could certainly improve my attitude, just for today, just for this one twenty-four hour period of time.

At least I could try, for once in my life, couldn't I?

I guess my Higher Power had decided that the time was right for Wes to rejoin humanity.

Jim spoke to me then, "Hello, Wes, this is something of a surprise! I didn't expect to be seeing you here this morning, so what brings you back to the Hill?"

I doubted that this was exactly a surprise to him, as I felt fifty pairs of eyeballs boring into the newcomer, wondering no doubt what jackpot I had landed in.

"Hi, Jim," I replied, looking him directly in the eye, "I can't say that I'm exactly thrilled to be back here, but I'm beat and I can't fight it anymore. I'm just trying to find some peace of mind, that's all, just something to hold onto, because my days are numbered otherwise."

"Well, you've come to the right place for that, Wes, so stick around this time and don't give up on yourself, or on your sobriety. You know the drill by now - just take it a day at a time and everything will work out fine."

"I'm trying, Jim, that's all I can do."

"Well, let's all welcome Wes back, shall we?"

The room erupted then into applause and loud shouts of "Welcome back, Wes," "Keep coming," and "Way to go, Wes."

I sat there shaking, overwhelmed, with half of me wanting to run out the door in embarrassment and shame, while the other half wanted to hug every person in that room, and never let them go.

≈≈≈

I returned to my room for a few minutes after the meeting wrapped up. I had an appointment scheduled with a counselor by the name of Dave at 10:30 that morning, so I sat on my bed and began to scope out my "Recovery Plan."

I knew that the counselors would be expecting me to put one together at some point, so I decided to get proactive and start in on it before they "suggested" that I do so. After all, I'd been to this rodeo enough times in the past to know the rules of the game by then. They were simple to understand conceptually, but the devil was in the details and the actual doing.

The bottom line, however, was that life wasn't going to change, so Wes had to if he was to survive, and that scared the hell out of me, because change can be terrifying for myself, and probably for most alcoholics and addicts.

I had done things my own way for my entire life, considering myself to be the Master of my universe, dysfunctional as it might have been. So when the stuff hit the fan, as it inevitably did, I took care of my own private little pile of garbage. It might have stunk, but it was *my* garbage and I was perfectly comfortable wallowing around in it.

But what would become of me now that I had to step out into the real world and finally get honest with myself, and with other people? In the past I had put up a great big wall around myself that was full of noise, bravado and bullshit. That kept the world at bay, but it wasn't going to cut it anymore - the events of the past week had made that abundantly clear.

So, once again, I needed to keep things simple, and stick to the here and now. I was in a safe place, well cared for and having a general knowledge of what I needed to do, so it all boiled down to just taking first things first.

And that meant developing a recovery plan that would be manageable, and simple enough for this broken down drunk to be able to execute once I stepped back out into the real world.

Seconds later I rose up from the bed to retrieve a notebook and pen on my bureau. But then, before I quite knew what I was doing, or understood why, I did something that I hadn't done since I was probably five years old, when the bad times came - I got down on my knees, bowed my head into my hands, and I prayed.

I did not fully comprehend it at the time, but that prayer was the first tangible confirmation of my surrender to the disease of alcoholism, without any reservations whatsoever, because I was finally turning my will and my life over to a Power greater than myself. I had become willing to be humble, and to accept the consequences of my past and future actions:

"God, I don't know what I'm doing, or why I'm here, but I know that I need your help. So please, help me to remain sober today, and please make me teachable. My way isn't working, and I would be grateful for your guidance. Thank you, God."

It probably wouldn't get me inducted into the *Prayer Hall of Fame*, but it was a start, and it was all I was capable of. I already felt better as I rose and returned to the bed, like a giant weight had been lifted from my shoulders.

That first prayer was modified a dozen times over the years, and it evolved into a beginning and end of day ritual after that, and prayer has continued to be my first and foremost means of surrender and acceptance ever since that day. It has become my primary expression of humility, and it is one of the many tools I store in my 'God Bag' that keep me stable and relatively serene as the storms of modern life rage all around me.

It started that morning, and I know that I would not be sober today, nor alive, had I not made prayer to a Power greater than myself a part of my daily routine.

≈≈≈

I fell into a rhythm soon after that, as pieces of the jigsaw puzzle known as "Wes" began to fall into place.

It wasn't that I hadn't paid attention at various times during my previous institutionalizations, or at the handful of AA meetings I had reluctantly attended at the urging of family, friends and outpatient counselors. I had listened, but I remained skeptical, and I had rarely participated in any of the discussions at meetings, or in my treatment groups.

Worst of all, when I did participate I usually came across as sarcastic, superior, arrogant, the class clown hiding his fears and insecurities behind a wall of big words, bravado and wisecracks.

In other words, I had behaved like a petulant, frightened little child who was attempting to prove to the world how tough he was.

But over the years, without realizing it, I had picked up a great deal of knowledge about my disease, and I had been introduced to the basic tenets of sobriety – how to get sober, and how to remain sober.

The bottom line was that I knew what to do, but I just hadn't lost enough to motivate me to actually do it, because that would mean changing the person I was, and that had never been part of the plan.

Now, however, it was finally time to admit that I had run out of choices. The losses were piling up rapidly, and it was change or die, so I needed to get with the program.

The prospect of change can be daunting, even overwhelming, for any alcoholic. I wanted to begin the process, but I was terrified of losing myself somewhere along the way, and coming out the other side as an empty shell, with no identity, no purpose to my life, and with nothing to hold onto.

But hell, I didn't have all that much to begin with, so who was I kidding? I was already an empty shell, lost, broken, soulless, staring down into my own grave. I had bought a one way ticket off this planet, and unless I changed my ways completely I doubted that I'd last another five years.

I thought then of my favorite song of all time, Bob Dylan's "Like a Rolling Stone," with the iconic lyrics that I had made my mantra since I was fifteen years old:

"When you ain't got nothing, you got nothing to lose."

Well, that was me - spiritually bankrupt, bereft, washed up on the shore like human flotsam after the storm.

But then it occurred to me that maybe, just maybe, I had been delivered here for a purpose, and that I did have one tiny sliver of hope. It stood to reason that if I had nothing to lose, then I couldn't really lose, so what was I getting down on myself for? Even if I failed I couldn't sink any lower, so why not take a shot at the brass ring, because my life couldn't be any more miserable than it already was.

It seemed convoluted, but to my diseased mind there was a certain elegant logic to Dylan's words that only a beaten down alkie like me could understand.

My man Dylan was correct, because for Wes there was no way to go but up, or all the way out.

I glanced at my watch - it was time to head over to my counseling session.

"This ought to be interesting," I thought, and then, unbidden and without any effort on my part came my plea, "and please, God, help me to be willing to change."

"Damn, now where did that come from?" I asked myself, shaking my head in wonder as I rushed out the door.

≈≈≈

I poked my head around the entrance to Dave's cubicle and cleared my throat to announce my presence. He looked up and smiled, nodding at me to enter, so I walked in and sat down on a folding chair in the cramped space next to his desk.

I recognized him from my earlier stay at the Hill. He had been a moderator at several seminars I attended, but we didn't have any direct interactions back then.

Dave had a calm, relaxed way about him, and I didn't detect any bad vibes in the air, so I dialed the threat level back down to DEFCON 3.

"Greetings, Wes, so how are you feeling today?"

"Hi Dave," I said, managing a half smile, "I'm doing okay, considering."

"We were all surprised to hear that you were back. Do you want to talk about it?"

"Well, there's really not that much to say. Things were going pretty well for a while, but I slacked off on meetings, didn't get a sponsor, didn't go to counselling, screwed things up with a woman I met up here, and when everything hit the fan I didn't call anyone to talk about it. I just drank, a lot."

"Yup, that's pretty much the perfect formula for a relapse," he chuckled, then added seriously, "sounds like you knew what to do, but decided you didn't want to do it. A little case of self-will run riot?"

"More like a big case. It felt like I was in a slow motion train wreck that I couldn't stop, or didn't want to."

Dave latched on to that last statement, like a leech going for blood, "Oh? And why wouldn't you want to?"

"I don't know. It's been the story of my life. There were some really good things happening, especially with the woman, but every time things start looking up I self-destruct. It's like I have a death wish or something, like I don't want to succeed."

"Or maybe you don't think you deserve to have good things happen to you?" he asked, his brows furrowing.

"I don't know, maybe," I muttered.

"Don't you think that we all deserve to have a happy and productive life, Wes?"

"I wouldn't know, Dave, it never worked out that way for me, so I don't bother to think about it all that much - I'm not a big fan of fairy tales."

"Well, then maybe that's where we need to start. Maybe you do need to think about it, because perhaps it's time to do a little attitude adjustment here."

"Whaddaya mean?" I asked, becoming defensive, not liking where this was heading, sensing that terrifying little dirty word "change" sneaking up on me.

"Well, you came back here, correct? You voluntarily picked up the phone yesterday and asked for help, so I think that deep down you really do want a good life, and to be happy, or you would have given up a long time ago. You keep coming back, but something keeps getting in your way, and that's what we need to work on."

"Something? What something are you talking about?" I asked suspiciously.

"Well, that's what we need to find out, so are you willing to do some work?"

"Do I have a choice?"

"We all have choices, Wes, every day that we wake up we have free choice, that's what makes us different from animals. For those of us in recovery it's just a matter of trying to do the next right thing, and to say no to the darkness that's always waiting right around the corner."

He had a point. I had to admit that I was a master of self-sabotage, and that I had a miserable attitude. It was almost as if I had been programmed to make the wrong choices at every important juncture in my life. The worst of it was that I always knew they were the wrong choices, but I took them anyway, arrogantly believing that I was larger than life, or just not giving a damn.

"Okay, so assuming I do trash myself too much, what do I do about it? I mean, it feels like it's hardwired into my brain most of the time."

"Well, you know what it's called – stinkin' thinkin' – plain and simple, and every alcoholic does it because it justifies their drinking. I oughta know, because I was a master at it myself, but unfortunately, if we do it long enough it does get wired in, and then it becomes a self-fulfilling prophecy that we don't know how to escape from. So, we end up running around like rats on a treadmill, making the same mistakes time after time."

"Where's it come from?"

"Well, that's what we're going to have to work on, if you're willing. Do you really want to change?"

"Yeah, I do. I just don't know where to start, and I'm not really into self-mutilation."

Or was I?

"You let me worry about that," he said, then asked, "Did you ever hear the saying in the program about peeling off the layers of an onion?"

"Yeah, I heard it a couple of times."

"Good, then you're the onion, and that's where we'll start, with the basics, and we'll keep peeling away the layers until we find out what makes Wes tick, and then we can get to work on changing your wiring."

He paused, then went for the close, "So, are you willing to do the work?"

Damn, I was getting nervous now, because it was clear that this guy knew me better than I had hoped, and he was no doubt going to take me to some spooky places that I didn't particularly look forward to visiting.

But what choice did I really have, because I knew that my days were numbered if I didn't break this deadly cycle, and there weren't many more particles of sand left in the hourglass.

So then I did something that I had rarely done in my life, except with Blue Eyes - I placed my trust in another human being.

"Okay, I'll give it a try, but I'm not liking it a whole lot right now."

"Don't worry, Wes, nobody likes it, so that's why it's called work, not fun. But I'll guide you through it, and we'll go at your pace. Okay?"

"Okay, I'll do it… I'll do anything at this point."

And with those words, unbeknownst to me at the time, I began to peel off the layers of the onion known as Wes.

≈≈≈

Dave wrapped up our first session twenty minutes later, and then instructed me to return at the same time on Wednesday.

Just as I began to walk out of his cubicle he asked whether I had a Twelve Step book.

"Yeah, I brought it from home."

"Good, then I want you to read Step One, and we'll talk about it Wednesday. Like I said, we're starting with the basics, so we're taking everything from scratch, which means working the Steps right out of the gate."

"Okay."

"Oh, and smile, will you, you look like you're going to your own execution."

"Whatever you say, boss," I replied, but what crossed my face was more grimace than grin.

I was somewhat wired after the meeting, so I walked out to the smoking deck, had a quick cigarette, and then returned to my room to take a nap before lunch. I was still plodding through the physical part of my detox, and I realized with some trepidation that the mental part always took longer than the physical to get wrung out of my system.

And now I had an additional concern - this was like the first day of school, and this damned "change" thing scared the hell out of me. I was intimidated by the Steps, because it was clear that I would need to take a long, painful look at my life. Step Four of the Twelve Steps reads, "Made a searching and fearless moral inventory of ourselves," and God only knew what I would find there.

But, once again, what choice did I have?

The answer to that was simple enough – none, so the Onion laid down on his bed after dinner that night and began to read Step One.

≈≈≈

The *'Twelve Steps and Twelve Traditions of Alcoholics Anonymous'* constitute a remarkable spiritual philosophy and mode of living for those of us in recovery, if for no other reason than the fact that they were conceived by a mere handful of recovering alcoholics in the 1930's who, but for the grace of the God of their understanding, should never have survived their disease.

Even more remarkably, those founding fathers - Bill Wilson, Bob Smith, and the Good Oldtimers - not only survived the ravages of their alcoholism, but were restored to happy, healthy, productive lives.

It is estimated that they, and their successors, have unselfishly passed down the legacy of their sobriety to countless millions of desperately ill and suffering individuals from around the globe over the past eighty plus years.

Their courage, compassion and stories of their personal experience, strength and hope were the touchstones that began a movement that has transformed the lives of so many otherwise hopeless individuals, including myself.

And, as recovering alcoholics, we understand that we share a common responsibility that, "We can't keep it unless we give it away," so it is through our unconditional love for our fellow alcoholic that our society strengthens and grows to this day, "passing it on" to one new recovering alcoholic at a time.

The first section of Chapter Five of the 'Big Book' of Alcoholics Anonymous is titled 'How It Works,' and in just over two pages it introduces the alcoholic to a program of recovery known as the 'Twelve Steps.' These steps trace out a precise blueprint for the alcoholic's adoption of a new manner of living that relies upon the maintenance of rigorous and unconditional honesty both with ourselves, and with the people we interact with in our daily lives.

In essence, by studying and adopting the 'Twelve Steps' we will be able to surrender to our disease, turn our will and our lives over to a Power greater than ourselves, make a searching and fearless moral inventory of ourselves, ask that Power to remove all of our defects of character, attempt to make amends to all the people we have harmed, seek through prayer and meditation to increase our conscious contact with that Power *as we understand Him* (or *Her*), and carry our message of experience, strength and hope to other alcoholics who are still suffering under the lash of this heinous disease.

Those two short pages, in other words, describe the process for a spiritual transformation of the alcoholic that is profound and life-altering., and the Twelve Step program, taken as a whole, becomes the vehicle for our survival and rebirth as emotionally and ethically healthy, functional human beings.

And that was what Dave would be working with me on as one of the central pieces of my counseling sessions.

≈≈≈

As I looked back on my twenty-five year history of insanity, I realized early on that I had led a self-absorbed, undisciplined life. My existence had been focused upon getting high, avoiding pain, shunning responsibility, making any and all compromises I needed to make in order to protect that sad, pathetic lifestyle that kept the world at bay.

Of ethics, morality, fair play and love for my fellow human beings I knew nothing, and cared less.

So the Twelve Steps were intended to be the game changer - my attitude adjuster - because my adoption of them could open the door to a new way of life that would enable me to be reintegrated into human society.

Recovery via Step study is not accomplished overnight. It is a long, arduous, oftentimes painful appraisal of the havoc that we have wrought upon ourselves, and upon the people we have come into contact with over a lifetime of addiction. We will never graduate from Step study, for there is always more work that we can do to improve our outlook on life, and to repair our relationship with the world at large.

Many of us attend Step studies regularly, over many years. I like to call it getting my tune-up and oil change, which insures that my engine, my sobriety, is running at peak efficiency.

In the years leading up to this last trip to Beech Hill I had attended a couple of Step meetings, but I had never committed myself to making it a regular practice. Step study intimidated me, because I was overwhelmed by the scope of my problems, and by the scale of the work that I would need to accomplish in order to effect any significant improvement in my attitudes and actions.

There was also something daunting about walking into a roomful of people I hardly knew to expose all of my faults and human frailties for their inspection. I had been shy all of my life, and had hidden my fear of people by constructing a perpetual wall of noise and arrogance around me that was impenetrable, and which served to discourage people from venturing too close.

Simply put, however, behind all of that bravado the reality was that I was terrified of letting the world see the real Wes.

Yet never once had I stopped to consider that every person in that Step meeting was just the same as me, harboring the same fears, doubts and insecurities. We were all in it together, and it had finally become clear to me that we would have to stand together as one in order to survive and recover.

So now that the rubber had met the road, I realized that I would need to rethink my entire philosophy about life, my relationships with people, and my spirituality. Needless to say I was intimidated by the magnitude of the task I was facing.

But at least I wouldn't be embarking on this journey alone. There's a popular saying in the program that goes, "We did what I couldn't do," so Dave, for better or worse, would be my tour guide during the early days. I admitted to feeling a certain sense of comfort in knowing that, because I figured that if we could tackle some of the major issues that kept standing in the way of my getting sober, then maybe I'd feel more comfortable about attending Step studies, and about going to counseling when I returned to the World and had to face life on life's terms.

So after all was said and done it was pretty straightforward. All I had to do was quit drinking and drugging, and then change my entire freakin' life, and the Steps could play a major role in opening the door to that.

Pretty simple, eh? Just another brick in the wall.

Yeah, right. Irony of ironies, I realized then that I would need to utilize the same self-will and stubbornness that had gotten me into this fix to get me out of it, because anything less than a one hundred percent commitment to getting sober would result in failure, and no doubt an early grave for Wes.

≈≈≈

I finished reading Step One that night, and slipped away into a dream. In it I was a child again, it was summer, and I was lying in a meadow that was overflowing with tall, waving grass and flowers. There was a cloud of butterflies floating around me, and honey bees droning about. The wind blew softly, as if whispering to me as it cooled my skin. I was content in the knowledge that there was no other place I would rather be, weeping the sweet tears of joy that only an innocent child can know. I felt like I was home, safe and protected, free from worry or fear.

And then in my dream I prayed to God that someday I would be returned to that field.

It would be many years later, on a magical summer's day, when I realized that He had listened to my prayer.

≈≈≈

I became acclimated to the routine at the Hill very quickly this time around, and I adapted to the rhythm and flow easily, without any significant cultural shocks. I knew the layout and the staff, and what was expected of me, and I made a conscious effort to participate in group discussions and activities.

I also made some fledgling friendships, usually while hanging around the smoking deck before and after meals, or in the evening. I was doing more than two packs a day back then, so it was natural that I would make "the deck" my second home.

One of my first friends this time around was a guy named Eddie, who also came from Massachusetts. He had brought his guitar with him, so a dozen of us would sit out on the deck most evenings, talking and listening to his great music.

We called him "Guitar Man," and he was good, and it became a sing-along most nights out under the stars.

I felt comfortable here, talking, laughing and sharing stories with people I inherently understood. I was even beginning to establish a bond of trust with several of them, which was no easy feat for me.

I also figured out pretty quickly who to stay away from. They were the energy drainers, the "denial aisle" crowd with the negative attitudes who were just marking time until they got clean enough to go back out into the World and start running their games all over again. They were easy enough for me to spot, because they were exactly the type of person I had been every time I rolled into a rehab – smug, arrogant, angry, cold-blooded and very much into myself.

My weight and physical strength came back rapidly this time around. Treatment centers and detoxes always go overboard on the food, because by the time a drunk makes it into a facility his or her body is usually pretty well broken down, and in my case I had lost about ten pounds during my binge. The Alps weren't the place for *Lean Cuisine*, so the food was high in calories and fat, with lots of rich desserts for a chocaholic like me to feast on.

Ironically, I had to begin walking the trails of the surrounding forest after two weeks, because my weight had rebounded so dramatically that I began to develop a gut.

I also discovered anew that hiking in that cool clear mountain air was as good for my head as it was for my body. It was then that I realized how far I had strayed from Nature over the years, so I made a vow to myself that I would one day return to it, and I have kept that promise.

But first things first, however. I needed to get sober, and I needed to learn how to live my life sober on a continuing basis, so that had to begin with my attitude, which quite frankly stunk.

But like they say its progress, not perfection, so I had to start somewhere, and this was a far better and safer place than most.

≈≈≈

The days began to morph into each other by the middle of my second week in the Alps. I had settled into a comfortable routine, and I soon discovered that Dave, my counselor, was very adept at keeping me focused on my priorities.

Over the course of the first week we had progressed steadily through the first three Steps, and had also begun to peel off the layers of the Onion.

Unfortunately, it was not very long before I remembered to my dismay that the act of dismembering onions oftentimes leads people to tears.

It turned out that I was no exception to that annoying little fact of life. Wes, the great and all-powerful Lone Wolf, bawling like a baby into his pillow at night as he surveyed the path of wreckage and heartache that he had left in his wake during a lifetime of addiction - go figure.

But with each new revelation, painful as it might have been, my liberation grew closer, and my attitude healthier. I had a long way to go, but I sensed a new strength, and for perhaps the first time in memory I felt the initial stirrings of hope. I might not have loved myself, nor particularly liked myself, but at the very least I had stopped hating myself. It was a start, anyway, and more evidence of that "progress, not perfection" stuff that they were always talking about at meetings.

And every morning I got down on my knees and asked God to help me remain sober, and every evening I got down on my knees and thanked Him for keeping me away from a drink and a drug for that day.

So that was Wes, the Onion, a work in progress, but certainly not perfection.

≈≈≈

On the Thursday of that second week I found a message slip pinned on my door when I returned to my room after lunch. It was from Blue Eyes, asking me to call her. She was planning on coming up for visiting hours that Sunday if it was permitted.

My heart skipped a beat, because there was no one on the planet I wanted to see more than her.

I called her right back from a pay phone in the lobby, and she picked up immediately.

"Hey, it was nice to get your message. How are things back home?"

"They're pretty good, busy with work and my daughter and all. How are you doing? Are you taking care of yourself?"

"Yeah, I'm doing pretty well for a change. Just trying to take care of my business - it seems to be going okay."

"So I'd be able to come up?"

"Yeah, I'm allowed visitors and I'd love to see you."

"Good, I have some errands to run in the morning, so I should be up there around 1:30."

"Perfect, I can't wait, I miss you!"

"Me too. See you then!"

As I hung up I couldn't help but think, "Hmm, maybe this getting sober stuff has some benefits, after all, and maybe my luck's finally changing."

Well, perhaps, but I hadn't yet been introduced to another AA'ism, a very simple one that states, "Be careful what you ask for, because you just might get it."

Yes indeed, my friends, be very careful what you ask for.

≈≈≈

I had been looking forward to Saturday evening all week. That was the night that one of the local AA groups from down in the valley came up to the Hill to put on a commitment for the residents.

Commitments were a staple of AA meetings in many parts of the northeast in those days, and I'd been introduced to them during the three or four years that I had been occasionally dropping in on meetings.

The concept was simple — four or five members of a local group would come up to the Alps, and each person would speak from the podium for about ten minutes. Each individual would relate his or her personal story about what it was like before, and what it was like after they got sober, and by so doing they would pass on their unique experience, strength and hope to us.

This was a win/win situation, because it gave the visitors an opportunity to motivate us in our recovery, and it reaffirmed and strengthened their own recovery.

I was always enthralled by the power of the messages that these speakers freely gave of themselves.

I will admit, however, that I was incredulous that anybody would have the courage to stand up in a roomful of complete strangers to tell an intimate and often degrading story about themselves, regardless of its ultimate outcome.

The great majority of those visitors weren't public speakers, just everyday Joe's and Jane's. Many were clearly nervous, and they often had a difficult time remaining on track, but that made the event even more genuine for me.

These were courageous people, and I shuddered to think what I would feel like if I ever had to walk in their shoes to the podium.

As I stood on the deck, smoking a last cigarette before the meeting, I couldn't help but thank God that I would just be one of the sheep tonight, sitting way up back in the cheap seats, taking it all in, getting some free inspiration.

So thank you, God, for this meeting, and thank you for letting me remain a passive observer!

≈≈≈

I really have to hand it to my Higher Power! He's got one heck of a sense of humor, and He was in rare form that evening, as He reminded me that there's no such thing as a free lunch in WesWorld.

We were just finishing our smokes, about to step into the dining hall where the meeting would be held, when the assistant director of Beech Hill walked up to us. His eyes caught mine, and for whatever reason I sensed impending doom. He just had that certain look about him, and let's face it, I was still a paranoid, suspicious drunk who was two weeks off the juice, so I could smell a rat a mile away.

My threat level went immediately to DEFCON 3, and my heart started banging in my chest.

Michael, the AD, touched my arm then, and spoke, "Wes, I wonder if I could have a quick word with you," he inquired confidentially, nodding his head for me to follow him to a more secluded area of the deck.

Bingo, and here we go straight to DEFCON 2!

"Yo, God? What's up here, God? You're still my friend, right? Yes? God?" was all I could manage to think.

It was then that I sensed that somewhere far, far away the halls of Drunk Heaven were reverberating with riotous laughter as I followed Michael to a more private area of the deck.

The executioner got right to the point.

"Wes, I need to ask you a favor. The commitment came up one short for speakers tonight, so they asked me to check whether any of the residents might like to speak. I know you've been around the halls more than most everybody else, and that you're working hard this time around, so would you be willing to speak for maybe ten minutes? I know its last minute, but..."

And then he went silent, fixing me with an expectant stare like all good car salesmen do when they're ready to "close" the unwary rube.

The rules of the game become simple then – the next person to speak loses.

I was a salesman, and I had learned this fun little game inside and out, so all I had to do was keep my big mouth shut, for once in my life, stare him down, and this potential nightmare would just go away.

It was really that simple.

"Don't be an idiot, Wes," I pleaded to myself, "just don't say a word and this whole thing will disappear, like the bad dream it is. Do NOT play his game!"

The man looked like a sad little lost puppy at that moment, staring at me, his big wet eyes almost begging, and then came a voice that seemed to arrive from miles away, "Hmm, this is a surprise, Michael. Geez, I don't know what to say," the Onion mumbled, the train wreck complete, and with those words I sealed my doom.

Bingo! DEFCON 1 - we have a winner!

≈≈≈

Ten minutes later I found myself seated with the speakers from the Valley group, shaking and vibrating worse than when I came out of my blackout two weeks previously.

There were approximately ninety people sitting in that room, eighty-nine of whom were happy, bored, energized, inspired, or whatever, and then there was the big bad Lone Wolf, sweating profusely, ever the pathetic, self-destructing narcissist in denial.

It was at that point that I considered making a quick run to the nursing station to see whether they had any extra pairs of Depends lying around, but I doubted that my legs would stop shaking long enough for me to get that far.

And, besides, even if I did somehow make it, there was a high probability that I would just keep right on going until I made it under my bed.

But no, this was finally my adult moment. Like it or not, I was about to become a man at the emotional age of twelve. And that, beyond all rationalization, was the real reason I had spoken up to Michael. I just needed to be convinced that it was time for Wes to walk the talk that I had been so blithely throwing around for two weeks. I just needed that little extra push, and my Higher Power gave it to me.

However, my mind was now going blank - I couldn't for the life of me think of anything to say after "I'm Wes, and I'm an alcoholic and addict," and that wasn't going to fill ten seconds, much less ten minutes.

They dragged out my torment for forty-five minutes while I sat, frozen in place, as the four speakers told their inspirational stories of defeat and rebirth.

I had to hand it to them - now that I was up there on the firing line I truly understood the courage and dedication that recovering people are blessed with when they step to the podium. Those people spoke from the heart, with a certain raw truthfulness that couldn't be doubted or imitated, and it was a beautiful thing to observe up close.

In fact, a part of me hoped that they would keep right on speaking until the meeting timed out, but that was not to be the case. God obviously had other plans for me, and He was sticking to them.

Finally, the dreaded moment arrived, and the chairperson stepped to the podium, "This evening we're going to do things a little differently. One of our speakers couldn't make it tonight, so one of your fellow residents has graciously agreed to step in. Would you please welcome Wes to the podium?"

Everything went into slow motion at that moment. I felt like I was floating in suspended animation, alone in the Universe, deaf, numb, focused only on making it six steps to the podium.

Surprisingly, however, a measure of calm overcame me as I made my way up front. The pounding in my temples and chest slowed noticeably, as my mind began to form thoughts and react to the loud applause and hoots and hollers from my fellow residents.

Even some of the locals from down in the Valley were joining in, as were my fellow speakers.

I doubt that those kind, gracious people ever realized what their support meant to me that evening, but I will remember those moments with gratitude until the day I die.

Somehow I managed to stagger the final steps to the podium, white knuckled its sides for dear life, took a great big breath and began to speak, "Good evening, I'm Wes, and I'm an alcoholic and an addict."

"Hi, Wes," the crowd responded enthusiastically.

"I suppose that you're wondering why I invited you all here tonight," I said, always looking for a cheap laugh.

And that's what I got – one cheap laugh amidst the chorus of groans.

The next ten minutes of my life are a blur. I know that I told the basics of my story, and spent a good deal of time recounting the activities of the prior weeks, right from the moment I came out of my blackout. I stumbled a few times, had a couple of brief lapses of silence as I fought to find the proper words to express myself, but the audience was on my side, and I received quite a few laughs from what I considered to be rather embarrassing episodes in my drinking career.

I realized then that every person in that room had walked a path much like my own, that we were all one, and that there was nothing unique about Wes. I was, after all, just another bozo on the bus, a sick person trying to get better, a lost soul trying to find his way home.

Mercifully, I eventually ran out of things to say and finished up with a thank-you to everyone in the room, then shivered in relief at the loud applause that followed.

For myself, I graded my drunkalogue a straight "B," which wasn't all that bad for a rookie who was just fourteen days off the juice.

I spent the next hour out on the deck, basking in the glow of my newfound popularity, on a rush, a high that was better than any I had ever experienced while I was using.

And, more than anything, I was exhilarated by finally having met and defeated one of my lifelong demons, my fear of public speaking, which after all is just another form of fear of intimacy, something that had plagued me for my entire life.

And now I was pulsating, liberated, celebrating my victory over fear. It might have been a baby step, one of many I have taken in recovery, but that talk convinced me once and for all that I could be alright if I simply put one foot in front of the other, and did the next right thing.

≈≈≈

I retired early that evening, but lay awake until almost dawn. I was far too energized to even attempt to sleep, because I knew that this had been a major step forward in my fledgling sobriety, and that I was not the same person I had been when I awoke that morning.

I sensed a new confidence coursing through me now, and I realized that it had been a gift from a Power greater than myself, timed to arrive at the exact moment when I was ready and open to receive it.

I thanked God for having given me this gift, and then drifted off into a brief but deep REM sleep. My last thought before the darkness closed in upon me was that I now had the confidence and strength to accept anything that came along in my life.

Little did I know, however, that in just eight short hours my confidence would be tested more strenuously than I had been expecting, because my Higher Power was about to give the Onion another growth opportunity, and not of the particularly welcome variety.

As the saying goes, "The Lord giveth, and the Lord taketh away," and I was about to get a painful but well deserved lesson in humility and human relations.

≈≈≈

I woke just after dawn, surprisingly refreshed after my brief sleep. I was still on a high from the prior evening's activities, so I jumped out of bed and immediately hit my knees to ask my Higher Power keep me sober for that day, and to help me accept His will for me.

I shaved and took a long, hot, soaking shower, then headed down to the dining hall, where I dove into the Sunday brunch. I spent about an hour there, packing on the calories and talking with several of my new friends.

We didn't have any formal counseling or group meetings to attend on Sundays, so we soon moved out to the deck to smoke and continue the conversation.

It was a warm, brilliant June morning in the mountains, with a gentle breeze blowing up from the southwest that promised perfect weather for the day.

I might have been running on the residual energy left over from my debut at the speakers' podium, but as the morning progressed my attention was rapidly transitioning to visiting hours, and to Blue Eyes' much anticipated arrival. I was nervous and apprehensive, but for the most part it was a good feeling, the sensation of butterflies in the stomach that a little kid has when his favorite playmate is coming to visit after a long absence.

I will admit, however, that I wanted her to be more than a playmate, and I was concerned that I had ruined any chance of that by relapsing and going silent on her, so my enthusiasm was somewhat tempered by a nagging fear in the back of my mind that I had failed her, and us.

But all I could do was pray that I might accept whatever the outcome would be from her visit, and I was going overboard on those prayers.

≈≈≈

At one o'clock I found myself sitting out on the deck in the warm sunshine, smoking and talking with Guitar Man, Bob D., Susan F., and Jimmy M., with my back facing the entrance to the building's lobby.

One moment everything seemed perfectly normal, as if it was just another perfect spring day in the mountains, but then in a heartbeat it was like time had been frozen in place. One by one my friends' faces went blank, all conversation ground to a halt, and then each of them stared off into a spot somewhere over my left shoulder.

In fact, it appeared that most of the discussions at the nearby tables had also stopped.

It didn't take long for me to figure out what had happened - Blue Eyes always had that effect on people.

I turned around then, and sure enough, there she stood in the doorway, scanning the deck for me.

My breath caught in my chest then, because she had outdone herself that day. She was a vison of loveliness, dressed to the nines, her funky hair and beautiful features done to perfection, projecting a quiet sensuality that always reminded me of Ingrid Bergman in the movie 'Casablanca.'

And then there were those great big killer blue eyes.

I rose, took two steps, and then we came together in one of those hugs that I had been missing for so long. We remained entangled for what seemed like forever, before finally pulling apart so that I could introduce her to my friends, who were just recovering their voices.

We socialized for twenty minutes, with Blue Eyes receiving most of the attention. Then I suggested that we grab a coffee from the dining hall and take a walk around the grounds, and she quickly agreed.

≈≈≈

A few minutes later we were strolling along a path that encircled a large pond, which was situated out on the edge of the forest, with a great view to Mount Monadnock.

We were walking hand in hand, and had been silent for a few moments, but then I spoke, "I want to thank you for coming up here today. You're a sight for sore eyes. I've missed you, a lot, you're always in my thoughts."

"Oh, it was nothing. I wanted to see you, also, I've been worried," she said, a quiet smile crossing her face, revealing once again the shy vulnerability that had attracted me to her since day one, a vulnerability that I also knew a lot about.

"No, it was a big deal, just like how you came down to keep me company two weeks ago. I wish you'd never had to do that, but you'll never know how much it meant to me - you probably saved my life."

She just smiled and squeezed my hand.

"How are you and your daughter making out these days?"

"We're good. She's out of kindergarten, a big girl now! She starts 1st Grade in August," she said, beaming with pride.

We continued on with our walk for another ten minutes, enjoying the warmth of the sun on our faces and catching up on the past month's news. It felt wonderful to be spending this time with her, but I was growing apprehensive because I knew that there was an invisible wall between us now, and it was a wall of my own making. I understood that I would need to be the one to tear it down, and I was searching for an opening.

We were almost through our second circuit around the track when I thought I saw my opportunity, so I began, "Listen, I need to…"

But then I stopped abruptly as I saw her glance at her watch, a look of surprise crossing her face as she noticed the time.

"Uh oh, I'm so sorry, Wes. I didn't realize it was getting this late - I have to run. I'm meeting a friend later this afternoon on the way home. He and I have been kind of spending some time together recently."

"Oh, umm, a new friend?"

"Yes, it's a long story. I met him at a meeting a few weeks ago. He's a really funny guy," she said, and then she giggled, her eyes sparkling.

And what did that make me, chopped liver?

"Well, actually," I thought, "yeah," because when a woman giggles like that she's telling you everything you need to know. You snooze, you lose, and I certainly had it coming.

"Hmm, uh, so that's kind of a surprise… are you, like, dating him?"

"Well, no, not right now, I guess not, anyway, but he's really nice, and he's had a hard life and we just seem to have a lot of things in common. He makes me laugh a lot," and then she giggled again, blushing.

"Hmmm, I don't know what to say," the Onion mumbled.

We were approaching the back of the main building, and the adjacent parking area. Blue Eyes hugged me tightly, then said, "I'm sorry, I really do have to run. It was good to see how well you're doing, so please stick with it, Wes, I'm so happy for you! Let's stay in touch and maybe try to get to a meeting when you get home, OK?"

"Sure, will do. Drive safe and give your daughter a hug for me. I, uh..." and then my words trailed off as she went rushing to her car.

I remained motionless for the next five minutes, while the dust that had been kicked up by her vehicle settled.

And that was that. Her visit had been a work of surgical precision - clean and decisive. I could hardly tell where I was bleeding, although I sensed it was in the vicinity of the left center of my chest.

≈≈≈

Blue Eyes and I got together many times over the years, but things were never again quite the same between us. We remained close friends, although mostly at a distance, but whenever we did meet up it was always as if we intuitively knew each other's thoughts, as if we had just seen each other last week rather than a year previously.

She was the one I let get away, and for that I will always feel a deep sense of pain in a secret part of my soul.

But, beyond the pain, there was a valuable lesson to be learned by my experience. AA is full of acronyms to fit just about every situation that an alcoholic might face in recovery, so I realized that I had just become the recipient of my first official "AFGO" moment, for I had just received "Another Freaking Growth Opportunity." It was one of many that I've experienced over the years, and it hurt badly, but through it I grew, learned a valuable lesson in acceptance, and never once did I consider drinking over it.

To the contrary, this loss became an opportunity for me to channel my efforts toward becoming healthier, stronger, more ethical, and more honest with myself, as well as with the people who came into my life.

The Onion was finally becoming an adult, even if it hurt like hell sometimes, so thank you for that Blue Eyes!

≈≈≈

And so, for the second night in a row, I didn't get much sleep, although this time it was for all the wrong reasons.

I was accustomed to rising shortly after dawn, but on that Monday morning my roommates had to give me several loud shouts, and a kick at the base of my bed, before I groaned and struggled out from under the sheets.

I felt listless and washed-out, like my head was full of sand, and I wasn't looking forward to the Monday morning "wake-up" meeting.

I was also dreading my counseling session with Dave, where among other fun things we would be tackling the Fourth Step, which for a newcomer can be one of the most daunting of all the Steps.

I recognized the symptoms then - I was suffering from an emotional hangover, and it had the potential to be as debilitating as any of my alcohol and drug-induced ones had been.

That being the case, I understood that I would need to take the proper steps to insure that I didn't resort to the cure that I had always used in the past to kill my pain, and that I would have to work my nascent program of recovery harder than ever.

As I knelt down to pray many of the phrases that I had heard over the years began bombarding my thoughts, as if on cue from above. "First things first," "Just don't drink, no matter what," "One day at a time," and many others started rolling through my thoughts, one after the other, rapid fire.

I realized then that my Higher Power would be watching over me, whether my life was going good, bad, or totally off the rails. And that made my job simple – just ask Him for help as many times as necessary until I was back in the groove, back to living from heartbeat to heartbeat.

At the end of the day it all came down to acceptance, and to being willing to change the person I had been.

And so I began my daily ritual, "Good morning, God. Thank you for delivering me to this place where I am safe, and please help me to accept my life exactly as it is today…"

Whereupon I commenced another day of "trudging the road to Happy Destiny."

≈≈≈

I sat up front at the Monday morning "Wake-up" meeting, listening attentively despite my fatigue. I didn't participate to any great extent, but I took careful note of the key elements of discussion, which emphasized the AA slogans, and the sage advice that newcomers attend "meetings, meetings and more meetings," once we returned to our homes.

I understood from painful experience that showing up at an occasional meeting, hanging around the periphery, and never interacting with other group members was a perfect set-up for failure, so I would need to immerse myself in the Fellowship if I was to have any hope of remaining sober. That would mean reaching out my hand to introduce myself, asking for guidance from fellow members, and perhaps taking a job to make the coffee, or set up chairs.

Bottom line, I had to become proactive in my own recovery, and to become humble, neither of which were my strong suits.

Fortunately, however, AA has hundreds of slogans that are meant to fit common everyday situations that we might run into. Two came to mind immediately during that session, and I was grateful to realize that something had stuck with me during my haphazard exposure to meetings over the years.

The first slogan was, "Stick to the ABC's – ashtrays, brooms and chairs," which meant stick to the basics, don't complicate things, volunteer for a job to help out for the common good, and be willing to get my hands dirty.

The second was, "Many meetings equals many chances, few meetings equals few chances, no meetings equals no chances."

That too was a no-brainer, and I had merely to look at the tailspin my life had gone into over the past five years to figure that little nugget out.

The good news was that I was finally beginning to understand the hard-won wisdom that lay behind all of the slogans, and that AA worked because its members believed that it would work for them under any and all circumstances they might encounter in their sober lives.

But then, just as the meeting was about to wrap up, there arrived the most terrifying of all the suggestions that newcomers were urged to follow, and which always sent a chill up my spine:

"Sponsorship."

That one little word might have sounded innocuous enough on the surface, but I had always resisted the concept, considering it to be too intimate to be adopted by any respectable lone wolf who made up his own rules about how to conduct his life.

Simply put, AA recommends that the newcomer ask an established member of the Fellowship to be his or her sponsor, whereby we become willing to share all of the details of our past with this person.

Experience had taught that the establishment of a bond of trust between a sponsor and a newcomer could pave the way for the new member to embark on a rigorous study of the Twelve Steps of recovery, make amends for his or her past actions, adopt healthier lifestyles, and most importantly have an ally who could assist in extinguishing the brushfires caused by festering issues that might threaten our ability to remain sober.

That might have sounded really nifty on paper, but sharing my innermost thoughts, fears and inadequacies with some guy I hardly knew had never been at the top of my list of fun things to do. I had always cringed at the thought of asking someone to be my sponsor, because that introduced a very scary word into the mix - intimacy – or in other words opening myself up to another human being at a more personal level than I had ever been capable of doing.

The bottom line was that sponsorship meant becoming vulnerable, honest, transparent and humble, all of which were attributes not ordinarily associated with this particular onion.

But then, right on cue, along came my new pal, the Energizer Bunny, banging on his drum again and reminding me once more, "But what choice do you have, Wes, if you want to survive?"

As difficult as it was to admit, my answer was simple: none.

So I decided that finding a sponsor would need to be my highest priority when I returned home.

Intimacy? Seriously? Grrrrr… what had I gotten myself into this time?

≈≈≈

"Made a searching and fearless moral inventory of ourselves."
(The 4th Step of "The Twelve Steps and Twelve Traditions" of Alcoholics Anonymous).

My trust in Dave, my counselor, had grown steadily over the prior weeks. We had worked on many of my relapse issues, and he had become a valued guide as I worked my way through the Twelve Steps.

But now, on this day, we would be tackling Step Four. This was, for me, the most intimidating of all the Steps, because who wishes to make a rigorous and honest appraisal of their character defects when they're barely two weeks off the sauce?

Not I, quite frankly, but fortunately Dave made it clear that he wasn't going to force-feed me the entire Step at one sitting.

I had begun to notice that Dave's smiles grew wider in direct proportion to the degree of my discomfort, as we peeled more layers off the Onion, and now he broke out into a wide grin as he sensed my dis-ease.

"Okay, take a deep breath and relax, Wes, we're going to take this little by slow - you got it?"

"Yeah, I guess," I muttered.

His smile widened further.

"Alright, I want you to consider your stay here to be the beginning of a long, brutal war that you'll be fighting against your disease for the rest of your life. You have a terminal illness, and it will never stop working on you, but you can receive a daily reprieve simply by staying away from a drink and a drug for twenty-four hours, by attending your meetings, by doing the next right thing to protect your sobriety, and, if the opportunity arises, by helping another alcoholic. You with me?"

"Yeah," I grunted.

He chuckled, then resumed, "You're here now, in treatment, and this could be compared to being triaged in a war zone. You've been terribly wounded, so we're keeping you safe and alive, attending to the worst of your injuries, but this is a field hospital, and it's just the start of your recovery. We can introduce you to the basic concepts, and point you in the right direction, but the real work will start when you get home, and when you hopefully get a sponsor and go into counseling. That's where the rubber meets the road, so your time here is just a tune-up for the main event."

He grinned at the expression of relief that appeared on my face when I realized we wouldn't be immediately delving into all the gory details of a life gone tragically astray.

Then he continued, "Yes, this is an important Step, and it can be intimidating, even for people who've been in the Program for years. But this is just the start of a lifetime of self-examination that will help you to understand your disease, and to take the actions you need to take when you detect the warning signs that you're getting a little off kilter."

He paused, then said, "Let me emphasize, you don't need to work on all your defects of character at once, but you do need to at least start the process immediately!"

I nodded and said, "Understood, Dave. It's just that I don't know where to begin."

"Do you trust me?"

"Yeah, I do, you've played it straight the whole way, which is a rarity for me."

"Okay, then that's a start, right?"

"Yeah, I guess, if you put it like that, it is."

"Good, then you just learned one of the most important things about the 4th Step, which is that you're capable of trusting other people - especially AA people."

"I don't get it. I thought this Step was about looking at all of my failings and moral weaknesses."

"That's where most beginners go off the track," he said, "so think of the 4th Step like you're making a business inventory of the shelves, and you're counting up the debits and the credits, the full shelves and the empty shelves. But instead of cans of soup, the AA inventory is all about determining our strengths and weaknesses, the credits and debits, the good, the bad and the ugly, and understanding that none of us is all bad, or all good."

He paused to let me think about that, and then continued, "Alcoholics tend to think in extremes, that everything is all black, or all white, that there's no middle ground. But that's our disease talking, because we're all just human beings, here for a very short time in the scheme of things, just trying to get by. So what we need to do is seek out and emphasize the good in ourselves, while recognizing and correcting our flaws wherever possible."

"I never thought about it like that."

"Newcomers usually don't, and for that matter some of the longtime sober folks don't either. But I believe that Step Four is critical for beginning the healing process, and for maintaining a sense of emotional balance and ethical orientation in our sober lives."

"Well, I'm having a tough time finding anything good about myself right now, Boss."

Dave chuckled, then said, "Ok, that's not surprising, so let's play a little game. Whenever you bring up a character weakness that you believe you possess we'll discuss it, but then you have to tell me something that's good about Wes. Because, remember, life is never all black, or all white."

I just stared at him skeptically, and he broke out into another wide smile, because he knew that I, like most newcomers, would have a difficult time coming up with even one positive attribute about myself.

So then we played our little game. Whenever I brought up one of my weaknesses of character we would talk about it, and then Dave would instruct me to mention one of my strengths.

In the beginning I found plenty of negatives, but I would hem and haw, stammer, or go silent while I struggled to find anything whatsoever that was good or redeeming about Wes.

So then Dave would prompt me.

"Did you ever have a pet when you were a child?"

"Yeah, a dog, and a rabbit."

"And did you love them?"

"Yeah, I guess, why do you ask?"

"Because you just told me that you are capable of love, which is the most important and enabling of all the human emotions."

"Well, yeah, but they were animals."

"That's not the point. You told me that you are capable of loving, and you didn't put any limitations on it. But okay, while we're on the subject, have you ever loved a human being?"

Damn, now he had me squirming.

"Well, I dunno, maybe, yeah, I guess I have, a couple of times possibly."

"But wait, I thought you told me that you're a big bad lone wolf, and that the rest of the human race doesn't matter, so how could you possibly feel love for another person?"

"Well it doesn't matter for the most part, but maybe once or twice I guess I loved somebody, a little anyway," I stammered, trying not to think about how I had made such a mess of things with Blue Eyes.

"Ahah! So you have just admitted that you are capable of loving another person! Now think about that the next time you get down on yourself. You see, whether you care to admit it or not, you're capable of experiencing the highest order of human emotions, of loving and, I might add, of allowing yourself to be loved, because you can't have one without the other!"

"But..."

"But no buts, period."

And so it went for another twenty agonizing minutes before Dave mercifully ended our session with a request that I continue to play the good cop/bad cop game until we met again on Wednesday.

"Oh, and I want you to make a list of what you consider to be your character defects, but only the major ones. Those will be the ones that have caused you the most trouble over the years, and they're the ones that are most likely to threaten your sobriety once you get home. But for God's sake, don't be too hard on yourself - this is meant to help you change the person who crawled in here just over two weeks ago, and to heal, not hate yourself back into a bar!"

≈≈≈

I began working on my list that evening, and soon began to see the patterns emerge as I connected the dots that marked my descent into Hell over the past forty-one years.

It became clear very quickly that arrogance, greed, and especially self-centered fear had been major factors behind my addictions, and I was overwhelmed by the memories of all the people I had harmed as a result of those flaws.

The memories began flooding back, and soon I was lying in what was becoming my customary nighttime position, my head stuck under the pillow, trying to hold back the tears as I surveyed the wreckage of my past one more time.

Damn, this getting sober stuff was turning me into a broken faucet, but damned if I didn't feel just a little better about myself, because you can't fix a problem until you acknowledge that you have it.

≈≈≈

Soon the days began to meld into one another as I settled into my healing routine.

Summer had arrived, and a heavy, warm, hazy blanket of air had settled quietly over the Monadnocks.

The daytimes were filled with group meetings, one-on-ones with Dave, and regular light exercise that consisted primarily of long, relaxing walks through the surrounding forest. Sometimes I walked with friends, but oftentimes I sought out the solitude and peace that I was rediscovering in Nature.

Many of those solo treks led me into quiet contemplation as I lay on the big rock next to the Money Tree, where I had first realized that I was falling in love with Blue Eyes.

I had begun, then, to sense a yearning that bordered on disquiet, a growing knowledge that my days in the classroom must soon draw to a close. I realized that I was fast approaching the moment when I would need to cut the umbilical cord, and to venture back out into the real world to commence my life anew.

I was becoming restless, agitated, somewhat like the highly trained athlete who has left his blood, sweat and tears on the practice field, and who knows in his heart that the only way he will be able to progress to the next level is to step into the arena and compete for all the marbles.

I cringed as I looked back at the prior six months, and at the war of chaos, pain, and terror that I had waged against the world, and upon myself, and I shuddered as I recalled the trips into treatment, the false starts and the many failures.

But, more importantly, I acknowledged the hard-won lessons that I had received through all of the blood, sweat and tears, and the growth that I was experiencing as I came through to the other side.

I had spent nine weeks over the past six months in treatment facilities, and in my heart I knew that there was little more to be learned in these antiseptic environments.

This phase of my life had been a trip I wouldn't wish on my worst enemy, but I had come out alive, surviving by the grace of God and the unconditional love of countless courageous people.

And now I found myself growing physically stronger by the day, emotionally grounded and spiritually aware for the first time in my life.

Even my socialization skills were returning. I had developed a bond of trust with many of my fellow residents, and the sing-alongs with Guitar Man had become a regular nightly feature. Soon I found myself taking an interest in the lives and hopes and dreams of my fellow residents, as we got to know each other out under the stars.

A strange thing began to occur then, because as I revealed a little of myself to them, they reciprocated, and soon an element of relaxed, comfortable intimacy was entering into our talks. I suppose that this was a natural developmental stage for most children when they're around eight years old, but at the ripe old age of forty-one it was a remarkable and invigorating new social dynamic for a lone wolf to experience.

I mean, really, who could have known?

Several staff members had also introduced me to the basics of meditation and deep breathing, which could be utilized as a means for letting go of daily stress, as well as for becoming more centered and contemplative. I began practicing them during my walks, and when I was alone out on the smoking deck just after sunrise, and now they were paying big dividends.

So as I grew healthier, I grew stronger, and as I grew stronger, I grew more optimistic. My confidence in myself and in the program of Alcoholics Anonymous grew apace, and a quiet feeling of calm overcame me, infusing me with a sensation of inner peace that I had never experienced before.

Finally, half-way through Week Four, I realized that I could forgive myself, a little, and that the only way I could continue to grow would be to return to the outside world and carry on my education out there, where everything was real and for all the marbles.

I knew then, beyond the shadow of a doubt, that the time to move on was fast approaching, that I was finally ready to engage the world on the world's terms, and it was at that moment when I knew it was finally time for Wes to come home.

≈≈≈

Any patient's decision to go 'AMA' is vigorously discouraged by treatment facilities, and usually for good reason. The acronym stands for leaving "Against Medical Advice," and practically always means that a resident has decided to exit the facility prior to his or her projected departure date.

At most treatment centers such as the Alps the prescribed stay for a resident was thirty days, which in the early 1990's generally coincided with the amount of time that an insurance company would pay the tab for an institutionalization.

That had been the duration of my stay at the Hill several months previously, and it was what had been authorized by the insurer this time around.

I knew that the staff wouldn't be thrilled by my decision, nor could I blame them. This was an extreme action for me to take, even though I was only shortening my stay by four or five days, because let's face it, I hadn't exactly been the poster boy for maintaining successful recovery habits over the prior five years.

So yes, lost revenue aside, the folks who ran the Hill had every right to be concerned about my motives.

But I hadn't made my decision in haste. It came after several long days of soul searching and deep introspection, and what it finally boiled down to was a thorough examination of my motives. Was I trying to escape *from* something that I was afraid to face, or was I attempting to go *to* something that could help me grow as a recovering person?

The answer, for me, was clear. I was convinced that my journey had gone as far as it could go here at the Hill, and that in order to take the next step along the road I would need to make a leap of faith.

And now, for the first time in my life, I possessed that faith. It had arrived as a calm sense of confidence in myself, in the program of Alcoholics Anonymous, and in my motives.

I understood, finally, that my destiny was beckoning to me from out *there*, sober, telling me that I had finally been liberated after a lifetime of struggle, that I was now free to explore, experiment, grow, evolve, laugh, cry, love, make mistakes, contribute, and never stop trying to become a better person.

Yes, it was finally Wes's time to join the World.

≈≈≈

It was Friday morning, July 3, 1992. The staff had reluctantly arranged for a cab to pick me up, and to drive me over to the Trailways terminal in Keene, New Hampshire, where I could catch a bus for the trip to Boston.

I was prepared, but I knew that saying my goodbyes to my fellow residents would be the toughest part of my decision.

When I made my 'AMA' announcement to the senior staff the previous afternoon their reaction had been predictable – they held out little hope for my sustained recovery. Then they laid out all the arguments on me that I had already laid out on myself. I remained true to my convictions, however, and responded honestly, expressing my gratitude to them for all of their help during my two stays at the Hill.

I had a private talk with Dave, thanking him for helping to give my life back to me. I told him that I would never forget him, or Donna, or the rest of the staff, and I haven't.

I felt a moment of regret when I finally broke the news to my friends. It wasn't that I didn't want to leave, or that I had second thoughts, but I feared that my early departure might give them a false sense of security, that as a result of my going 'AMA' they might also harbor thoughts of leaving prematurely.

That was the last thing I wanted, but then I realized that we all have free choice, that we all have our own path to follow, and that at the end of the day we must all look at our own 'Man in the Mirror.'

I was just another drunk trying to get better, so it would be the epitome of arrogance for me to believe that I had so much influence over others.

So I said my goodbyes to everyone, and spent a couple of extra minutes speaking with Guitar Man. We had developed a strong friendship in four short weeks, and it would continue for another several years, until he and his wife left the Boston area.

Then the cab arrived, so I tossed my duffle bag into the back seat, climbed in after it, and we drove down the hill.

I didn't look back, for my life lay ahead of me.

≈≈≈

The cabbie dropped me off at the Trailways terminal in Keene at 9:30 that morning. I paid my fare, tossed him a fin, then grabbed a coffee and a donut and picked up a newspaper that somebody had left on the bench. It was the first paper I had seen in more than a month, so I intended to read it front to back while I killed the two hour wait until the bus departed.

But after five minutes I realized that the world was just as screwed up as it had been before I went off the deep end, so I concentrated on the sports and funny pages. As it turns out, I've pretty much stuck to that reading agenda for the past twenty-six years, with no discernible ill effects, and I have discovered that newspapers do indeed wrap fish quite efficiently.

We began boarding at 11:00 a.m. I was gratified to see that there were only about a dozen passengers taking this leg of the trip, so I slung my duffle bag over my shoulder, proceeded to the rear of the bus, tossed the duffle into the overhead, and settled into a window seat.

My luck held, because it was almost deserted back there. After residing in a therapeutic community for four weeks I was hesitant to get crowded in close to other people, particularly somebody who might tend towards being of the chitty-chatty persuasion. I may no longer have aspired to being a Lone Wolf, but being exposed to a motor-mouth was a bit of a stretch for someone fresh out of a four week gig in an alcohol rehab, if you catch my drift.

I soon slipped into a nod, lulled under the spell of the droning tires as the bus rocked gently and lumbered down the winding country backroads toward Route 2, and its ultimate destination of Boston.

≈≈≈

That was all I remembered until the bus shuddered several times, and then I heard the release of pressure from its airbrakes as it began to decelerate. Groggy, I felt a momentary sense of panic as I tried to orient myself to my new surroundings, and just then the driver shouted "Concord, Massachusetts, two miles, last stop before Boston."

I rubbed my eyes, then peered out the window just in time to note that we were passing the stark concrete walls and barbed wire barriers of Concord Reformatory, one of Massachusetts' medium security penitentiaries.

I couldn't help but say a silent prayer of thanks to my Higher Power for keeping me on this side of those walls, because I knew that I had probably been fortunate more times than I could count.

But for the Grace of God go I.

Moments later we rolled into the parking lot of a Howard Johnson's motel and restaurant. I grabbed my duffel bag and, still somewhat disoriented, stumbled down the aisle and out into the parking lot.

I needed a cup of real coffee, strong and hot, not the tasteless, watered down decaffeinated swill that they feed you at detoxes to prevent you from getting all wired up and excitable, and I needed a payphone to call a cab.

HoJo's had both - thank you, God!

The coffee revved me up quite nicely, and ten minutes later the cab drove up to the front of the building. I tossed a couple of bucks on the counter, grabbed my duffel and a refill of coffee, then walked out the door just as the cabbie was stepping out of his vehicle.

He looked like your typical hack, about my age, medium height, average build, with short hair and a mustache, dressed in jeans, a tee shirt and high top sneakers. I noticed, however, that he appeared somewhat nervous as he sized me up and inquired whether the duffel was my only baggage.

I answered in the affirmative, and informed him that I was headed for Norwood, about twenty-five miles distant.

He appeared to make note of that, but was slow to respond.

Then I inquired as to what the fare would be. He appeared hesitant, almost as if he was deciding whether to make the trip, so I asked again, somewhat more insistently this time. He stared at me for a moment, then at my duffel, and then he relented and told me that the fare would be forty dollars.

Highway robbery, literally, I thought, but I didn't have any alternative, so I tossed my bag onto the back seat and climbed in after it.

The cabbie slid into the driver's seat, fired up the engine, and we were soon cruising east on Route 2 toward Route 128, the notorious commuter highway. I remained silent, staring out the window, happily nursing my coffee refill.

A couple of minutes later I happened to look up front, and noticed that the cabbie was eyeing me somewhat suspiciously in his rearview mirror.

"Now what the hell is this all about," I wondered, recalling the similar look he had flashed a couple of times while we were discussing the fare.

He finally broke the silence, "Uh, so where are you coming from?" he asked tentatively, his eyes flicking back and forth nervously between the rearview mirror and the windshield.

I wasn't about to tell him that I had just been released from an alcohol and drug treatment facility, and, besides, I was beginning to build an attitude against him, so I simply stated, "Oh, back up the road a little ways," and tilted my head in that general direction.

My response didn't exactly loosen him up - if anything, he became more tense and fidgety.

"Just up the road?"

"Yeah."

I was having a difficult time figuring this guy out. Why the paranoia and questions? He was acting like I was a criminal, for God's sake.

And then it hit me - he *did* think that I was a criminal! The prison was just a couple of miles up the road from where he had picked me up, and I fit the bill – a single guy, a little rough around the edges, wearing beat up jeans and a work shirt, appearing out of nowhere with just a duffel bag.

It stood to reason that the HoJo's was probably a waystation for many of the newly released prisoners who were heading back to the Boston area. Some probably had good intentions as they began a new chapter of their lives, but in all likelihood there were just as many who planned to pick up right where they had left off before a judge gave them a time-out.

I had to admit that I had the general appearance of someone who had just been released from the 'joint.' For all I knew he probably thought I was already planning my next crime spree, and that I had lined him up to be my victim, because cabbies generally carry a big wad of cash in their pockets.

Oh, this was sweet! My first instinct was to play with him a little bit, but then I remembered why I was there. I had just spent nearly a month trying to change the miserable, deceitful and angry person I had dragged into Beech Hill, so now it was time to put myself in his shoes, calm his concerns and walk the talk for a change.

Humbled, I was about to explain that he didn't have anything to worry about, but just then something caught my eye. It was a large brass coin, dangling on the keychain that hung from the ignition, and it was glinting in the sunshine that flooded in through the passenger window.

There was something vaguely familiar about that coin, now where had I seen it before?

And then the final piece of the puzzle clicked into place. This guy was in the Program, and I was staring at his AA anniversary medallion, a brass coin designating the number of years that the holder had remained sober. You receive them annually, on your sobriety anniversary, and most people keep them close by, like a good luck charm, in their wallet, or near their bed, or as this guy had done, on his keychain.

And what better place for a recovering person to "remember when" than on a keychain, reminding you of what you could lose if you drank again?

With that I broke out into loud, hysterical laughter - the irony was just too rich!

But the driver was freaking out now. I thought he might run us both off the road by the way he was looking around at me, panicked, his head almost spinning, probably figuring that his ride was not only an ex-con, but an insane ex-con to boot.

Finally I regained my composure, dialed things down, and asked, "So, how many years have you got?"

"Huh? What do you mean?" he asked, still intimidated by the looney in his back seat, and probably thinking I had him pegged as an ex-con out on parole also.

"Your medallion. You're in the Program. I'm in the Program. How many years do you have sober?"

"You are too? You aren't a...?" and then his voice trailed off. He was clearly embarrassed that he had made a rash assumption about me.

"Nah, I didn't just get out of the prison, I'm actually coming home from a treatment center up in New Hampshire, newly clean and sober."

"Holy crap! I don't believe this, where were you up there?"

"Beech Hill, in Dublin, it's a nice little garden spot out near Keene," I chuckled, "so how long have you been sober?"

"Six years."

"Damn, I've never made it longer than two months, so that sounds like forever, how'd you do it?"

"You just have to take it one day at a time, and remember, don't sweat the small stuff, because it's all small stuff."

"I hear ya. What's your name? I'm Wes."

"I'm Bob. Nice to meet you, Wes, and really sorry about misjudging you like that. It's just that I got beat for fares a couple of times by the cons."

"Nice to meet you also, Bob, but don't give it a second thought. With all the nonsense stuff that I did over the years I'm probably fortunate that I'm not coming from there myself."

"Hah, I know what you mean," he chuckled.

And then it hit me, and I felt something catch in my throat. This had never been meant to be some random, improbable meeting - it had all been part of a plan much larger than me. I had been destined to meet Bob out here, a mere three hours after leaving the safety of the Hill. This had been a gift from my Higher Power, telling me that Wes was going to be alright if I just continued on the path, and did the next right thing.

The Big Guy just wanted to let me know that He was always at my back, and close by if I ever needed Him, and it was a good feeling.

Bob loosened up quickly after that, and became my sobriety guide for the next forty minutes, compliments of God, and we talked AA and recovery the entire way to Norwood.

I handed him a fifty when I exited the cab, and thanked him for sharing his experience, strength and hope with me.

Then we wished each other well, and parted ways.

≈≈≈

I have learned many things during my years in the fellowship of Alcoholics Anonymous, but the most valuable lesson of all is that if I put one foot in front of the other, and remain humble and grateful for my recovery, then my Higher Power will always be watching over me, giving me exactly what I need.

So thank you God, and thank you Bob the Cabbie.

Damn, as I'm proofing this the sweet tears of joy are coming again – twenty-six years in, and it's still brand new.

≈≈≈

I was somewhat reluctant to turn the key to the front door of my apartment. It had been almost a month since I abandoned the place, and after tacking on my week-long blackout I was fearful that I had adopted an entire community of weird little many-legged critters during my vacation from reality.

I was happily surprised, however, for despite the dank, stale air that still held the smell of heavy cigarette smoke, everything appeared to be in halfway decent order.

Then I remembered that Blue Eyes did some straightening up while I was making my last check of my wardrobe, and she had dumped a trash bag full of empty bourbon bottles, cigarette butts and a half eaten pepperoni pizza in the dumpster out behind the building. I was grateful for that, because it meant that I wouldn't have to deal with five empty bourbon bottles that no doubt still carried the scent of my favorite escape vehicle.

Yes, I had a growing confidence in my new sobriety, but I wasn't thrilled by the prospect of handling empties just yet.

It was obvious that the apartment would need a complete once-over, but that could wait until the next day. It was around four o'clock, and I just wanted to take a nice long nap, and then a hot, soaking shower, so I opened some of the windows to air the place out, then stretched out on my bed and was out cold in two minutes flat.

I had big plans for the evening, so I needed my rest. I was planning to hang out with a bunch of drunks – sober ones!

≈≈≈

I awoke from my nap feeling revitalized and alert. I shaved, grabbed a quick shower, then pulled on my last pair of laundered blue jeans and a tee shirt, and was walking out the door by six o'clock.

I arrived in Medfield fifteen minutes later, and stopped at a sub shop that I had discovered on one of my previous trips to a meeting over there. I ordered a roast beef sub with all the fixings, then drove over to the church where the meeting was being held. I parked in the lot across the street, smoked a cigarette, and stared at the church for a few moments, steeling myself for what was to come.

Not surprisingly, I was more than a little nervous. I hadn't attended this meeting for two months, and I was certain that most of the members knew about my relapse by then. It was one of a long string of failures I had put together over the past couple of years, so I was apprehensive about what kind of reception to expect.

So I prayed. I asked God to give me the strength to walk into that church with my head high, and to help me accept the outcome of my return, whatever that might be. Then I thanked Him for my newfound sobriety, and for delivering me to this place.

Finally, it was time to face my fears, so I grabbed my bag of food, walked across the street, took a deep, cleansing breath and entered the church.

≈≈≈

Tony was one of the regulars, and he was standing near the door when I walked in, serving as a greeter. He was about my age, and he had put together a long string of sober years. He was one of the first people to reach out to me early on in my occasional visits to AA, and now a smile of recognition crossed his face as he held out his hand to me.

"Hi Wes, welcome, it's good to see you again," was all he said, but those few words spoke volumes, because they told me that the past was the past, that regardless of my previous failures I was still welcome in the Halls, and that this moment in time was all that mattered.

"Hi Tony, thanks, it's great to be back."

"You look good. Wherever you've been, you look relaxed and healthy."

"Yeah, well I've been to Hell and back, but I'm here again, and hopefully some of the stuff that I heard up on the Hill will stay with me this time around, and that's all I care about right now."

"Oh, so things didn't get any better out there since I stopped drinking?" he laughed.

"I think you already know the answer to that, Tony, so just be grateful that I did the field research for you. I usually charge the big bucks for that stuff."

"Oh, I am, thanks very much, Wes," he laughed, "now stick around this time - we missed you!"

And with those words I realized that the Lone Wolf had come home.

In the next few minutes I ran the gauntlet, as half a dozen early arrivals came up to welcome me back and shake my hand. A couple of them even gave me their phone numbers, "just in case you need to talk to someone."

I was early for the Beginner's meeting that started at seven o'clock, so I went into the kitchen and wolfed down my sub between handshakes and salutations from other members who I recognized from my previous visits.

It felt great to be back, and great to be alive.

≈≈≈

Beginner meetings are just what the name implies - meetings designed to assist newcomers in becoming familiar with the program of Alcoholics Anonymous.

I know through personal experience that most new arrivals can feel somewhat intimidated by "regular" meetings when we first walk through the doors, so this is a good venue for being introduced to the program, asking questions, learning the ins and outs, and getting to know some of our peers who are just as new and shell-shocked as we are.

The word "beginner" can often be a misnomer, however, because many of us believe that we will always be a newcomer to sobriety, for we only have today to be concerned with, and therefore we must always keep our recovery fresh, and green, and in the present moment.

It's therefore not uncommon to see somebody with five, ten, even twenty years of continuous sobriety attending a Beginners' meeting. The newcomer learns a valuable lesson as a result, because he or she receives the benefit of hearing the experience, strength and hope of people who have remained sober for long periods of time, regardless of what challenges modern life has thrown at them.

Conversely, the regulars get a great reminder that they're only one drink away from being a beginner again, and that's if they're lucky enough to survive that drink. We must always remember that our disease has laid dormant these many years, doing push-ups and quietly waiting for us to become complacent, to let our guard down, because our disease wants us miserable, and dead, and it is very patient.

I too have attended Beginners' meetings many times over the years, and I find these visits a wonderful "remember when" to a time when I was new and struggling myself.

On this night there were approximately a dozen people in the room, mostly true newcomers, but also a few who had, like me, bounced in and out a few times, and who I recognized from my previous visits to this meeting. I hated to wish bad luck on anyone, but I will admit to feeling a certain sense of comfort in the knowledge that I had not been alone in my numerous half-hearted attempts to get sober.

But now the slate was clear, we were back, we were sober, and we each had a brand new life beckoning to us if we wanted it badly enough. I couldn't speak for the others, but I for one wanted it, and I was willing to do anything to keep it.

≈≈≈

Beginner meetings are usually moderated by a member of the "regular" group. That person will generally have a long period of sobriety, and he or she will suggest a topic for discussion that is of particular interest to newcomers.

That night's meeting was chaired by Mary P., and the topic was, "picking up that damned two hundred pound telephone."

Newcomers often feel uncomfortable about calling another member of the program for help when they're struggling – I know I did, anyway. Some consider it to be a personal weakness or character defect that they can't seem competent to take care of their own problems, while others are fearful that they might appear to look weak-willed, or inferior, and others are simply ashamed that they "blew it" again.

Mary began the discussion by speaking for a few minutes about her own inability to call other AA members when she was angry, frightened, and close to drinking in her early days.

She then explained that it was not until she realized that, "we're all in the same fix when we're first starting out," that she was able to overcome her embarrassment about asking for help.

She also mentioned that never once had she realized that somewhere out there was a person who actually wanted her to call, who had been through the identical experience, whose day would be brightened by having the opportunity to help another alcoholic get through a rough patch.

That was a new angle for me, this concept that I'd be helping somebody else by calling them to discuss my own problems. Through the fullness of time, however, I have discovered the wisdom in the concept, for I have grown and matured in ways I would never have believed possible whenever I found myself on the receiving end of one of those calls. As much as I had assisted the other person on those occasions, I had benefitted equally myself.

Mary broke into my thoughts then, "Hello, Wes, welcome back, we missed you! Would you care to give us your thoughts?"

Well, not really, Mary, but in for a penny, in for a pound I suppose.

"Hi, Mary. Okay, well, first off I'm grateful to be here. I just got home from treatment a few hours ago, so I'm kind of on information overload, but I know that for myself I've never been comfortable about picking up the phone when things were going down the tubes. It's like I didn't want to impose on other people with my problems, or that I was embarrassed. It made me feel queasy, talking about my weaknesses and failures."

"I understand how you feel, we probably all felt like that at times, but surely you must see how that has hurt you over the years. You've been coming here every once in a while, for maybe two or three years now, but never really participating, and look where's it's gotten you, right back at a Beginners' meeting. Did you ever think of calling somebody before you drank again?"

"No, all of a sudden I just found a drink in my hand, and I never thought to call anyone. I never realized that I might be helping someone else by dumping my stuff on them - it's a new way of looking at things."

"Well, give it a try the next time you're having a hard time coping with a problem. It's like we say, we're only as sick as our secrets, so just pick up that damned phone and call someone. You'll be amazed at how good it will feel to share what you're going through with another person, it's cleansing, and you might even discover that they went through the exact same thing themselves."

She paused, then said, "Now promise me that!"

"Okay, I promise, Mary."

And with those words the big bad Lone Wolf took one more baby step out of the wilderness.

≈≈≈

I sat up front, near the podium, for the regular meeting. I had run into a longtime friend, Lynn, at the refreshment table. She had attempted, to no avail, to help me get sober many times over the prior year.

And now, true to form, she was taking charge to make sure that I was situated close to the speakers from the commitment, rather than hiding out in the back of the room on "Denial Aisle," which had been my seating area of choice in all of my previous forays to Medfield.

We had partied hard together once upon a time, but now she had a couple of years of solid recovery, and it was clear that evening that she was going to make it one of her life's missions to shepherd me through the struggles of early sobriety.

She was tenacious, a force to be reckoned with, and I was helpless to resist her efforts. In fact, she pretty much kidnapped me, so based on past experience I knew that I'd be getting a lot of personal attention from her that evening, and that the Onion would soon be getting another shave.

"I want to hear all about your latest little adventure," she had demanded, as she grabbed me by the elbow and propelled me up to the front of the room.

She now had a cute little fretful frown on her face, the one that always made her look like she had just found a sick puppy and was nursing it back to health, but if you were to have looked into her eyes you would have seen a force and a determination there like no other you have ever experienced.

This sick little puppy recognized that expression, and knew that resistance would be futile, so Mr. Tough Guy followed her without a whimper.

"That's it, be a good little doggie, Fido," I told myself.

We talked for ten minutes, and I gave her the short version of my recent adventures, even mentioning that I had spoken at a commitment much like the one that was about to begin.

But, if I was hoping to snag a couple of brownie points for that one, then I was sadly mistaken.

Lynn just smiled mischievously, knowing that she had me trapped, and said, "Gee, that's nice to know, Wes. I happen to be chairing a commitment next Thursday over in Foxboro, so you're coming, no excuses. You can't speak until you have ninety days, but you can listen and learn. It'll be good for you, and it will make up for that time you bailed out on the commitment that I chaired over at the prison last winter," she purred, her voice all sweet and syrupy as her eyes bored a hole through me.

Ouch, I had forgotten about that!

Just then the meeting was called to order, we had a moment of silence for the sick and suffering who were still out there using, and then we recited the Serenity Prayer – saved by the bell!

≈≈≈

There's somewhat of an established rhyme and reason in the manner by which AA commitments are conducted, because the speakers and group members each have general guidelines, or rules that they will typically follow.

Speakers concentrate on telling their own stories. They talk about what their life was like *then*, when they were still using, and what it's like *now*, as sober, recovering persons. It is through this narrative that they heal, express their hope for another day of sobriety, and attempt to motivate other alcoholics to walk the same path as they have. By so doing they become a power of example, as they continue the lifelong process of acknowledging and cleaning up the wreckage of their past.

Meanwhile, the audience members concentrate on placing themselves in the speaker's shoes, thereby identifying with the speaker, and emphasizing their similarities, rather than pointing out their differences. Whereas every person's story is unique, by comparing our similarities we discover more often than not that we are all alike in the manner by which our disease progressed and stole from us, and that we all had the same hole in our soul on the day we walked into our first meeting.

It is through this shared experience that we find the means to recover and grow as sober, responsible human beings, and we find that we never have to be alone again.

I have heard many thousands of stories over the years, and few are the ones that I couldn't identify with, at least in part.

Three men and two women told their stories of experience, strength and hope that night, and I was hooked from the very beginning. I found myself identifying with each speaker, as I recalled my inaugural talk at Beech Hill a few weeks previously. Each person spoke from the heart, with a candor that could not be doubted, nor imitated, and I now understood firsthand how difficult that can be.

The evening's visiting group came in from Newton, which was a close-in suburb of Boston that was approximately a thirty minute drive from Medfield. On this night each of the five speakers told a part of my own story, and sometimes it felt like they were reading my mind.

One man had lost a dozen jobs because of his drinking, and his wife had finally divorced him. That was easy enough for me to identify with, because I had lost nearly as many jobs, and several relationships due to my own drinking and drugging.

And then I wondered, fleetingly, whether I had lost Blue Eyes this time. I felt a pang of regret, because it sure looked that way, so yeah, it was plenty easy for me to connect with that guy.

One woman had lost custody of her children, another man lost his freedom, imprisoned for crimes he committed while under the influence of alcohol and drugs, and another guy lost his money and property because of gambling debts he made while intoxicated. His children never spoke to him again, even after he got sober.

All of those things had happened to me to one degree or another, or were "yet's" that I knew were waiting patiently right around the corner, biding their time and doing push-ups until I took another drink.

Finally, the chairwoman spoke. She told a story of great loss, heartache and shame, and my heart went out to her. But it wasn't until she realized that she had lost herself – her hopes and dreams and dignity and innocence – that she could find the strength to surrender to her disease.

That one hit me right in the gut, because I have never felt so lost, empty or alone as I did that fateful day when I crawled out of my last blackout and stared at the broken man in the mirror.

Yes, I too had lost myself, and now I was searching for my way home.

≈≈≈

After the meeting wrapped up Lynn and I made plans to attend the Tuesday night Discussion meeting. She and her husband and kids were heading down to the Cape for the 4th of July weekend, so she took that opportunity to hammer home the fact that I needed to spend every possible waking moment at meetings over the next few days.

Unlike the past, her advice fell on eager ears this time around.

Holidays, particularly those that occur on long weekends, can be treacherous times for recovering alcoholics and addicts, particularly newbies like myself. Many of us partied hard on such occasions, often around the clock, or even longer if we were addicted to coke or speed, so we can find ourselves in quite a bit of mischief when left to our own devices on a long holiday weekend such as this 4th that I was facing.

Truth be told, I was looking forward to the weekend with mixed emotions. It would be great to have some time to myself without the regimentation that was a twenty-four hour feature at the Alps, but I was concerned that I might become bored quickly now that the regimentation was absent, and boredom was my mortal enemy.

Lynn came to my rescue, however, and ran down a list of popular weekend meetings that were in the general vicinity. She also reminded me that there would be an "alcathon" in Dedham, which was several towns away and not too far from where I lived. It was scheduled to run around the clock, from dawn on Saturday morning until Sunday at eight a.m.

Alcathons are a blast. They're celebrations, generally held on holidays, joyful gatherings of recovering persons from many towns, backgrounds and lifestyles, around-the-clock meetings where alcoholics can drop in for a dose of AA no matter what the time of day or night. They're also safe havens, serving as welcoming beacons for many of us who might feel an extra sense of discomfort as a result of our prior holiday drinking and drugging habits.

These celebrations are structured like "open meetings," and commitments from nearby groups often take one hour slots, or more, and individuals can fill in the open spaces to share their own experience, strength and hope.

Food tables abound, especially ones containing deserts, so if you're a chocaholic like me you will think that you've been transported to Heaven - there's just something about that special bond between recovering alkies and sweets. They say it's related to the sugar fix, but I believe that it's more about comforting the soul, and evidently I have a lonely soul that requires a lot more comforting than the average person.

And, because these meetings attract recovering people from many different communities, you're also likely to meet a whole bunch of strangers who may soon become new friends, as well as learn about interesting meetings in nearby towns.

I had already scoped out my meeting plans at the Trailways station before I took my bus ride down from New Hampshire. I planned on attending the Saturday morning discussion meeting in Medfield, then give my apartment it's much needed clean-up. Lynn's suggestion that I attend the alcathon was a great addition to the list, because I could get there whenever I wanted, and stay as long as I wanted, so I was planning to plant my fanny at that meeting and hang on for as long as it took to keep me safe and sane.

And, last but not least, I planned to hit the Sunday night Step meeting in Medfield – that would wrap up the weekend on a high note.

≈≈≈

I arrived back at my apartment around ten o'clock, and was gratified to see that it had aired out nicely during the evening.

It was time for one last smoke, and then I hit the sack, stopping first to get down on my knees to thank my Higher Power for keeping me sober, and for delivering me safely back home.

I was out cold ten minutes later - mission accomplished for another twenty-four hours in the life of the recovering onion known as Wes.

≈≈≈

I was up and drinking my first cup of coffee just after seven the next morning. The weather was sunny and warm, and it held the promise of a magnificent day awaiting me - it felt like the first day of summer vacation when I was a little kid.

Come to think of it, I guess I was just a little kid again.

I had already said my morning prayer, splashed some water on my face, and decided that I would tackle the first stage of the cleanup before I headed over to the Medfield meeting. It started at ten o'clock, so I began to bag the remainder of the garbage and detritus that was left over from my binge, then started in on the refrigerator.

One hour later I tossed a Hefty into the dumpster out back, then drove over to Friendly's restaurant in Medfield. I ordered coffee and English muffins, and was just taking my first bite when a guy I recognized from the halls came over, held out his hand and said, "Hey, Wes, good to see you again. How you doin' these days?"

It was my buddy, Andy, who I had met the previous summer when I came dragging my butt back into a few of the Medfield meetings after another in that long string of relapses.

Andy was a young guy, in his early twenties, and he began drinking when he was still a kid. He and I had both grown up in Westwood, which had the dubious reputation for being a big party community, so the drinking and drugging had started early for us, as well as for many of our peers.

Andy was hard to miss, because he always towered over most of the crowd. He was a big, tall, rugged kid, checking in at around six foot three inches and weighing in at two hundred and forty pounds, most of which was muscle. He always spoke softly, politely, but you knew that there was a powerful young man behind his words.

We shook hands, and I said, "Hey, Andy, please sit down, nice to see you, how've you been?"

"I've been good," he smiled, "all in all doing pretty well. I haven't seen you at meetings for a while, everything okay?"

"Well, I did a little more field research, you can probably guess how that turned out, but I'm back, and feeling pretty good about things."

"I've been there, also, so just try to keep it one day at a time, it's been working for me," he said.

"So far, so good, I'm hanging in there, its meetings, meetings and more meetings on the agenda."

"Just go easy on yourself Wes, whatever you do, and don't beat yourself up," he said, then added, "I've been reading the 'Big Book' every day, and it's really helped me. You may want to give it a try, and there's also a 'Big Book' meeting in Medfield on Monday nights that I've been attending. There's some incredible wisdom in the AA literature – the Old Timers really got it right back then."

"I'll do that, thanks."

It was good to see him, and I was pleased to hear that he had remained sober, because that meant he was coming up on his one year anniversary. I said a silent prayer that he would stick with his program, because if you're a sober young kid who has put the booze and drug wars firmly behind you, then you have a great head start on life. You've been through the hard stuff, and survived, learning many of life's toughest lessons, and you will have developed a maturity and a wisdom and a strength of spirit well beyond your years that will guide you safely through all of the storms and challenges that are thrown in your path.

For myself, I was now in my early forties, so a part of me regretted all the wasted time, unnecessary losses, and trail of sadness and hurt that I had left behind me. But there's a saying in the program that goes, "we should not regret the past, nor wish to shut the door on it," so I knew that if could remain sober I could make my amends to the people I had harmed, make peace with my past, and look forward one day at a time to a brand new life full of hope and opportunity.

It might very well be that I could even find some peace of mind, that one elusive commodity that I had been searching for my entire life.

≈≈≈

I did not know it on that quiet summer morning, but Andy would become one of my best friends for life, one of the people in AA who I forged a deep and enduring friendship with that has survived the decades. We've been through a lot, good and bad, even teaming up on some business ventures, and I have been blessed by my Higher Power to have known and learned from him this past twenty-six years.

His is a kind and gentle soul, and he carries a quiet spirituality that is both calming and inspirational. He has traveled the world extensively, his wanderlust taking him throughout the United States and to many foreign countries, where he has plied his trade as an electrician, inventor and writer.

And, best of all, his travels have given him the opportunity to attend AA meetings around the globe. What a gift, and what an opportunity to experience the universality of this program that has saved the lives of millions of people in the far corners of the Earth.

≈≈≈

Andy mentioned that he was also on his way to the morning meeting, so we paid our tabs, went out to our cars, and drove over to the church.

≈≈≈

It was just like old home week when I walked up the front steps of the little parish house under the elms. There were several people from the prior night's meeting hanging out, smoking and talking, and there were also four or five others who I remembered as regulars at this meeting.

So once again I was besieged by handshakes and hugs, then had to give a brief recap of my past month's fun adventures all over again.

Soon it was time to go inside, so I entered the small building and headed toward the back of the meeting room, hoping for a little anonymity.

Fat chance of that!

Walter, who was chairing that day, noticed my entrance and called out to me to come up front. He was pointing to a seat right next to him that had evidently been set aside for me, and it was the seat that was ordinarily reserved for the guest speakers.

Uh oh, I wasn't sure that I was ready to be put on display, but my Higher Power evidently thought I was, so who was I to argue? Besides, I had a sinking feeling that I knew what was coming next, so why try to avoid it?

I took a deep breath and walked over to Walter. We shook hands and I took the seat next to him. This was a smaller, more intimate group than many in AA, and on this day there were approximately twenty people sitting around in a circle, talking and laughing before the meeting started.

"It's nice to see you back here, Wes," Walter said, "I was worried."

"Thanks, Walter, I guess I'm just more pigheaded than most, so I needed to test the waters one more time."

"Well, I'm glad you made it back in one piece, because many don't," he said, then added, "So, would you care to be the guest speaker today?"

Gulp. Gee, what a surprise, but it wasn't like I could say no, and truth to tell I was becoming comfortable about telling my story by now. So, no big deal, because if my HP thought that I needed this, then I really didn't have much of a choice, and it was probably better to get it over with earlier, rather than later.

"Sure, I'll speak Walter, I'm getting used to it."

"Great, thank you," he said, then called the meeting to order and led us through the Lord's Prayer and the Serenity Prayer.

Walter led off the meeting with a five-minute version of his own story, then introduced me to the group. I recognized nearly every face in the room, so I didn't have much of a case of the butterflies, and I started right in, "Hi, my name is Wes, and I'm an alcoholic and a drug addict."

"Hi, Wes," came the response from the group, with a couple of "welcome backs" tossed in for good measure.

I spoke for ten minutes, first giving a quick recap of my crash and burn, then talking at length about my surrender that began in Bill's car, and which culminated with Donna in the peaceful garden on the mountain.

I got choked up for a moment, but recovered quickly and spoke about my experiences "up on the Hill," then mentioned my gratitude for all the unselfish people who had helped me on my journey over the past month.

I finished up by relating my adventure with Bob the Cabbie, and said, "That, as much as anything, told me that I was on the right path, and that my Higher Power was always going to be at my back."

Surprise, surprise, I even spoke briefly about my feelings, which had always been off limits, and I noticed that I didn't break out into a cold sweat this time. That was major progress for me, because like many others who were born in the early 1950's I had grown up in a household where feelings didn't exist, period, then used alcohol and drugs to kill whatever took their place every time they tried to peek out from behind the veneer.

So score one for Wes, because here I sat on Independence Day, 1992, sweating it out but talking about my feelings - go figure.

I finished up by thanking everyone in the room for their support over the years, then turned bright red when the next round of handclapping and "welcome back" started up.

≈≈≈

I hung out on the parish hall's porch for about thirty minutes after the meeting, smoking and getting reacquainted with a half-dozen people who I knew from my previous visits to Medfield meetings.

It was good to see George, Paula, Debbie, Christine, Eddie, a second friend named Lynn, and several others, all of whom had reached out to me in the past. Each had given me their number to call if I was hurting, or told me how they had handled the rough spots that any recovering alcoholic faces sooner or later, or simply held out their hand in friendship, assuring me that I was going to be alright.

I felt comfortable, relaxed and accepted in this quiet little sanctuary under the elms. It was a nice feeling, and one that I found myself becoming accustomed to. I planned to make this one of my core meetings, along with the Friday nighter, because they were two great venues for greeting the weekend - each of them was already beginning to feel like home to me.

Then I drove back to my apartment, spent a couple of hours finishing up the cleaning, and collapsed onto my bed, where I fell into a deep sleep for several hours.

I needed my beauty rest, because I was going to a bash that evening with a bunch of friends who I had never met.

≈≈≈

I could feel the raw energy emanating from the church in Dedham as soon as I parked my car, and as I walked toward the building on that warm, humid evening I could already sense that it was buzzing with activity, the air around it vibrating with anticipation.

There were well in excess of one hundred people already on hand, judging by the number of cars parked nearby, and the size of the crowd hanging out in front of the church.

Many had probably been there for hours, and it was a good bet that the attendance would double as the evening wore on.

I stubbed out my cigarette, then walked inside to the large meeting room. I recognized a couple of people from the various meetings that I had occasionally dropped in on over the years, and there were even a few familiar faces from the Medfield meetings that I had attended during the past twenty-four hours.

It was gratifying to see every person in that room, because every one of them reminded me that I had many sources of support wherever my travels took me. Here were people just like myself, standing quietly and anonymously in the background, but always prepared to step up and give me a hand, or advice, or a friendly pat on the back whenever I feared that I was alone in the wilderness.

And, over the years, I have added hundreds of those kind, generous people to my extended AA family.

≈≈≈

First things first, I made a beeline for the long dessert table at the rear of the room, grabbed a couple of chocolate chip cookies and some chocolate cake, and then found a seat.

For the next two hours I sat anchored to my chair while a dozen speakers related their stories of experience, strength and hope. I got up briefly to take a bathroom break, grab another coffee and hit the dessert table one more time, but other than that I was locked on like radar to the speakers' podium.

I was fascinated, once again, by the stories. Man or woman, young or old, rich or poor, healthy or frail, each person who stood at the podium that evening told a story that was unique unto themselves, but in a way it was as if each was speaking on my behalf, because they all touched upon the same feelings that I had experienced as I struggled through the barren wastelands of addiction, and into the flowering gardens of sobriety.

Each had, in their own time and place, peered into the mirror of their soul and had their epiphany. They had survived their terrible disease, surrendered, and were now recovering, one day at a time, by the grace of the God of their own understanding.

No one had it easy, no one had found a short cut to the Promised Land, but each person who stood before me that evening, or at the two thousand plus meetings I have attended since, spoke from a language of the heart that was sincere, humble and inspirational.

These were people whose sobriety had survived the tests of time and life, and they were here tonight providing me with a roadmap to a future that could be full of hope and promise, one day at a time.

For perhaps the first time in my life I understood the true meaning of gratitude, and of the security that comes from belonging to something that is far larger than oneself.

And once again it came back to one simple concept: "We did what I couldn't do."

≈≈≈

There was a fifteen minute break at eleven o'clock, so I stepped outside, lit up a cigarette, and spoke with some people I recognized from various meetings in the area.

I realized then that I was physically exhausted, and that I was on information overload from all of my adventures since leaving the Hill the previous morning, so I decided to hit the road and get a good night's sleep.

As I walked slowly to my car on that warm, muggy evening, I noticed that summer was settling in, and I realized that for the first time in weeks I was no longer in a hurry to get anywhere.

I stopped then, stared up at the three-quarter moon for several minutes, and realized that I was right where I was always meant to be at that one brief, perfect moment in time.

There was then for me no past, nor future, just the here and now, and it was a good feeling.

≈≈≈

I awoke from a deep, dreamless slumber at nine o'clock on Sunday morning. I felt rested, refreshed and strong as I rolled out of bed and hit my knees to say my morning prayer.

I realized then, with some surprise, that my twice-daily prayer sessions had become an automatic reflex. This simple act of surrender was now wired in, just something I did, like breathing or brushing my teeth. There was no conscious thought process involved, and I considered that to be a giant step forward in my fledgling recovery.

I had no big plans on tap for the day, with the exception of attending the Sunday night Step Meeting over in Medfield, so I decided that I'd just take things slow and easy, and let life decide what I was meant to do that day.

I put on a pot of coffee, placed a couple of English muffins on the broiler rack, tossed down a half dozen vitamins, and then began scanning through the stack of bills that had gathered during my absence.

Ahh, reality was returning, but for once I didn't worry about minor details.

It was like I had heard up at the Alps, "Don't sweat the small stuff, because it's *all* small stuff."

Okay, God, if you say so, I'll buy it.

I savored my breakfast, taking the time to enjoy every bite, then took my second cup of coffee out onto the patio. Along the way I grabbed my "Twelve Steps and Twelve Traditions" book, and settled into my lounger.

I decided that there was no better place to commence my new life than at the beginning, so I opened the book to Step One, "We admitted we were powerless over alcohol - that our lives had become unmanageable," and began reading.

This is where it all begins, because this is where the alcoholic admits complete defeat, and embarks on the lifelong process of healing.

I thought back with gratitude to my own surrender in that serene garden on the top of the Hill, with Donna, where I had finally stopped fighting life and the bottle.

Me, Wes, experiencing gratitude - what a strange sensation, and what a miracle.

≈≈≈

I soon became acclimated to the rounds of handshakes and "welcome backs" at the Medfield meetings. I had forgotten that there were so many people I had occasionally crossed paths with over the years who also attended those meetings, including a few who I had done some serious drinking and drugging with at one time or another.

It was these latter individuals who always seemed to catch my attention, because the fact that they had survived, made it into AA, and were thriving in sobriety convinced me that I too had a chance, if I could just manage to stick to my program.

≈≈≈

I was in for a surprise when I sat down in the large circle of chairs at the Medfield Sunday night Step meeting. There, sitting directly across from me, was Pat, the clinical coordinator who I had met during my one week stay at the Framingham Detox back in January.

Pat had conducted my outtake interview on the final morning of my stay. He told me several years later that he had arrived at the not unlikely conclusion that I hadn't been quite done with my drinking and drugging career when we wrapped up our little discussion.

Geez, Pat, I'm deeply wounded, because I did stay clean and sober for an entire week that time!

He looked up just then, noticed me staring, and gave a slight nod and smile. I wasn't sure whether he recognized me or not, but for whatever reason I made a mental note that he was a straight-up guy, and that if I ever needed some help down the road he would be right at the top of my call list.

Little did I know that I would make that call three years later, and that it would save my life.

≈≈≈

I was right back on my knees ten hours later, asking God for help in keeping me away from a drink and a drug, and remaining reasonably sane for one more day.

Then I brewed a pot of coffee and sketched out my plans for the day.

My highest priority was also the most intimidating one. Dave had given me the name and telephone number of a woman who was a counselor at one of Beech Hill's Greater Boston facilities, and he had strongly urged me to give her a call to set up private counseling sessions as soon as I returned home.

"Don't wait, or put it off," he warned, "or you'll never get around to it, and then I can almost guarantee that you'll be right back up here, or maybe dead, six months from now," was his sage, optimistic advice.

Gee, I guess that for some strange reason Dave thought I still had a little more work that I should attend to - go figure.

Well, so maybe I couldn't exactly argue the fact, but I wasn't looking forward to going through the process of breaking in another counselor - this would make four, or was it five, in the past six months.

Okay, and maybe I was a lot more nervous about having to open up to another human being who might know me better than I knew myself, and who would no doubt dredge up all of my character defects, fears and doubts one more time. This poking and prodding to find out what made Wes tick was always intimidating, no matter how many times I had to go through it, and some of the revelations were downright spooky.

But the bottom line was that I couldn't go back to the place in my head where I had been just one short month ago, because I knew that I wouldn't survive for more than a few years, so I reluctantly concluded that the Onion had no choice but to forge ahead one more time.

In retrospect, I'm grateful that I made the call.

≈≈≈

"Hello, this is Eileen," came the woman's voice, "how can I help you?"

"Uh, hi Eileen, my name is Wes H., and I believe that Dave, my counselor, told you that I'd be contacting you."

"Oh, yes, hello Wes, I've been expecting your call."

"I just got back Friday, and I guess Dave thinks that I should go into counseling as soon as possible."

"Well, he did recommend it, but what do you think?"

I paused, then bit the hook, "Yeah, I think he's probably right. I've been doing really well since I left 'the Hill' Friday, but usually I can't seem to stay sober for very long after I get out of treatment. This last time really broke me, and I don't want to relapse again. I'm not sure that I have another recovery left in me if this one fails. "

"Well, then let's make sure it doesn't! I have some available time this week, maybe Wednesday or Thursday, if you'd like to get going on it?"

Damn, out of the frying pan and into the fire, I thought, but to say the least my choices were limited.

"Would you have something Wednesday, in the morning?"

"How would 11:00 be?"

"That would be fine."

We discussed the fee structure, which was fair, then Eileen gave me directions to the office, and that was that.

"Okay, God, please don't give up on me, at least I'm trying," I thought, as I hung up the phone.

≈≈≈

I met up with Andy again over at the Medfield Big Book meeting on Monday night.

We talked at length afterwards, and he suggested several other meetings that I might benefit from. He, like Lynn, was a big fan of the Medfield Tuesday night discussion meeting, so I agreed to meet him there the next night.

Andy and Lynn – here were two great chaperones for keeping Wes out of trouble, and I would go on to develop lifelong bonds of friendship and trust with these two wonderful people.

≈≈≈

I realized that I had found "my" meeting from the moment I walked into the Medfield Tuesday night room. Everything just seemed to fit like a glove, the room, the atmosphere, the people, and the energy. It all came together, and it was clear to me that this was where I was always meant to be at this one unique moment in my life.

I saw a dozen familiar faces smiling in recognition, and I knew then that I was home.

The Tuesday nighter became my go-to meeting for the next ten years, until I moved out of the area. I rarely missed it, nor the Friday night and Saturday morning meetings, and the many friendships and support that I found in those rooms were a gift from my Higher Power that I will be forever grateful for.

≈≈≈

If you haven't noticed, we have a lot of sayings in AA, and one that is close to my heart is, "When you've been to too many meetings, go to too many more," which I did, in spades.

And so it was that those three core meetings marked the beginning of my total immersion in recovery activity through AA. I began planning my days around a meeting, and during my first year in sobriety I developed a discipline whereby I attended almost three hundred and fifty meetings, stood at the speaker's podium to relate my experience, strength and hope at a dozen commitments, and met one-on-one for counseling with Eileen more than thirty times.

I would need every one of those meetings, because I knew that my life depended upon them.

≈≈≈

God rang me up a couple of days after I returned home and said, "Welcome back, my son, so I trust that you had a fruitful trip?"

I got a big kick out of that, for I knew that He knew that it had been.

"Yes, thanks God, it was an eye opener, that's for sure."

"I take it that you enjoyed my choice of cabbies for the last leg of your journey?" He asked, chuckling.

"That was you? Geesh, I should have known that you'd pull something like that."

"There's a lesson there, my son, because cab driving is a noble profession," He said, and then added, "so you may wish to consider that line of work somewhere down the pike."

God is great with the puns, but I took the high road and replied, "Well, thanks God, but I'm a professional salesperson, so I'll stick to what I'm good at," I said, with just the slightest touch of arrogance.

God just chuckled again, wished me well on that beautiful summer day, then went off to build a galaxy somewhere out beyond Orion's Belt.

In retrospect, I suppose that I should have known He was setting me up for something – to be polite, I'll just call it another one of those irritating little "growth opportunities."

≈≈≈

I knocked on Eileen's office door at precisely eleven o'clock on Wednesday morning.

"Come in, Wes," she called out.

I entered her office, sensing that I was going to my first day of school all over again.

As it turned out I was, because I had a lot to learn about life, sobriety, and the onion known as Wes.

Part Three: Life on Life's Terms

"Chop that wood
Carry water
What's the sound of one hand clapping
Enlightenment, don't know what it is"

From the song "Enlightenment"
by Van Morrison

"Let it go, Wes."

"Let what go, Jack?" I'd sigh in exasperation.

"Just let it go, Wes."

"Aww, geez, Jack, not again, let *what* go, damn it?"

"Just let it go, let it all go."

"What the hell, Jack, let what go? Always with the riddles, let go of what?"

"Just stop fighting it, Wes, you're going to be alright, so just let it all go!"

And then his eyes, dark glowing embers, would burn a hole through me as he jabbed his finger into my chest and half-shouted, "And just don't drink, no matter what, just don't drink, Wes, you never have to drink again!"

The mantra was always the same, and no matter where we started, or what we talked about, it always came full circle back to that frustrating little conundrum that drove me nuts – what was "IT," and how in the name of God was I going to be able to let go of "IT," if I didn't even know what "IT" was?

≈≈≈

Jack was my AA sponsor in the early days after I returned home from Beech Hill. I asked him to be my sponsor because I believed that he was certifiably insane – in other words, I sensed a kindred spirit.

He'd been a fighter pilot in the Korean War, and God only knows what he must have experienced over there. I knew one thing however – I sure wouldn't have wanted to be lined up in his gunsights when he was having a bad day, because he was one wild old bird.

I'd also heard some great stories about his drinking escapades when he returned to the States, so I sensed a common bond between us. Bottom line, I considered Jack to be the second craziest person in the AA rooms, after myself, so I figured in typically naïve newbie fashion that we could be pals, just two crazies hanging out at meetings, having a few laughs and a grand old time "getting sober."

Wrong!

It turned out that I was just straight out of the looney bin crazy, but Jack was crazy like a fox, with twenty years of hard-won sobriety under his belt, and he had my number from Day One. Of course he did, because he had been just like me twenty years ago, but he had survived, remained sober, and flourished by the grace of God and the fellowship of his friends in Alcoholics Anonymous.

He, as it turns out, had solved the grand cosmic mystery, and had let go of "IT."

And now, out of the goodness of his heart, and with no ulterior motive other than an unconditional love for his fellow alcoholic, he was taking the lessons he had learned through his own blood, sweat and tears, and was working them on me, albeit with mediocre success so far.

I was sober, but I was struggling, so Jack kept hammering away on the dual concepts of surrender and keeping things simple, just taking the day in bite-sized pieces.

What it all came down to was acceptance, and about how we looked at life and the world around us. Jack accepted his life, and the world, exactly as they were at any particular moment in time, whereas I didn't – I was still fighting them at every turn.

Jack was happy – I was miserable.

Jack was optimistic – I was negative, defensive, perpetually sensing impending doom around every corner.

Jack understood life, and his position in the grand scheme of things, while I was lost and floundering, still fighting life, the world and myself.

But at least I was sober. Well, stark raving sober, anyway, because I certainly wasn't floating around on one of those pink fluffy clouds of joy that some lucky souls appeared to have discovered in their own early sobriety.

To tell you the truth, however, I thought that I was doing just swell, and that it was those happy, chirpy, gee-whiz newbies who had the wet brains.

Wrong again, Wes. They had simply let go of "IT," and I hadn't, so the Lone Wolf was still lost, marooned somewhere out on the edge of insanity, howling at the moon.

≈≈≈

There's a saying in the halls that goes, "Meetings, meetings and more meetings, when you've been to too many meetings, go to too many more."

I took that sage advice to heart during my first months back home, but I still felt like I was running on a treadmill, going nowhere, but going very fast nevertheless.

In my defense, it wasn't that I didn't care, or that I wasn't committed, because I was attempting to work my program of recovery harder than I had ever worked any job in my life.

I was attending seven, eight, even ten meetings a week. I was reading the 'Big Book' almost daily, and attending Twelve Step meetings, painstakingly working through the first three Steps. I was going to one-on-one counseling with Eileen once a week. I was hanging out with AA friends after the meetings, talking and knocking down hot fudge sundaes at Friendly's, going on commitments to other groups, and even picking up Mary's two hundred pound phone every once in a while to talk with other recovering alcoholics when I was having a bad day – which, of course, was every day.

I was doing everything that had been suggested to me, but there was still something missing, and for the life of me I just couldn't figure out what it was.

Jack knew, and probably the rest of AA knew, but I didn't, and therefore I couldn't let go of "*IT*."

It should have been simple to figure out, I guess. After all, I'd been drinking and drugging myself to the brink of death for twenty-five years, so could I really expect to just click my heels together, chant some inspiring phrases, and "get sober" in two short months?

Well, with the alcoholic's need for immediate gratification, guilty as charged – after all, what's an alkie's favorite "wine?"

Simple – "Whaaaah, I want it NOWWWW!"

And so, like the emotional infant I was, I needed everything right here, and right now, including sobriety, and I hadn't yet learned about that simple four letter word that we go into mortal combat with from the moment the doc smacks us on the butt and says, "Go forth and prosper!"

TIME – Things I Must Earn.

That, for me, was the cruelest word in Webster's dictionary.

≈≈≈

By midsummer my frustration had grown to the extent that one of the more astute members of the Medfield Saturday morning meeting had arrived at the conclusion that, "Wes is a candidate for spontaneous combustion."

I'm certain that most of the Fellowship would have readily agreed with his assessment.

As it turned out, however, he wasn't too far off the mark. I didn't realize it at the time, but a lifelong case of undiagnosed depression was making itself felt in a very big way, and it was just adding to my misery.

It would be several months before I learned that one of the primary reasons for my suicidal drinking and drugging habits had been in the futile hope that I could somehow self-medicate that depression, and kill all of those negative emotions.

But now all the toys were gone, and I was standing naked on the shore with a lifetime of repressed feelings bubbling up and overwhelming me.

I had been a decent pitcher when I was a youngster in Little League, but one day I wasn't doing so swell, and had loaded the bases with none out. One of my coaches had then shouted from the bench, "Just get mad, Wes, get mad," and I had, whereupon I proceeded to strike out the side.

Lesson learned, that statement had become my fight song over the years.

"Just get mad, Wes," and so I did every time that life went against me, which seemed to be every twenty minutes.

So now, where the rubber met the road, all I could do was get damned pissed off, and stubborn, and keep trying to work my program, just keep doing what I had been told to do by Jack, Eileen, and dozens of other kind and caring AA members.

Call it white-knuckling, if you wish, but nevertheless it was all I had to work with, so I held on tight, gritted my teeth, got mad and kept driving on.

But, despite my best efforts, I couldn't seem to let go of "IT."

≈≈≈

Blue Eyes and I remained in touch after I returned home from Beech Hill. She was still seeing her new beau, but we spoke on the phone weekly, and attended a couple of AA meetings together in July.

She appeared to be doing well, and her relationship with her daughter was strong and loving.

She had told me some rather disturbing things about her boyfriend that concerned me, however, but I was in no position to be her relationship counselor, so I would change the topic whenever she brought him up.

I was conflicted in my feelings about her at the time. I realized that I still cared deeply about her, perhaps more than I had ever cared for any woman I had dated, but I had been hurt by the manner in which she delivered the news to me. I shouldn't have been, of course, because I was the one who had relapsed and disappeared out of her life, so how could I have expected a different outcome?

And, besides, being dumped while you're in an alcohol rehab is probably the safest place for an alcoholic to be dumped, so whether she realized it or not she had done me a big favor.

Nevertheless, it hurt, a lot, and I didn't have my alcohol and drugs to anesthetize my raw, wounded ego, so I missed her, and the pain of losing her just added to my frustration about not being able to let go of the all-powerful and omnipotent "IT."

To sum things up, my life wasn't exactly a box of Whitman Samplers during my first six weeks home from the Alps.

But regardless of my emotional turmoil I was still sober, and that was a miracle, so thank you God for watching over this sick and suffering alcoholic – as always, you gave me what I needed, when I needed it.

≈≈≈

I hadn't recognized Eileen when I walked into her office for my first counseling session the week after I returned from the Alps. She was a member of the Friday night Medfield meeting that I had occasionally dropped in on during my last couple of drinking years, and although we never had any direct interaction I had nevertheless noticed her from a distance.

Well, actually I recognized her mostly by the back of her head. She always sat up near the front of the room, close to the speakers' podium, amongst the more serious members of the Fellowship, whereas I had always grabbed a chair way out back, either on "Denial Aisle" or "Skid Row." Either of those strategic positions had granted me plenty of anonymity, as well as quick egress to the back door, the smoking area, and the parking lot whenever I got too squirrelly, or heard things that made too much sense.

My first impression back then had been that Eileen was a quiet and committed recovering person who attended meetings for the sole purpose of maintaining her sobriety, rather than out of any desire to belong to a social club.

"What a novel concept," I had thought at the time, "although somewhat boring."

What I hadn't realized, however, was that she was coming up on twenty years of sobriety, and had many years of counseling experience, so she could spot a phony like me from a mile away. She was formally educated in the field of substance recovery, and had witnessed every variety of sick and suffering alcoholic and addict who had come trudging through her door.

Needless to say, she had learned a lot about human nature and the disease of addiction, so she could detect a BS artist from a mile away, and that didn't necessarily bode well for Wes, the Onion.

≈≈≈

Eileen took control of the meeting from the moment our introductions and the establishment of the ground rules had been completed, and I had signed a boilerplate agreement to abide by the rules of proper conduct, and to pay my fees on time.

"I've had a chance to review the records that they sent down from Beech Hill. You've had quite the adventure this past six months," she began, "so do you want to talk about it?"

Then she went silent, her eyes boring into me.

And thus with one simple "open" question she had taken control of the conversation, and put the onus on me, so there would be no nice chitty-chat opportunity to delay the forensic examination that she was about to conduct.

Well played, Eileen!

"Well, then you probably realize that I never seem to get it," I began cautiously, still attempting to hold back just a little in order to see where she was coming from. This was a dance I had performed with a half-dozen counselors previously, so I had learned early on that it was wise to listen a lot, and speak a little, at least until I got the lay of the land.

Unfortunately, Eileen knew all of the dance steps a whole lot better than I did.

"Why do you think that is, this 'not getting it' thing? It's not like you haven't seen what happens when you drink again – you always end up in the same place, or worse!"

"I don't know. I always try at first, but after a while I get frustrated. It's like nothing ever changes, like I'm not getting anywhere, and then I get down on myself and start trashing AA, like it's okay for some people, but not for me."

I noticed that she made a quick entry on her notepad – swell, that was never a good sign!

"How long do you think you can keep going like this, Wes, with the constant relapses," she queried, "because each time things seem to get worse."

"To tell you the truth, I don't think I have any more chances, this last run was the worst ever."

"I'm surprised you've survived as long as you have, your insides must be made of cast iron."

"I'm trying, Eileen," I said, "I worked really hard up at the Hill, and I did everything they asked of me."

"I know. I've read all of Dave's notes, and it's clear that you worked hard up there. But I need to ask, why did you leave early, why did you go AMA, because a cynical person might think that you were intentionally setting yourself up for failure again."

"I left because I knew that I was ready, that I had progressed as far as I could, and that it was finally time for me to face the world on its own terms."

"Fair enough, but as I'm sure you're aware, you're on rocky ground, so you need to make sobriety your number one priority, in fact, your only priority. Nothing else matters, Wes, not jobs, not money, not friends, not a woman."

Her eyes bored into me on that last one, and it was clear that Dave had dropped a dime to Eileen about Blue Eyes and me – swell, again!

"I'm doing everything I can, Eileen, and I wouldn't be here otherwise."

We talked for another thirty minutes, concentrating on my childhood years, and on my introduction to alcohol and drugs back in the mid '60's, and then she called it a day. She suggested that I come in once a week, because we had a lot of ground to cover, and I agreed.

It had been a painful discussion at times, but I found myself trusting Eileen, at least as much as I was capable of trusting any human being at that moment.

Then, just as I was standing up to leave, she made a curious statement:

"I noticed a pattern in your relapse history, so I want to watch you for a while. You seem to go along fine, but then you get to a certain point where nothing seems to get better, so you get frustrated and start using again. I might have an idea why that is, but I want to take it slow and just see what happens this time around."

She paused, then added, "You seem committed to your sobriety, so just keep doing what you're doing, Wes, and stick close to AA. You need to hit as many meetings as you possibly can, and sit up front this time!"

I walked out of Eileen's office feeling a little tired and beaten down, but nevertheless hopeful. The Onion had peeled off another layer, but dear God, how many more were there to go?

≈≈≈

I walked up to the podium at the Medfield Friday Night meeting on the evening of July 10, 1992, and the Chairwoman handed me a little red poker chip that signified my one month of continuous sobriety. It might have looked like a trinket made of cheap plastic, but to me it was as valuable as gold. I had paid a lot of dues to earn that chip, and had gone through a lifetime of pain and suffering for it.

My knees were knocking slightly as I stood at the podium, but I wouldn't have missed that experience for the world. This marked a turning point in my sobriety, because it was the first tangible acknowledgement that I could actually remain sober if I continued on my path, and did the next right thing.

The other members of the group were clapping and shouting out congratulations, and for perhaps the first time in my life I felt like I really belonged somewhere.

I would go on to receive many more chips that year, and eventually began receiving my annual brass medallions, but that first little red chip was the special one.

I had a difficult time falling asleep that night, just as I had after my inaugural talk at the Saturday Night meeting up at the Hill. My thoughts were racing as I looked back in wonder at the changes that were occurring in my life. Here I was, just one week shy of my forty-second birthday, and I was finally beginning to feel like an adult.

It was clear that I had a lot of catching up to do, but for that one perfect moment in time I felt only gratitude.

≈≈≈

Misery loves company, or so they say.

For the first few months after my return home I often felt like I was wandering aimlessly through a strange, alien landscape that I knew only as "Sobriety World," and I'd ask myself the same nagging question a dozen times a day – would I ever fit in, or would I always be the outcast, forever doomed to live in a nether world somewhere out on the border between sanity and chaos?

Much of it was my own doing, of course, because I tried to maintain a certain distance from most of the longer term members of the various meetings that I attended, although I appreciated all of the kind-hearted people who went out of their way to hold out their hands in welcome, telling me "nice to see you, Wes, and keep coming!"

I also enjoyed hearing their personal stories of experience, strength and hope that had seen so many of them through terrible hardships while they struggled through their own early sobriety, as I was now doing, and I identified with every one of them.

These wonderful people instilled in me a certain degree of hope that I could also get better, and I doubt that they ever realized how much their personal attention meant to me.

But I was nonetheless intimidated by them, because these veterans had crossed the Rubicon to a wonderful new way of life, while I was still fighting against the tide.

I mean, let's face it – I had been lost in the wastelands ever since I was in my mid-teens, so I had developed very few social skills over the years. As a result, I now found myself painfully self-conscious, embarrassed by my relapses, and cautious about opening myself up too far with these relative strangers.

They had something that I wanted, but I was too new and insecure to ask for it, so I kept most of them at arm's length that summer.

≈≈≈

In the end I did what most newcomers did – I kept a low profile and hung out with other beginners, usually outside in the smoking areas. We were raw, had a lot in common, and it was easy for me to identify with most of them.

We even coined a name for ourselves: The Class of '92. There was Bryan, Dave, the two Debby's, Roger, Paula, Dan, several other newcomers, and my buddy Andy, who was technically in the Class of '91, but we made an exception to the rules for him.

Eventually several of us began to hang out together on those nights when we didn't have a regular meeting to attend. Andy, Dave and I took a few road trips to check out various meetings in several surrounding towns, which gave us a good cross-view of AA in the area.

We'd occasionally hit a meeting in Walpole, or Norwood, or Millis, and always hit the Friendly's in Medfield to get our sugar fix at the end of the night. It was a great way to build a bond between us, and it also exposed us to the larger world of AA.

The three of us made a good road crew. We all had similar backgrounds, having hit the substances hard at an early age, lost a lot, and finally come crawling back into reality broken, angry and full of testosterone and attitude. We inherently understood each other, and often times words weren't necessary because only another drunk or addict could understand where we came from. We knew each other like brothers, so when one of us was talking ragtime the others always knew it, and the tough love came in fast.

Ironically, every once in a while we'd hit a new meeting, and I'd run into somebody who I had known back in the drinking and drugging years. Those people seemed to have disappeared from the bars at some point, and I had occasionally wondered whether some harm had befallen them.

But no, the answer was often much simpler – they had surrendered to their disease, gotten sober, and dropped off the map into a wonderful new life. Who could have known that such a thing was possible?

Certainly not I.

I didn't care to admit to it at the time, but at the ripe old age of forty-one it appeared even to my own skeptical eyes that I was developing a modicum of social skills. Better late than never, I suppose, because even though I might not have been planning to win a blue ribbon as a ballroom dancer anytime soon, those formative days were nonetheless the start of this alcoholic's re-integration into society.

Dear God, despite all of my stumbling and bumbling, was I finally coming out of the fog? Had I finally stopped fighting life? Was I finally beginning to let go of "IT?"

Well, hopefully God knew, because I surely didn't.

≈≈≈

By mid-summer I had a love-hate relationship going with Eileen, my counselor.

On the one hand, she had been adept at enabling me to open up and begin the process of confronting all of the fears, doubts, insecurities and demons that had reinforced my addictions.

That was a good thing, to a point, because it demonstrated to me that I was just another bozo on the bus, sick but not evil, and certainly no different from any other alcoholic, or so I prayed anyway.

On the flip side, however, her success at getting me to bare my soul had introduced an element of intimacy into our professional relationship that I was unaccustomed to. I had run away from intimacy in all of its forms ever since I was a little kid, but now it appeared that I was expected to open myself up to varying degrees with my counselor, my sponsor, and every time I spoke at a meeting.

And everybody wanted one thing from Wes – they wanted me to hand over my feelings to them on a silver platter. That was the terrifying part, because it put me on the defensive, fearful and vulnerable, and the last thing any alcoholic ever wants to feel is fear or vulnerability.

Self-centered fear is, after all, the root cause of why we drank and drugged in the first place, because at the bottom line the disease of addiction is the disease of fear – of loss, of success, of love and hate, of change, intimacy, rejection, and so much more.

This Lone Wolf knew that better than most, because fear of intimacy had ruled my life ever since I was a young child, but now I evidently had to accept it as one of the first baby steps to my survival and recovery.

To make matters worse, I was finding it difficult to transition from an anger and greed-based lifestyle to that of a love-based philosophy, but that is the path a recovering person must take, because love for my fellow alcoholic is the key to my own survival and redemption, and I must "give it away" before I can receive it.

They say that we're only as sick as our secrets, because they can kill us if we don't confront them, and thereby take away their power. So now I was walking a thin line, because I had to trust another human being with my innermost feelings, and with my life, and that scared the bejesus out of me.

But, again, what choice did I really have?

The answer to that was simple enough – none, at least not if I wanted to survive.

So week after week I did what was expected of me, like a good little boy – I dragged my sorry ass into Eileen's office, painted on my best smiley face, and puked up some more of my feelings for her forensic examination.

I guess that's what the Big Book means by "trudging the road to Happy Destiny."

Yeah, well, whatever, so maybe I hadn't exactly arrived in "Happychirpygeewhizland," but I wasn't drinking, either, and that was a miracle in itself, so score one for the Onion!

≈≈≈

All work and no play makes Wes a dull boy, so sometime around my two month anniversary I decided that it was time for a road trip.

I had been working my program of recovery hard from the moment I left Beech Hill, so I figured that it was time for a short break from the routine. I wasn't looking for anything big or extravagant, just a night off to smell the roses and catch my breath.

I had always wanted to get a tattoo, but it was just one of the many "bucket list" items that I had never quite gotten around to, usually because I ended up spending all of my paychecks on alcohol and cocaine.

After all, we need to stick to our priorities, don't we?

Tattoo parlors were also illegal in Massachusetts back then, an extension of the 'Blue Laws' days, and I had been too lazy to drive forty miles down the road to Rhode Island, where there were dozens of shops.

So instead this sophisticated world traveler glued his lazy ass to a barstool and talked about getting one, but never got off his butt to do anything about it.

Now, however, I was sober, and bored, so one night in mid-August I happened to mention my interest to several friends during the smoke break at the Medfield Friday night meeting.

Jeannie, a young lady in her mid-twenties, with a year of sobriety, spoke up excitedly.

"Wes, I've been wanting to get one also! I found out about a guy in Watertown who does them at his house. It's obviously illegal, but he's supposed to be good, and he doesn't charge a lot, so what do you think?"

"Do you have his number?" I asked.

"I can get it. I'll call him, and maybe we can go over one night next week?"

"Super, I'm all in," I said, thrilled by the prospect of playing hooky for one night.

≈≈≈

Jeannie and I had a nice dinner in Waltham on the following Wednesday evening, then drove over to the tattoo artist's home. He was situated in your typical middle-class neighborhood in Watertown, just outside of Boston, but that didn't diminish the invigorating sensation that we were doing something illicit.

We weren't exactly Bonnie and Clyde, but nonetheless I felt a certain rush from the knowledge that we were stepping just a little bit over the line.

John, the ink man, led us into his living room. In attendance was his girlfriend Cathy, a cat, a dog, a rabbit in a cage, and a monkey that wasn't in a cage. If nothing else, that menagerie created an interesting backdrop to the crime scene.

We socialized for a couple of minutes, discussed his fees and what artwork we were interested in, and then John asked, "Okay, so who wants to go first?"

Jeannie and I had talked it over in advance – she was slightly more nervous than me, so I stepped up.

John pointed to a chair and handed me a modesty towel. I unbuttoned my jeans, rolled them partway down, and covered my front with the towel. I adjusted my position so that my left hip was elevated and exposed, and then John pulled up his chair and switched on the needle gun.

John's girlfriend went over to the stereo, put on the Stones' *Beggars Banquet* album, loud, and soon *Sympathy for the Devil* was pounding throughout the room.

Jeannie, Cathy and the dog watched intently as John banged the needle into my hip. The cat slept, the rabbit scampered around its cage, and the monkey scrambled up to the top of a bookcase and chattered away at us.

I, on the other hand, gritted my teeth and clenched my fists. The pain was excruciating – it felt like John was carving through my hip with a serrated steak knife.

Jeannie noticed the expression on my face, so she reached over, grabbed my hand, squeezed it hard, and just that small amount of human touch was enough to help me tolerate the procedure.

And the testosterone rush from the Stones' music took care of the rest.

John shut down the needle gun thirty minutes later, swabbed my hip liberally with a clean, damp towel soaked in antiseptic, and that was that. I was now the proud owner of a chubby little "Sparky," the comic book devil, replete with an impish grin and a pitchfork.

John took a ten minute break, so I walked around the room to stretch a little, while the monkey screeched at me from the bookcase and Jeannie pumped me for information, primarily about the pain.

Naturally, being the macho recovering drunk that I was, I lied my ass off.

"Nah, nothing to it, I hardly felt anything at all."

She didn't believe me for a second, of course, but she was a trooper and had no intention of backing down anyway.

≈≈≈

Jeannie was lying face down on the couch five minutes later, her jeans pulled down just enough to expose her right buttock, and John was inking a cute little tropical fish, blowing bubbles, onto her butt.

She was squeezing my hand so hard that I feared she'd cut off the circulation.

John completed his artwork thirty minutes later, switched off the gun, and it was mission accomplished. Jeannie now owned a cute little 'tat on her bum and, like me, she carried a special memory about an unconventional gift of recovery.

We sat around and talked with John and his girlfriend for a few minutes, and he gave us instructions on how to care for our artwork. With that we said our good-byes and headed back to Medfield, where Jeannie picked up her car, and then we went our separate ways.

This had been a night to remember, and a defining moment in my recovery. I had finally stepped out of my mundane Walter Mitty shell for the first time in memory, and had dared to live.

It was exhilarating!

When I hit my knees that night I thanked my Higher Power for giving me the courage and willingness to change. That night had been a gift I have never forgotten, and will always be grateful for. It may just have been a baby step, and not a particularly orthodox one, but after all you have to start somewhere, so why not right here, and right now?

I realized, then, that I had missed out on a lot of living during my twenty-five year binge, but now, on this special evening, I had learned that I could have fun without drinking or drugging.

As I drifted off to sleep I made a pledge to myself that things were going to change from now on, and that I was damned sure going to participate in life, come hell or high water.

≈≈≈

I would be remiss, however, if I didn't mention that there are many addictive activities in life. It turns out that getting tattoos, for certain personality types, is one of them – just ask me and any number of my friends from AA. I will leave it at that, except to mention that there is a psychological condition known as OCD – Obsessive Compulsive Disorder – that many alcoholics, addicts and tattoo freaks share in various iterations.

Thus, I often find it prudent to recite a simple prayer, "Please, God, keep me away from a tattoo parlor, just for today!"

And sometimes He listens, and sometimes He doesn't.

≈≈≈

Eileen and I had been dancing around the elephant in the room for six or seven weeks. I suppose that by unspoken mutual agreement we had decided that the topic of Blue Eyes was better left for another day, perhaps when my recovery was more established and stable.

In the beginning I had maintained a cavalier attitude on the few occasions that Eileen brought up the subject, and I had even been able to brush it off with a combination of nonchalance and humor.

It turned out, however, that she had never bought my game, and things finally came to a head in mid-August.

"So," she finally asked, "do you want to talk about her?"

A chill ran through me – I knew who she meant, of course, but I feigned ignorance anyway.

"Huh? Who do you mean?"

"Oh, come on, Wes," she said in exasperation, "you know exactly who I'm talking about, so don't try to avoid the subject. Blue Eyes is renting space in your head, big time, and that's a dangerous situation for somebody with your relapse history!"

"Aww, come on, Eileen! It's no big deal, you're making too much out of it. Blue Eyes and I are friends, that's all, and I'm fine with that. She's been seeing some other guy, and I wish her all the best!"

"I'm calling BS on that, Wes. This *is* a big deal, and you're just kidding yourself if you seriously think she isn't a threat to your sobriety. That's just denial, plain and simple!"

"Geez, why don't you tell me what you really think?"

"You know what I think, Wes, so stop playing games! You need to stay away from her, or you'll end up drinking again," she said, "and I doubt that you have one more shot at sobriety left in you, so this could kill you! Do you understand that, or do you just not care?"

She paused for a moment, but before I could reply she added, "And I'm not just talking about Blue Eyes - that goes for dating any woman at this point! You're two months sober, emotionally immature, and in no position to enter into a healthy adult relationship with anybody - you'd need a year, or more, before you'd have enough sobriety and personal growth for that!"

"Of course I care, Eileen," I shot back defensively, "but you're wrong about us! We met at Beech Hill, developed a great friendship, and hung around a little when we got home. Then I relapsed, which had nothing to do with her," I lied, "and she met another guy. I guess they had a hot time for a while, but she broke it off with him a few weeks ago. Yeah, she called me, all bummed out, so I went up to her place, like any friend would, and I held her hand for a couple of hours while she talked it out, and then I left. No big deal, and I haven't spoken with her since. She made her choice!"

What I had failed to mention was that Blue Eyes had been in rough shape that night. She had discovered that her boyfriend had been feeding her a constant stream of lies, including the big one, that he was single, when in fact he was married, with a couple of kids, and that almost everything else that came out of his mouth was also a lie.

She hadn't taken it well. She was deeply hurt, and had gone into a shell, so my guilt kicked in when she called, and I drove up to her place in an attempt to comfort her.

We sat out on her front steps for a couple of hours, and I let her talk it all out while I massaged her neck and shoulders. They were rigid, knotted up and frozen, and try as I might I couldn't relax them.

Eventually she told me that she had to go next door to pick up her daughter, who was playing with friends, so we hugged and parted.

The bottom line was that my seemingly complacent attitude was just a flimsy disguise. I was hurting for her, and probably just as much for myself, and I knew that Eileen knew it.

She glanced at her watch, then said, "Our time is up for today. I want you to think about this whole situation – there's a reason why we tell people not to get into relationships in their first year of sobriety. If it goes bad, one or even both of the individuals could end up using. Do you want that to happen to you, or to Blue Eyes?"

Then she stared directly into my eyes and said, "This is the most serious threat to your sobriety there could possibly be, and with your track record it could kill you! I mean that, Wes, this could kill you, so you have some decisions to make – now, not later!"

She snapped her notebook shut, then ended the session with, "I'll see you next week at the same time. Get to your meetings, talk to your sponsor, and do what's right for Wes for a change. Please!"

She was correct as always, I was definitely at risk and I knew it, and it was killing me.

Damn, this being an adult stuff sucked!

≈≈≈

Letting go of Blue Eyes was the most difficult thing that I ever had to do in early sobriety, and losing her was the price I paid for my emancipation.

There were times in those dark, empty nights when I felt haunted, wondering whether my loss had been worth it. But then I realized that if I remained sober I might be able to help others to do likewise, and perhaps by virtue of their sobriety they might find true and everlasting love in their lives.

So, in the end, wouldn't my loss be worth it, no matter the pain I felt?

I guess only God knows the answer to that, because I surely don't, but that's where my trust in the fellowship of Alcoholics Anonymous keeps me on the path, and grateful for the life I have today.

I'm also grateful to add, however, that Blue Eyes and I have remained friends to this day, although mostly at a distance. Call it kismet, or serendipity, but somehow we remained in each other's orbit. We would occasionally talk on the phone, she came to a sober New Year's party that I held that winter, and we got together for "catch up on life" dinners a few times, but we never dated again.

Ironically, we also ended up living thirty miles apart from each other in Florida ten years ago, so we get together a few times a year for dinner and a movie. She's still the only person I have ever known who I could talk to a year after our last contact, and it would be like we had just spoken the previous day.

We always had that special connection, and I'll cherish that forever.

≈≈≈

Eileen finally dropped the bomb on me one morning in early September, just after I had filled her in on my activities from the prior week.

The Onion was about to get peeled again.

"Okay, Wes, I want you to keep an open mind about what I'm about to say."

With that, my mind closed and the hairs on the back of my neck stood up.

She paused, for effect, then said, "Now don't get nervous, but I think there's a possibility that you're suffering from a mood disorder. You've been exhibiting a number of the symptoms that are typically associated with the disease of depression."

"Huh? Whaddaya mean, Eileen," I blurted out indignantly, "do you think I'm crazy, or something?"

Her comment had set off alarm bells, and as usual I had jumped to conclusions. I didn't choose to mention it at the time, but I knew a couple of people, including a close family member, who had been hospitalized with serious cases of depression – serious enough that it had landed them in locked wards. I had visited them, and it had been a spooky experience each time. So now a chill ran down my spine at the mere suggestion that I might be suffering from a similar condition, and I had no desire to end up in anything even remotely similar to a locked ward.

Unfortunately, however, I had just the slightest inkling that there might be some truth to her words.

"No," she smiled, "I don't think you're crazy, and I told you not to get all worked up! Depression is a very common condition that occurs in people who have suffered significant emotional trauma, or who have a long history of substance abuse, or both. Alcohol is basically a depressant, and except for the cocaine most of your other drugging activity was with downers. It's possible that without realizing it you were using those substances to cover up or kill emotional pain."

"Well, what makes you so sure that its depression?"

"I didn't say definitively that you do have it. However, you exhibit certain characteristics that are usually associated with people who suffer from it. It's not a diagnosis that I can make, but I'm thinking it probably wouldn't hurt to have you talk to a professional."

"What professional?" I asked, as if I didn't know.

"I have a psychiatrist that I sometimes refer clients to. He's very familiar with the disease of addiction, and he understands its direct relationship to the disease of depression. I think he'd be a great person for you to speak with."

"Oh, okay, I get it, so now you think that I'm some kind of a whacko who needs a shrink?"

She scowled in frustration and said, "There you go, proving my point. Every time I try to open you up to new concepts you get negative and defensive."

"Well, what do you expect, Eileen? You're basically telling me that I'm a nutjob!

"Oh, good grief, Wes, I'm saying no such thing! I'm merely suggesting that there is a direct relationship between the diseases of addiction and depression. Basically, many alcoholics use alcohol and drugs to self-medicate themselves, and thereby kill or cover up the emotional pain they're in."

She paused, then said, "To me, you're a perfect example of that. It's in the way you talk, and look at life, and even in your body language. You've been coming in to see me for almost two months, and even though you're sober, it's clear to me that you're not happy. I see a good person who's in a lot of emotional pain, and has been for a very long time, maybe from before you even started drinking. So, I think it's time to have you speak with a professional who can evaluate your condition, and what harm could that do?"

What harm? Well, for starters, I thought again about Jack Nicholson in that final scene of "One Flew Over the Cuckoo's Nest," but I considered it prudent not to give her any ideas.

No, this was just another one of those junctures in life where Wes realized that the next person to speak would lose. I knew it, I thought about it for a couple of seconds, and then true to form I spoke up anyway.

"Alright, so let's just say you may have a point. I don't seem to find a lot of joy in my life these days. I'm working my program as hard as I can, but it feels like I'm not getting anywhere. Yeah, it's frustrating to have to sit in a room with a bunch of happy, chirpy people who are upbeat and optimistic, while I'm dying inside. But really, a shrink?"

"Wes, he's a mental health professional, and you're a person in a lot of emotional pain. What would you do if you were to break your foot? Wouldn't you rush to a doctor? So what's the difference here?"

"Well, for one thing there's the stigma attached to it - people don't want to hang out with a psycho!"

"Oh, please, Wes, what stigma? There's only a stigma if you announce it to the world, which I strongly suggest that you do not do. This is just another medical condition, like addiction, and it's an anonymous condition, unless for some reason you decide to make it otherwise. And for God's sake, stop calling yourself a whackjob, or a psycho, or a nutcase, or whatever, because you're just proving my point!"

And so it was that I was faced with another one of those annoying little adult moments that I was really beginning to get an attitude about. I knew that Eileen didn't have the licenses to formally diagnose me with any disease, including depression, nor could she prescribe medications should they be indicated.

So, bottom line, she would need to refer me up the stack.

And, besides, I knew how bad I felt on the inside, that I was at risk, and that this depression thing may have led to at least some of my relapses, so did I really have any choice?

No, not if I wanted to get better, so once again it was time for Wes to man up, and I threw in the towel.

Grrrrrr.

"Okay, what's his name and telephone number?" I growled.

She gave me his information, then asked, "Geesh, was that so hard, Wes? Why is it always like pulling teeth with you, can't you just go along with the flow once in a while?"

"Hey, I'm paying the big bucks for this, Eileen, so I figure you've gotta earn your pay."

Now it was her turn to scowl at me – that alone was worth the forty bills I was dropping on the meeting.

≈≈≈

One week later, and with more than a little trepidation, I walked into a psychiatrist's office in Rockland, Massachusetts. I had sat in my car in the parking lot for fifteen minutes before finally saying a prayer to my Higher Power, asking Him for help in accepting the outcome of my decision, whatever that outcome might be.

I was scared stiff, because I knew that the Onion was about to shed a great big layer of skin this time, and I wasn't sure that I wanted to discover what lay beneath it.

But in for a penny, in for a pound. I had already made my leap of faith when I surrendered to Donna in the serene garden on the mountaintop in New Hampshire, just three short months previously, so now it was time to walk my talk and let the chips fall where they may.

As it turned out, that one little act of humility probably saved my life.

≈≈≈

The psychiatrist's first question after we exchanged greetings was, "So, Wes, how long have you been sober?"

His query surprised and impressed me, because it meant that he understood the need most newcomers have to keep track of their sobriety date - it is, after all, one of the only things of value we have to hold onto in the early days. I knew that most of his colleagues wouldn't have bothered to ask, or even to care, so score one for the Doc.

It turned out that this guy was okay. He was low key, non-assuming and professional, with a relaxed, quiet manner that put me at ease. At times it even felt like we were having a scholarly discussion about the weather, rather than a forensic examination of a life gone tragically astray.

At other times, of course, he hit some pretty deep nerves, and it was on those occasions that I noticed his notebook pages were filling up rapidly.

After about fifteen minutes he pushed my folder aside and said, "Okay, Wes, thanks for your candor. It's clear that you've had quite the adventurous life, but you survived, and you're working hard to get better. I see a lot of people who come in here suffering from the effects of various addictions, and many of them share a common characteristic - it's pretty clear to me that you do also."

He paused, then asked, "Do you know what 'PTSD' stands for?"

I knew a little about 'PTSD' because I had been in the Army during the Vietnam War. I hadn't served overseas, but I had a number of friends who did, and some of them came home carrying some pretty ugly baggage.

A couple of them had been diagnosed with 'PTSD' and were still struggling to get their lives back on track twenty years later, but what did that have to do with me? I hadn't fought over there, and all I'd done was drink and drug myself to the brink of death for twenty-five years.

"Yeah, sure," I said, "it stands for Post-Traumatic Stress Disease, or something like that. But I don't get it, I thought that was for guys who got screwed up in combat, so why are you asking me that?"

"You're close, it's called Post-Traumatic Stress Disorder, not disease, but it affects a much larger segment of the population than just combat veterans. It also includes victims of serious accidents, crime victims, abuse survivors, and, here's where you come in, many individuals who suffer from addiction."

"I don't get it, why would people with addictions be included in this category?"

"Look at it this way. The human body has a wide spectrum of chemicals that provide defenses for dealing with excessive stress, or physical threats. They're known as neurotransmitters, and a primary one is called cortisol – that's what is known as our "fight or flight" chemical. When we sense a threat to our physical or emotional well-being our body floods the system with cortisol, and it simultaneously reduces the production of the "feel good" neurotransmitters, such as dopamine and serotonin. This is a self-defense mechanism that we can't control, it takes over the reins and enables us to react to the particular threat that we're facing."

He paused to let that sink in, then asked, "Are you with me so far?"

"Yeah, I think so, it's like when I'm about to get in a fight, it's why I get all jacked up?"

"Yes, exactly," he said, then continued, "over a lifetime of substance abuse your body has become addicted to alcohol and drugs. It needs those chemicals in order to feel "normal," so when they're no longer available your body panics, and then it reacts by producing more cortisol. At the same time it reduces the production of the "feel good" neurotransmitters. Its automatic, nothing you can control - when your drugs of choice are taken away, your body chemistry immediately sends you into panic mode, and you become a drug seeker who needs his fix, whatever that drug might be."

"So that's what happens when I've got the DT's, and I'm "jonesing?"

"Yes, it's why you develop a craving and experience the delirium tremens. Think about it, Wes, for the past twenty-five years you've basically been at war with the world, isolated, out of control, full of self-hate and anger, a slave to a bottle and a whole slew of drugs. Think of the losses you've endured, such as jobs, friendships, relationships, finances, and the more you've lost, the more you've isolated yourself, and the more you've killed your emotions with drugs and alcohol. You've been way out on the edge, it's been a vicious cycle for all of your adult life, a twenty-five year disaster."

He paused again to let that sink in, then asked, "So, if you're curious about why I classified you in the same category as war veterans, tell me, doesn't your background remind you of someone who's been waging war for the past twenty-five years? It's just that you've basically been fighting life, and yourself, rather than another country."

He had me on that one. In retrospect it all looked so crystal clear - how could I have been so full of denial that I missed it? I had indeed been at war with the world, and with myself, from as far back as I could remember.

I finally understood – alcohol and drugs were the Grand Illusionists, they had hijacked me mind, body and soul, and I never stood a chance.

"Okay," I said, "so maybe that explains why I've been so crazy and jacked up since I got home from Beech Hill - my body and head have been sending me messages? So what do I do about it?"

"Well, you're on the right path now, and I congratulate you for that, because I know how difficult it is to remain sober, particularly in the early days. Eileen tells me that you've been attending a lot of AA meetings, and you're showing up regularly for your sessions with her. That's all good, keep it up, but there are some additional things that could help you."

"Okay, I'm listening."

"First and foremost, continue going to your meetings, and keep speaking at them. Just talking and sharing your thoughts can be very cathartic when you're getting positive feedback and support from your peers. Regular exercise is also very important, because it helps to produce the "feel good" neurotransmitters. Also, eat well and healthy, and get plenty of sleep."

"Well, I'm doing most of that, although I'm smoking two packs a day, so I'm a little slack on the exercise."

"That's okay, you can try to quit the smokes when the time is right, but I strongly suggest that you not attempt it now. You already have enough on your plate, and going through nicotine withdrawal is very stressful and could send you right back to the drinking - there's time enough for quitting later. So for now get some fresh air, maybe try walking around the block a couple of times a day, or go to the beach and swim, or just float in the water, or read a book, listen to music, anything that relaxes you would help."

"Okay."

He smiled, paused, and then said, "I guess that I hit you with a lot of technical stuff today. Basically what it all comes down to is that your mind and body have become so accustomed to receiving a regular supply of alcohol and drugs that they don't know how to function without those substances. So then the cravings begin, because when you've been denied that daily supply of chemicals, the cortisol levels rise, and your "feel good" hormones, the serotonin and dopamine, go into a deficit. The end result is that you experience intense nervousness, cravings, anger and depression."

"Well, I guess that pretty much describes me."

He hesitated, then added, "In your case you're struggling, and Eileen is worried, particularly because of your relapse history. I agree with her, so I want to talk to you about medications that can help people who are suffering from clinical depression, which it's clear you have."

"Meds?" I asked. I hadn't seen that one coming, or had I just rolled out my usual wall of denial?

"Yes. I described the connection between all of the different brain and body chemicals that affect mood, but sometimes, no matter what you do, the things we talked about aren't sufficient to restore the brain chemistry to a healthy balance."

"Okay, that makes sense, that's me, my recovery doesn't feel like its hitting on many cylinders."

"Well, give yourself some credit - you've already made a good start. Look at what you've accomplished - you stopped the drinking and drugging, you're attending a lot of meetings, and I urge you to get to as many as you possibly can. You're going to counseling, and you have a very big supporter in Eileen. You're socializing with people in AA, and staying away from your old friends who are still using. That's one hell of a great start!"

"Yeah," I said, "but I still can't find much to look forward to. I feel like nothing's ever gonna change."

"Well, not to worry, there's hope. We have a new class of drugs that has recently been introduced, and which has been shown to be very effective at treating depression in cases such as yours."

"Oh?" He had my attention now – I hadn't thought that I'd ever feel "normal" again.

"The technical name for this group is, "Selective Serotonin Re-uptake Inhibitors," but we just call them "SSRI"'s for short. In laymen's terms they help maintain your "good" chemicals, especially the serotonins, at acceptable levels. The result is that you're able to experience a certain degree of happiness and well-being, emotionally capable of handling the challenges of early sobriety, and your mood swings, those big ups and downs that you've been experiencing, should moderate."

"Sounds too good to be true," I said.

"Well, they're a good additional tool that should reinforce everything else you're doing, but they're not a substitute for attending your meetings and counseling, maintaining a strong program of recovery, and sticking close to your sponsor and friends in the Fellowship."

"Understood, so what else do I need to know?"

"Well, there can be some side effects," which he then discussed, "and I will need to see you every few months, just to be certain that things are remaining on track."

"Okay, so when do we start?"

"Well, we can start right now. I'll let Eileen know, and she'll be monitoring you closely. I'll want to see you in six weeks, also, to do a follow-up eval."

With that he pulled out his prescription pad, scribbled on it, handed me a scrip, and with that the Onion took another leap of faith.

≈≈≈

The next morning I said a prayer to my Higher Power, asking only that I be able to accept the outcome of my decision to take this step, regardless of what that outcome might be, and thanked Him for keeping me sober, and for bringing the people I needed into my life.

Then I jumped, pulled the ripcord, and swallowed my first pill.

≈≈≈

It would be almost two months before I could discern any improvement in my mood, or outlook on life, but gradually the fog of my depression began to dissipate. In a way it was as if I had been trapped under water all of my life, and now found myself struggling to get back to the surface, fighting the tides and the currents, but nevertheless making slow, measurable progress.

I was starting from scratch, however, because I had no frame of reference to work from at the time. I had rarely experienced "happiness" or "peace of mind" since I was a child. Those were just words, constructs, intangibles, fleeting glimpses of a world that was nothing more than a charade to me, a world that I had never inhabited for any length of time, a world that I never understood.

But now, in so many ways, I was a child again, staring at the world through a brand new shiny prism, and many of those things that had for most of my life seemed incomprehensible were now within my grasp.

The meds weren't a magic concoction that solved all of my problems, however. There was no panacea, no Nirvana, no free "high," but nonetheless they gave me a fighting chance by chasing away the worst of my demons and negative emotions, while filling the void with a measure of hope and optimism, which were two attributes not ordinarily associated with Wes's personality.

I realized then that I had just been "talking the talk" since I returned from Beech Hill, but never actually walked it, and I had never believed that recovery could work for me. I had felt dead inside, but arose every day and painted on a happy face that was nothing more than a mask that might have been fooling me, but probably not the rest of the world.

Now, however, I had the initiative to redouble my efforts, to participate and share more at meetings, to be honest with myself and with others, to express my true feelings and emotions in an adult manner, to admit that I wasn't perfect, that I shared the same fears, doubts and insecurities as anyone else who was sitting in that room.

The Onion was finally becoming an adult at the ripe old age of forty-two - who would have thought it possible?

≈≈≈

I remained on the meds for approximately a year. They had some frustrating side effects, and they certainly weren't any kind of magical solution that solved any of my other problems, but nevertheless they accomplished their mission by balancing my brain chemistry, and by chasing away the worst of the dark clouds, negativity, hopelessness and fear that had ruled my life for forty years.

And, miracle of miracles, into that void came a measure of positive thinking, optimism, and self-confidence that I had never previously experienced.

I now found myself on a level playing ground with the rest of the world, and it was a gratifying sensation.

For me, the SSRI's were simply one of a dozen tools that helped me to remain sober, and to perform the work I needed to accomplish in order to grow emotionally and spiritually. Over the years, however, I would go on to discover many other activities, including exercise, which could accomplish much the same thing as the SSRI's.

In 1995, while recuperating from back surgery, I stuck a nicotine patch on my arm for six weeks and stopped smoking. This not only helped balance my brain chemistry, and calmed my nerves, but it also led me back to aerobic and strength training exercises. These were activities that I had stopped participating in when my drinking and drugging went out of control in my late teens.

I soon found myself running five or six days a week, and lifting weights, and the endorphin rush that I received from those activities was far better than any alcohol or drug high I had ever experienced.

"A runner's high?" you ask? Oh, yes, and there is no better sensation on earth.

Also, for readers who think that jogging is beyond their physical ability or comfort zone, I would suggest that a brisk walk is just as therapeutic, and you'll enjoy the scenery more. I have hiked the hills and mountains of central Vermont, the beaches of Florida, the back roads of Boston's western suburbs, and I have experienced a sense of peace and well-being wherever I have ventured.

I have also practiced meditation and yoga, and likewise discovered a measure of serenity and peace of mind in these pursuits. I have been a massage therapist, and have found that the art of simple human touch can release serotonin and dopamine in much the same way as exercise, and is beneficial for both the client and the therapist.

Massage therapy is even beginning to find its way into alcohol and drug treatment centers as an adjunct to medications during the physical withdrawal process.

The point is that if we are diligent, and willing to expand our horizons, then all recovering people can find that one special activity that will relieve the stresses of the day, and transport us to our own special comfort zone, where the body, mind and soul can find peace and balance.

For me, saying hello to Bullwinkle or Yogi on a mountain road in Vermont, or reading a book in a hammock, or floating on a gentle sea in southwest Florida as a wedge of pelicans comes skimming across the waves are all gifts of sobriety beyond anything I could ever have hoped for.

And wherever I find that special haven where my soul is at rest, it has become second nature for me to recite a few simple words of gratitude: "Thank you, God, for delivering me unto this place."

≈≈≈

The magical day arrived almost before I knew it.

I was there! I made my ninety days without a drink or a drug on Saturday, September 5th, 1992, which was the longest stretch of time in twenty-five years that I had ever gone without using substances! It was truly a miracle, almost beyond my ability to comprehend.

But when I hit my knees to pray that morning I stuck to the basics, because they were what had gotten me that far.

≈≈≈

I thanked everyone at my Saturday morning meeting for helping me to reach that milestone, and a few of us celebrated with hot fudge sundaes at Friendly's afterwards.

A certain degree of responsibility came along with this accomplishment, however, because it meant that I was now eligible to speak from the podium at the Friday night meeting, as well as to speak at commitments that we took to other groups throughout the Greater Boston area.

This is a big step up for any newcomer, because it's one thing to be able to speak, seated, in a small discussion group of ten or twenty of one's peers in the local church basement, but it's quite another to speak from the podium in front of fifty, a hundred, or even more people, especially when you're visiting groups of total strangers in other towns.

But I had an ace up my sleeve, because I had already spoken from the podium at that Saturday night meeting up at the Hill, just three months previously, so I had a measure of experience and self-confidence to work with.

It was clear once again that my Higher Power had been watching over me that evening in New Hampshire, that He had always had a plan for me, and that my job was simply to let go of the reins, and to allow Him to guide me along the next step of my journey.

So yes, I still had a few butterflies in the pit of my stomach, and probably always would. But they were manageable, and they were far outweighed by the sense of catharsis that I inherently understood I would experience when I stepped to the podium to take the next step on my journey.

≈≈≈

Six days later I walked cautiously to the podium at the Friday night Medfield meeting. My knees were knocking slightly as I looked around at the members of my home group, so I took a deep breath to calm the jitters, and began, "Hi, my name is Wes, and I'm an alcoholic…"

And with that simple phrase I trudged another step along the "Road to Happy Destiny." I realized then, in that one perfect moment in time, that my total immersion in the program of Alcoholics Anonymous was paying benefits, little by slow, in my Higher Power's time, not my own.

And, beyond a doubt, I knew that the Lone Wolf had finally come in from the wilderness.

≈≈≈

I fell into a routine shortly after I made my first talk at the podium. In addition to my regular Medfield meetings, and my occasional road trips with Andy and the guys, I now went on commitments every few weeks with various members of my Tuesday and Friday night groups.

I soon discovered that I actually enjoyed speaking from the podium, and that it wasn't a chore, nor particularly painful or intimidating. Rather, it was a means for spreading the message of Alcoholics Anonymous, with the added bonus of having the opportunity to meet hundreds of fellow recovering alcoholics and addicts throughout the Greater Boston area, and even down into Rhode Island.

It was through this process that I began to understand the power and scope of the program, its universality, its ability to heal, to save lives, to reunite families, to restore the alcoholic as a rational, functioning member of society.

Suddenly, AA wasn't a Beech Hill thing, or a Medfield thing, but rather a universal movement that was saving hundreds, thousands, perhaps millions of lives like my own. I was humbled by the realization that I was just a tiny but necessary cog in a worldwide movement of recovery, and this was a responsibility that I had no intention of shirking.

≈≈≈

It didn't take long for me to realize that weird math happened when I participated in commitments, because we were actually attending three meetings over the course of one evening – such a deal!

190

The first meeting occurred while we were driving to the host group. This was a time for bonding with members from my home groups, some of whom I knew, but many of whom were still strangers. I could participate in the conversation now that I was eligible to speak on the road, and I was no longer relegated to the back seat with a good natured but firm admonition from the night's chairperson to "Shut up and listen, Wes, you might just learn something."

It felt great to be treated like a peer, and I learned a lot about recovering people and the program of Alcoholics Anonymous on the rides to and from the commitments. I felt like I was back in school, and it was the rare trip to another group that failed to teach me something new about one or another of my fellow alcoholic roadies.

The second meeting was, of course, the actual commitment. I was somewhat fidgety the first few times I walked into a new hall, particularly the larger ones where there might be fifty to one hundred people, or more, in attendance. But the nervousness generally dissipated quickly, as group members came up to me and held out their hands in welcome. I have found AA folks to be friendly, outgoing and gracious wherever I have attended meetings – in some ways I've felt like I was being welcomed into a person's home, rather than into a church or meeting hall.

I suppose that's why we call our local members our "home group," because in a way we're all family.

I was gratified that the chairpersons went easy on me for those first few road trips, by placing me toward the end of the speakers' rosters. I appreciated their thoughtfulness, because I still had the wobbly knees in those days, so I needed a little time to put on my game face and practice in my head what I planned to say.

Soon enough, however, I was being called up to be the first speaker at the podium, and after several successful outings I felt very comfortable about telling my story to a group of complete strangers.

It turns out that I was an okay speaker. I learned how to pull in a few laughs along the way, and it was always great to see the hosting group members nodding their heads in agreement with my words. It felt good to know that I was being accepted, that people identified with me, and that all of us had walked the same long, lonely road out of despair and into the sunlight.

I was also amazed by the number of people who walked up to me after the meetings to shake my hand and thank me, a perfect stranger, for speaking. And, more often than not, they would tell me how much they identified with my story, and would go on to relate similar occurrences in their own recovery.

So I soon learned that there is no such thing as a coincidence in AA, and that realization never failed to send chills down my spine whenever I came across another example of how similar we all are as recovering alcoholics and human beings.

And then, finally, there was the third meeting of the night. This was the one I enjoyed the most – the ride back to Medfield with my companions, and the victory sundaes at Friendly's. On the return home we were always loose and relaxed, joking, laughing, experiencing that special bond known only to people who have opened up their souls to complete strangers, and who have been welcomed and accepted as equals.

For me, the return ride home was always proof positive of the power of renewal and redemption that AA grants to all who have surrendered and come in out of the darkness. I realized then that home is indeed where the heart lies, and that I need only walk into any Alcoholics Anonymous meeting anywhere in the world to experience that special sensation of belonging.

And there's not a better feeling in the world.

≈≈≈

Eileen decided to shake up my world in mid-October. I don't know whether she thought that I was becoming complacent, or that it was time for me to expand my horizons, but whatever her motivation, she had a surprise waiting for me when I walked into her office that Wednesday morning.

We had barely made it through the usual pleasantries when she said, "I think it's time for you to perform some public service work, Wes. You're working hard, and I'm pleased with your progress, but I think you're ready to give back to the community, you know, help others."

"Whaddaya mean, Eileen? I'm hitting my meetings, going on commitments, hanging out with AA people, isn't that enough?"

"That's all fine, Wes, you're doing everything you need to do to stay sober, but there's a larger world out there that I think you need to open yourself up to. There are a lot of people who are struggling, in many different ways, and most of them don't have the benefit of a program like AA to help them."

"Aww, geez, what people are you talking about?"

"I'm talking about the elderly, particularly the shut-ins who may never have contact with another human being for days, or even weeks at a time. They live in a twilight world, unnoticed, with no family or regular visitors, and some of them don't even have neighbors to check in on them once in a while.

She paused for a second, then continued, "Many of them feel isolated, cut off from society, and unable to fend for themselves, as a matter of fact, somewhat like you were not so long ago."

"But why me? I don't have any experience doing stuff like that. Who are these people, where are they, what would I do?"

I was becoming anxious now, because I could hear that spooky "change" word jingling somewhere in the background, but nevertheless curious as I nibbled at the hook.

"They're everywhere. Some of them have assisted living arrangements, but for the most part they live on their own in elderly housing, apartments, or in their private homes. Many of them can't drive, and don't have relatives or friends to run errands, take them to the doctor, or pick up something at the store. If they're lucky, they may have a case worker who drops in on them once every couple of weeks. Some are lonely and frightened, and some don't even have the ambition to fix their own meals."

"Well, I feel bad for them, Eileen, but I'm not a social worker, so I wouldn't know where to begin."

"You don't need to be a social worker, Wes. There's a volunteer organization called "Meals on Wheels" that delivers one nutritious meal a day to these people. They're always looking for volunteers to come in and help for two or three hours a day. You'd be delivering meals, checking in on the clients, spending a little time talking with them. And, if you sense that the client is having health or other difficulties, you'll need to let the staff know so that they can perform an intervention."

"Well, this comes as a surprise, can I think about it?"

"Oh, come on, Wes, what do you need to think about? You aren't working yet so you have plenty of free time, its local, and it's important to these people. What do you have to lose, it would only take three hours out of your day, five days a week, basically the same as a part time job, and you would be *really* helping these people. You may be the only human contact that they have in a week..."

She paused, like the great salesperson she was, then added, "This would be a great opportunity for you to look at the world from a different perspective. It would take you out of your own head for a while, and it would get you invested in people who are also struggling, just in a different way than you were."

Eileen was making a compelling argument, as usual. I wasn't working at the time, just living off my savings. I had initiated a part time job search, but I knew that it might be months before I found what I needed, and if I were to be honest with myself I was becoming bored. I had a full AA life, attending meetings or related activities nearly every day, but that still left plenty of time to do other things, and it sounded like these people could use some help.

So bottom line, what harm could it do to give it a shot?

"Well, okay, I suppose I could give it a try to see how it works out. When would they need me, maybe in a month or two, like after the holidays?"

"I've already spoken to them about you, and they need you immediately. Could you go over to their office tomorrow to have an interview? They mentioned that they'd like you to start on Monday."

"Aww, geez," I whined, "you don't waste any time, Eileen!"

"Wes, you're going to thank me for this," she said, her eyes twinkling.

And she was right, as usual.

I drove back to my apartment an hour later, wondering for not the first time who this strange new person was who was driving my car, then asked out loud, "Okay, God, what have you gotten me into this time?"

I could have sworn that I heard just the hint of a chuckle from somewhere very, very far away, and then the words of my friend Lois came back to haunt me, "We all seem to think we're so damned important!"

Yes indeed, Lois, don't we all?

Well, if there was one thing I had learned over the past several months, it was that when Eileen, God and Lois all ganged up on the Onion, it just wasn't worth arguing anymore.

≈≈≈

I drove across town to the "Meals on Wheels" distribution center the following Monday morning, and picked up my first supply of meals. Not surprisingly the prior week's interview had gone well, and the director had explained the basics of the job to me.

It was relatively simple - I would come in Monday through Friday at around 11:00 a.m. to collect thirty-five boxed hot lunches, and then distribute them to elderly clients on a fixed route covering the west side of Norwood and East Walpole.

In addition to delivering their meals I would be expected, over a period of time, to establish an unofficial type of caretaker relationship with these clients, in order that I might get to know them well enough to detect any worrisome trends in their health and living habits.

The main things to look out for were changes in attire, diet, housekeeping conditions, alertness, and any personality changes that might be evident.

Was a person who was usually neatly dressed now coming to the door in their pajamas, their hair disheveled, or with a three day growth of beard? Was a friendly, talkative person suddenly quiet or withdrawn, or acting confused or depressed? Was a normally neat apartment now full of dirty dishes scattered around haphazardly, or were there piles of crumpled clothes strewn about on the floor?

All of these anomalies, and many others, might have a logical explanation, or they could be warning signs that the resident was experiencing any number of potentially serious difficulties, so it was my responsibility to get to know them well enough to detect a red flag when I saw it.

I soon learned, however, that reality is often far different than one's expectations. I had been viewing my role merely as that of a part-time, unlicensed caregiver, whereby I'd be performing a simple two or three hour chore before heading home to get on with my life.

I did not expect, nor seek, anything else, and I certainly didn't think that I was capable of becoming emotionally invested in any of my clients. This was intended to be a job that would keep Wes occupied and out of trouble for a few hours a day, and to keep Eileen happy, and nothing more.

That mindset lasted about two hours, however, because only halfway through the first day's route it became clear that I shared several personality traits with many of my clients, whose lives were ruled primarily by loneliness, isolation and fear.

I could certainly identify with them, because for the prior twenty-five years my life had been dictated by those very same emotions, so it was natural that I would feel empathy for these people.

And, once I felt empathy, it logically followed that I would also become emotionally invested in their welfare.

Within a couple of days I realized that I was taking ownership of this venture. I was learning responsibility, taking the initiative to reach out to my clients, because these people were depending on me not only for their food, but for something just as important - a human connection. I might have been the only contact with the outside world that they would have on any given day, or week, so I considered it my mission to spend a few minutes with each client, talking about their children, their hobbies, their lives.

And my reward for this simple task? Every day I drove home feeling like I might have made a difference in a person's life.

And then one day I realized that I had made a difference in my own.

≈≈≈

I visited "my" clients every weekday for several months, until I began working full time after the first of the year, and during that period I had one instance where I had to report my concerns back to management.

That case concerned a man who stopped coming to the door when I knocked. I couldn't hear any sounds emanating from the apartment, so after two days of silence I contacted my manager, and she took over from there. I didn't deliver to his apartment after that, and I learned later that he had been hospitalized.

I never learned the outcome of his illness.

In those days most AA groups in Massachusetts handed out brass medallions to group members when they reached their annual sobriety date. That was the medallion I had noticed sparkling on Bob the Cabbie's key chain when he picked me up in Concord the day I left Beech Hill. I had seen other members' medallions as well, and had noted the inscription on the back of each coin – three words arranged in a triangle – Unity, Service and Recovery.

These were the three words that embodied the essence of AA's philosophy, and I realized that once again, little by slow, the more I reached out to others, the more I was healing myself.

My volunteer service work was certainly important to my elderly clients, and I was grateful for that, but it was equally important to my own recovery.

I was finally becoming responsible, a contributing member of humanity, and that is a powerful motivator of change - for a person, as well as for a society.

≈≈≈

The Thanksgiving and Christmas/New Year holidays had always been rough patches for me to endure during my drinking career. I'd been a loner all of my life, so it was customary for me to party hard during that time of year, and by so doing kill the crushing depression that I always experienced during those "happy, merry" weeks.

My annual theory, which was nothing more than a pathetic case of bullshit and denial, was that I would experience a brand new start to my life if I could just hang on by my fingertips until the New Year was rung in.

Because, after all, "Next year will be your year, Wes! Things will change, you'll see, you're about to realize great happiness and success! Hell, you might even be able to cut back on the drinking and the drugging next year! Yes indeed, you'll see, everything's gonna come up roses - this is gonna be your time to shine, so hang in there Big Guy, stay high, keep out of any jackpots, and just paint on your happy face!"

Fat chance of that! My dis-ease always worked overtime on me during the holidays, so the bottom line was that the low-life stinkin' drunk who closed out the old year was the same low-life stinkin' drunk who rang in the new one.

Not surprisingly, my life went spiraling further down the crapper every time that damned calendar rolled over, so in reality the only thing that ever changed after the holidays was my traditional fight song, which always went straight from "Jingle Bells" to "Poor me, poor me, pour me another drink."

Oh, and before you ask, let's not get into a discussion about my New Year's resolutions, because I went 0 for 5 every year.

≈≈≈

And now, by mid-November, 1992, I was already sensing a growing uneasiness - the onset of my annual funk as the holidays crept ominously closer.

This year, however, I had the ace of spades up my sleeve. I had been sober for five months, and clear-headed enough to realize that I was entering treacherous waters.

And, fortunately, Jack, Eileen, and many of the other veteran members of the Medfield groups were quick to remind all of the newcomers that the holidays were hard on all recovering people, regardless of how long we had been sober.

It was comforting to know that I was not alone, but in and of itself that didn't insure my sobriety, so I had to raise my threat level and defense scheme just a little bit.

≈≈≈

I had given myself a goal when I returned from Beech Hill back in July – I planned to attend three hundred meetings in my first year. At the time I considered such a target to be practically impossible to achieve, but I figured that it would be a good motivator nonetheless, so why not shoot for the moon?

Part of the plan included doubling up on meetings over the major holidays, and the twin demons of Thanksgiving and Christmas/New Years were as major as it gets. Armed with that knowledge, I reasoned that the extra attendance would be sufficient to get me through the holiday horrors with a good head of steam built up as I entered the New Year.

The most important thing, regardless of how many meetings I eventually attended, would be to always keep the momentum going, no matter what, and to get to meetings even when I thought that I didn't need a meeting.

In fact, I needed to get to a meeting especially when I didn't think that I needed to get to a meeting!

Forewarned is forearmed, so I got proactive and began to double up on some of my meetings heading into Thanksgiving. Where I had been going to six or seven a week, I was now going to ten, and I was arriving at meetings earlier, and leaving them later than usual.

After all, a lot of the healing in AA comes in the discussions and camaraderie that take place before and after the actual meeting, so this is a rich feeding ground for meeting people, establishing friendships, and discussing some of our issues with a trusted member of the Fellowship one-on-one, rather than in a room full of twenty or thirty people.

AA, the organization, understands how dangerous holidays can be for recovering alcoholics, so the Central Service folks always make sure that there are extra safeguards in place, primarily in the form of additional meetings. These are non-stop, around-the-clock meetings, and we call them alcathons.

I had already attended my first one back on the 4th of July, and it had been a great experience.

Now I learned that the larger groups in my local area held three alcathons during the winter holidays, so I made it my mission to attend every one of them.

The first was a Thanksgiving meeting in West Roxbury, a nearby neighborhood of Boston, and it ran from Wednesday evening into Thursday evening. Another meeting, in Natick, ran from Christmas Eve into late Christmas day. The final one, which was sponsored by the same group in Dedham that had hosted the 4th of July alcathon, kept its doors open from New Year's Eve into late afternoon on New Year's Day.

I attended each of those meetings for various amounts of time that year, hung out with many friends from the Program, met many interesting recovering people, heard many strong, inspirational messages, and had a great time wherever I landed my butt in a seat.

For the first time in memory I felt a universal connection with the rest of the human race, and I finally felt like I was a part of something important, a contributor rather than a taker, or an outcast.

It was an enabling and gratifying sensation.

I also worked the phone a little harder, calling friends in the Program when I was getting down on myself or feeling lonely. I read the AA literature, particularly the personal stories in the Big Book, and I made sure to pray twice a day, asking only that my Higher Power help me to stay sober, and to remain grateful for what I had.

They say that you should "fake it 'til you make it," so I even feigned a gratitude that I didn't always feel, reminding myself that I was alive, in one piece, and that I had a fighting chance at experiencing a brand new life, if not today then someday soon.

And, finally, I would remind myself a dozen times a day to "just hang on, Wes, you can do this, just for today, for one hour, for one moment, for one heartbeat, or for whatever the hell it takes!"

And somehow, by the grace of God and the Fellowship of Alcoholics Anonymous, I remained sober during the holidays, for the first time in twenty-five years.

I called it my Christmas miracle.

≈≈≈

I finally stopped procrastinating a couple of days after New Year's, 1993, hunkered down, and initiated a full time effort to return to the workforce.

My last job, which had been as a marketing representative for an insurance company, had ended the prior January.

Not surprisingly, it hadn't exactly ended well, which was pretty much par for the course during my drinking career. I had some smarts, and I was great at schmoozing with the insurance agents and taking long, liquid lunches with them, but I was a lot less effective at handling the incessant administrative nonsense that my boss laid on me, or getting along with the nitpicking underwriters back at the home office.

In retrospect, I will humbly admit that there was just the slightest possibility that my problems at work weren't with them, but rather with Wes.

Okay, so let's say that was more than just a possibility.

I had only been employed at the company for about six months when things came to a head. I had just participated in another of what had become a long line of dust-ups with one of the more anal-retentive bean counters at the home office (that was my opinion of him, anyway), so I decided to stop at a bar for a quick drink on the way home from an appointment with a client.

That drink became a dozen, and that's all I remember until I came out of my blackout.

I would determine later, by means of a detailed examination of my credit card and ATM receipts that I had been "out there" for approximately three days.

It turns out that my boss and the HR people at the insurance company had been searching for me all that time, and they finally asked the Norwood police to stop by my apartment to check whether I was still alive.

By that time, however, I was already decked out in my ratty bathrobe and smiley slippers at the Framingham Detox, taking my well-deserved vacation from the world of high finance. So when the Norwood police informed them that their company car was safe, and locked up in the parking lot of my complex, my boss cut his losses, canned me, and began interviewing for my replacement.

The fact that I had gone missing appeared to have been of modest interest to the police, however, so they left a note on my personal car asking me to contact them, but as for my boss, meh, not so much as a quick phone call inquiring whether Wes was still alive.

In retrospect, I can't say that I blamed him.

But now, nearly a year later, and with some stability in my life, I knew that it was time to make an effort to return to the workforce. I felt a new optimism, a realization that this would be another major step in my return to the world, to participate in life, to rebuild my career, to develop a work ethic that was as strong as my sobriety ethic.

Oh, and yeah, I was also running low on cash, which is always a rather significant motivator of change.

≈≈≈

John and his wife, Debbie, owned a small insurance agency in the Boston suburbs. They were a nice couple, in their late thirties, with two children, and they had built the agency from scratch over the prior ten years.

John took care of the sales and marketing responsibilities, Debbie handled much of the administrative side, including the bookkeeping, and they had one employee, a middle-aged lady who performed the policy and claims processing functions.

John also had an entrepreneurial side, and he was fascinated by computer technology. In fact, he was so hooked on tech that he was writing software with a nifty new relational database program that could singlehandedly manage his client and policy data, all of his administrative and claims processing, client billing, word-processing, accounting and marketing.

It was a great tool for a small agency such as theirs, because it streamlined their management and administrative functions, as well as affording them a significant competitive advantage in marketing due to its relational database search/sort reporting capabilities.

And, best of all, it was inexpensive and could be installed on any IBM-compatible personal computer.

I had called on John and his wife regularly when I worked for the insurance company that I had crashed and burned from the prior January. They weren't drinkers, so they had never seen me in action, and we had developed a good business relationship back then, which now turned out to have been a blessing.

I happened to run across John's 'Want Ad' in one of the industry publications in the second week of January. He was searching for a salesperson to license his software program to other small insurance agencies that were planning to automate their own businesses, and that was exactly what I was looking for.

The prior decade had ushered in an exciting new era in computer processing technology. The world was experiencing a perfect storm, as the cost of computer processors fell in direct proportion to the increase in their processing power. It seemed like overnight computers had ceased being the exclusive domain of the world's largest corporations, educational institutions and governments, and were now opening up vast new opportunities for streamlining all types and sizes of Main Street businesses, including John's.

I had sensed the potential of the insurance automation trend ten years previously, and in 1981 had left a secure mid-level marketing position at a regional insurance company in order to sell computers into that hot new market.

I was a good salesman, and I made a great living selling computers. I was so good, in fact, that my company soon offered me a sales position in the Miami area, where they were hoping to expand their market.

Miami – what a perfect town for a thirty year old single guy to enjoy life, while selling groundbreaking new products into a hot new marketplace! I jumped at the opportunity, and arrived in Miami two weeks later.

Unfortunately, however, I hadn't yet been introduced to the riddle that goes something like this:

Question: What do you get when you take an out of control alcoholic out of Boston, and put him in Miami?

Answer: Simple - an out of control alcoholic in Miami.

Well, that was me, so it didn't come as much of a surprise when three months later my company fired me, and that was that. I had pretty much burned all of my bridges in Florida by then, so I headed back to New England with my tail between my legs.

You'd think that I would have learned something from the experience, but we have another riddle in the Program that goes like this:

Question: What's the definition of insanity?

Answer: Doing the same thing over and over, but expecting different results.

Well, once again that was me, the ever-hopeful optimist in denial, so I immediately jumped right back into the insurance automation marketplace and quickly secured another position selling systems to insurance agencies.

I fared better this time around, at least for a while. My new company had been developing some specialized proprietary insurance programs that were being well received in the market, so with my ten years of experience working for an insurance carrier I had some initial success at opening up new markets with regional insurance organizations.

I also conducted product demonstrations for large groups of insurance agents throughout New England, and I did some traveling for the company throughout the country.

The Gods of the Lost Drunks must have been watching over me in those days, because somehow or other I managed to avoid any major jackpots during my travels, and I brought in enough sales to keep management off my back.

Well, let me correct that... for the most part I stayed away from jackpots, although there was that one time at a convention in Miami where I hooked up with a couple of other vendors and partied hard. We called ourselves the "Doggie Baggers," because we stayed over for almost a week after the convention ended.

About the only things I remember about that little vacation are that one shouldn't attempt to swim in the hotel pool at three o'clock in the morning while wearing a brand new Ralph Lauren business suit, and that credit cards have a maximum limit for a reason.

But other than that I remained reasonably under control at that company, at least if you consider missing a day or so of work every week or two due to hangovers "reasonably" under control.

One year later I deserted them and joined another company that was taking the insurance software market by storm. They had the hottest new products, the slickest sales and marketing organization on the street, and their systems were selling like hotcakes.

I flew out to Chicago for an interview at their home office, where they wined and dined me the night before our meeting.

I must have done alright, because they offered me the job even though I woke up out of a blackout the next morning.

Then they told me that my territory would be all of south Florida, including my old stomping grounds in Miami – yippee!

Oh, by the way, did I happen to mention a riddle that goes something like this:

Question: What's the definition of insanity?

Answer: Doing the same thing over and over, but expecting different results.

Yes? Well, three months later I was back in Massachusetts looking for work again, but not in the insurance business - I had managed to burn all of those bridges for the time being.

But now, almost ten years later, and with six months squeaky clean and sober under my belt, I was planning to get back into computer sales to the insurance markets.

And this time I didn't intend for it to be déjà vu all over again!

≈≈≈

The interview with John and his wife went well. We had a long, fruitful discussion, and it was clear that our priorities were aligned.

We haggled a little over my compensation, then agreed on the terms of my employment. I would receive a base salary sufficient to cover most of my living expenses, plus a sliding scale commission program that increased in steps whenever I hit predetermined goals.

That was a standard arrangement for the industry in those days, and it gave me a terrific incentive to overachieve.

They wanted me to start the next day, and that was fine by me.

When I hit my knees that night I thanked my Higher Power for granting me this opportunity to return to the work world. I knew that I would never have had this chance if I hadn't been sober, and if I hadn't been humble, and willing to change, so I was one grateful Onion that evening.

≈≈≈

I threw myself into the job from day one. This was the first time in memory that I had entered into a new venture clean and sober, energized, my head clear, striving to succeed rather than attempting to slide by with a minimum of effort and emotional commitment.

I began working the phone from my apartment that morning, calling lists of insurance agencies that were members of various trade organizations.

Cold-calling is generally a long, frustrating and thankless task, albeit a critical one. The job requires tenacity, self-confidence and a thick skin, all of which were attributes I didn't possess back in my drinking days. Rejection rates are extremely high, so the caller shouldn't take dozens of successive "No's" personally.

In fact, cold-callers are often instructed to "love rejection, because that's just clearing out the dead wood and losers, and getting you one step closer to the next real buyer."

Well, that may sound nifty in theory, but in practice it's tough to endure, especially if one is an alcoholic in early recovery, and has only known defeat and failure over a lifetime of addiction.

But I had the wind at my back this time. I had experienced rejection, and knew how to combat it. I had suffered a lifetime of fear, doubt and insecurity, and I understood that those were merely tricks that an addict's mind plays in order to get him drinking again. I now had the gift of seven months of sobriety under my belt, and I recognized that all of the things I had done to remain sober had also been an ideal preparation for this new endeavor.

Where there had been fear, I now possessed confidence. Where there had been anger and self-hate I now felt gratitude for this opportunity. Where there had been doubt about my abilities I now experienced a sense of optimism and acceptance.

My mind was clear, my thought processes logical, and my ambitions were realistic and achievable.

Somehow, and without ever realizing it, I was becoming present, centered and aware, and grounded and mindful. It was then that I realized that the Promises of AA were coming true in God's time, not mine, just as Jack, Eileen and all of the Oldtimers had been telling me right along.

Within an hour I hit my groove, and by the end of the day I had made several appointments to visit small agencies in eastern Massachusetts that were planning to streamline and organize their businesses.

So, as had become my nightly habit, I thanked my Higher Power for granting me the willingness and ability to remain sober, and to put one foot in front of the other as I "trudged the road to happy destiny."

≈≈≈

Okay, so I suppose it's time for another witty little "AA'ism," which goes something like this:

"Be careful what you ask for, because you just might get it!"

What I asked for was success.

What I received was success.

So that's a good thing, right?

Well, yes, on the face of it, perhaps, but let's not forget that we're talking about WesWorld here, so things may not always turn out quite as anticipated. That's just how life is, and people in recovery who have been around awhile will be quick to remind you of that little nugget.

But the good news was that I was hitting on all cylinders within a month after beginning my new job. I had worked the phones hard, and had built strong momentum during my first week, so I began following up with sales presentations and price quotes for the warmest prospects during my second and third weeks.

I was thrilled by the acceptance we were receiving from these smaller insurance agencies. We had a product that was sized and priced perfectly for their needs, and it was a turnkey system, which meant that we would install it, train their staff on it, and support it as the agency grew.

And, because it was developed and supported by insurance agents, we had instant street credibility.

So what was there not to like?

Nothing that I could see!

≈≈≈

I made my first sale in late February, five weeks after starting my job. Needless to say I was thrilled, grateful, and brimming with self-confidence. I was selling a great product that I believed in, and I had a lot of respect for John and his wife, who had been supportive of me from the very beginning. They had given me a chance, and that was more than most business owners would probably have done.

I also had a great pipeline of prospective sales lined up, and I was certain that we were in the sweet spot of the fast growing "small agency" segment of the market.

Three weeks after I made my first sale I was already close to signing up a second agency, and a third wasn't far behind.

By then John had already installed the software on the first client's computer, and was halfway through the staff's training sessions.

Everything seemed to be going according to plan, so I went charging ahead with my sales calls.

This wasn't work - this was fun!

≈≈≈

This was also 1993, so those essential devices that we now identify as cell phones didn't exist in those days. John was a tech junkie, however, and he had run across a company that was selling a "mobile" phone that was a precursor of the modern cell phone, and he bought one for me to use on the road. It was about the size of a walkie-talkie, unwieldy and kludgy, and you often had to be facing in the general line of sight of your target, but I'll be darned if it didn't work reasonably well.

I called him from the parking lot of a restaurant, and he picked up on the third ring.

"Hey, John, great news - we snagged another one!"

There was a short silence, which I interpreted as a slow signal transmission, and then John replied in a monotone, "Hey, that's great, Wes. Another one already – and we haven't even finished training the first one. Way to go," he said, his voice trailing off.

"Yeah, there's a larger market out here than I thought, so we should be able to keep pulling them in at this pace, or maybe even a little faster," I said.

"Whoa, slow down," he said, then laughed nervously, "I'm just one man, and I have an agency to run also!"

"I understand," I said, still not getting the gist of his words, or perhaps I was just lapsing into denial about what I was hearing under his forced laugh. "Well, how's the training going? Are they up to speed now?"

"No," he said cautiously, "it's taking longer than I expected, and there's been some pushback by staff. Some people just don't like computers, they're too set in their ways, and they're terrified that they may lose their job to a machine."

"Well, I understand, but they'll get through the uncertainty, they always do," I replied, then added confidently, "otherwise, they won't be around in five years."

"I just hope that I'll still be," he said quietly, and it was then that I understood.

John, for whatever reason, was having some second thoughts about the venture, which didn't spell particularly good news for the Onion.

≈≈≈

It turned out that the pushback John had mentioned wasn't coming exclusively from the agency he was training - a fair share of the resistance was coming from his wife and their employee, as I soon discovered to my dismay.

I understood their situation. The insurance industry was by nature a conservative business, where change came grudgingly.

Even now, a dozen years after computers had been introduced into the large, forward-thinking, better financed agencies, they still weren't a business staple in most insurance offices. This was particularly true in the smaller "Mom and Pop" ventures that we were targeting, where computers were still considered more of a scary luxury than a business essential.

Yes, things were changing, especially as the price of systems fell, but it was a slow, painful process, where progress moved at a glacial pace.

I also knew that I would have to tread carefully here so as not to alienate John's wife, or their employee. I wanted to make them allies, and that meant getting them emotionally invested in the venture, and making sure that they had "some skin in the game."

I tried to paint on my happy face, but I knew that I would be fighting an uphill battle, because in the small business world family usually comes first, like it or not.

In this case I was correct. I called in to the office a couple of days later to check on the progress John was having in our first client's training sessions, and his wife picked up the phone.

Her friendly greeting trailed off ominously when she heard my voice.

"Hi Wes, what can I do for you?" she asked, rather brusquely I thought, then added, "You'll need to keep this brief, we have a lot going on these days."

"Hi, Debbie, I just wanted to check in to see how John's making out with the training for the new client."

"I wouldn't know, except that he's been spending way too much time down there. We have an agency to run here, and he's hardly ever around."

"I understand, but his program is solid, so once they're up and running completely you should never hear from them again, except to cash their maintenance checks."

"Well, I don't know about that. All I do know is that he's never around when we need him, and he's not spending enough time on the insurance business, which still pays all the bills."

"Okay, well please just let him know that I called."

"I will." Click.

And that was pretty much it.

≈≈≈

Things disintegrated rapidly after that, and it all came down to the simple fact that John was wearing way too many hats – insurance salesman, entrepreneur, programmer, staff trainer, treasurer of the local business association, husband and father. The list of his responsibilities went on and on, and the pressures on him must have been too intense.

We spoke by phone later that week, and he explained that he would need to "temporarily" apply the brakes to the software business in order to determine how much additional work would be involved in training and supporting new clients.

I mentioned that I had two more prospects who were getting close to coming into the pipeline, but he requested that I break off contact with them for the time being, until he could get a handle on his time requirements.

There wasn't much I could do to change his mind, and to tell the truth I didn't pressure him at all, because I didn't want to be the cause of conflict in his busy life. We all have our priorities, and his was clearly family first, then his existing business, and then way down the list came this risky new venture that was clearly taking up a disproportionate amount of his energy and attention.

I understood that, and I respected him for sticking to his priorities.

Unfortunately, however, this shutdown put me in a financial bind. I needed regular income by then, and I feared that it might be weeks, months or never before we got the software business back up and running again.

In the end I had to laugh at the irony of it all. Here, for the first time in memory, I was leaving a job because I had been too successful – you the man, Westie!

≈≈≈

One critical fact stood out from all the rest when I began to perform the autopsy on my latest boondoggle. It had been clear to me from day one that John's program was a good, but very basic administrative and marketing tool for small insurance agencies, and this failure to have a big run on it didn't change things in the least.

It was a mid-range, no-frills program that had some decent marketing features, and it was relatively easy to use. I had been able to garner interest from the agencies I approached because it was inexpensive, and would handle many of the repetitive daily chores that they needed to accomplish.

I knew, however, that this was a relational database program that held a lot of untapped power under the hood. John had written some decent beginner's programs, but he hadn't begun to scratch the surface as far as the software's potential went.

I had exactly zero programming background, but I had been around long enough to have looked over a dozen programmers' shoulders, so I understood that this was a groundbreaking tool that even non-programmers such as myself could make sing with a little hard work, and a good imagination.

I also knew that I didn't have a "no compete" clause in my contract with John. I certainly wasn't planning to solicit any of the insurance agencies that I had approached while working for him, but that still left an almost unlimited market for me to go hunting in.

And there was one other critical factor - this new breed of relational database development tools was very adaptable, which made them attractive to many different types of businesses. The potential end market that lay out there, ripe for the picking, was huge. It stretched from sales organizations such as insurance and real estate, to industrial, processing and servicing, retail, and to a score of other verticals.

This was a true cookie-cutter tool and, just like the program of Alcoholics Anonymous, its beauty lay in its simplicity. One elegant program, properly developed, could be introduced into hundreds of different small businesses with some simple re-engineering and tweaking for each unique market, and for each individual business within that market.

I thought then of Dr. Bob's final words of advice for Bill W. when he lay on his deathbed:

"Remember, Bill, let's not louse this thing up. Let's keep it simple!"

I shivered then, as I realized that my Higher Power had been watching over me all this time, and that He had delivered me to this time and place for a reason. It was now my moment to move on to the next waystation in my sober life, and my path was clear.

First things first, Wes, stay sober and keep it simple, and then shoot for the Moon!

≈≈≈

There's something exhilarating and enabling about closing one's eyes, taking your hands off the wheel and just going along for the ride. The thrill of the adrenaline rush can be great, if we survive, but the results don't always turn out the way we project in our secret little fantasy worlds.

In my case the old impulsive-compulsive Wes would have jumped into the programming head-first from Day One, then worried about the results somewhere way down the line. After all, that had been my modus operandi for many years, albeit with predictable and not always agreeable outcomes.

This time, however, my head was clear enough to understand that I would need to reorder my list of priorities if I was to have any hope of being successful in my fun, scary new adventure.

And then, like a bolt out of the blue, I remembered one of those age-old AA'isms that goes, "plan your work, and then work your plan," so for one of the few times in my life I stood back, thought it all through, and planned everything out.

And voila, like a lightbulb flashing, everything fell into place as it came down once again to "first things first," so I spent the weekend hitting all of my meetings, and drawing up my business plan.

≈≈≈

As soon as I returned home from my Saturday morning Medfield meeting I wrote out a short, concise laundry list of my priorities.

First, last and always came my sobriety, so my number one requirement would be to continue to attend all of my AA meetings and counseling sessions, because without my sobriety I'd have nothing except a pauper's early grave to look forward to.

Second on the list was my financial survival. I wasn't broke, but neither was I flush with cash, so I needed to find a part time job that would pay the bills, and would be flexible enough to allow me to do my programming while still attending all of my AA meetings and counseling sessions with Eileen.

The actual programming and related activities came in third place. I had already researched all of the small business relational database programs on the market and was certain that the 'Alpha 4' software was best of class. I had looked over John's shoulder enough times during product demonstrations to know that the programming was well within my skill set, so I had a high degree of confidence that I could make my product sing.

My next priority was sales and marketing, although I knew that I wouldn't be getting heavily involved there for probably six months. Nonetheless, I knew the importance of branding, so everything I did on the programming side had to fit into the brand – that would make it real, palpable, something I could anchor myself and my potential clients to.

So then I came up with a snappy name for my fledgling company of one, 'Phoenix Systems,' which was inspired by the mythical bird that had crashed and burned, then rose from the ashes to soar again. That was a no-brainer, because it represented the redemption of this grateful drunk who, by the grace of God, had been returned to the world of the living.

And last, but not least, I named the program itself. Its trade name would be "The Silent Partner." That too was a no-brainer, because I knew that my Higher Power was my partner, and it was through His grace that I had hope for a better life.

When I hit my knees that night I thanked God for helping me to stay sober, to have the willingness to change, and to possess that most precious of all gifts – hope - if I simply put one foot in front of the other and did the next right thing.

≈≈≈

On Sunday morning I attended a meeting at Southwood Hospital in Norfolk. This was the facility where NORCAP was situated, and where I had dried out several times previously.

I was gratified to see a few familiar faces of staff members who had tried to help me back then, as well as some other alumni who I had run into at various meetings in the area. That was one of the great things I noticed in my early recovery – the large number of people who kept showing up out of thin air to remind me that they, too, were sober and rebuilding their lives, putting one foot in front of the other just like I was.

It was then that I recalled the familiar saying, "AA isn't an "I" program, but rather a "We" program," and a shiver ran up my spine as I realized that the Lone Wolf never had to be alone again. What a blessing!

I did some more business planning on Sunday afternoon, then drove over to the Sunday night Step meeting in Medfield.

We did Step 3 that night: "Made a decision to turn our will and our lives over to the care of God *as we understood Him.*"

I didn't consider it to be a coincidence that we were doing that particular Step on that particular evening. Truth to tell, I pretty much didn't believe in coincidences anymore.

≈≈≈

On Monday morning I placed a call to the software company that had written the 'Alpha 4' development tool that I intended to build my programs on. I asked a few questions, received the answers that I expected, and placed an order for the software.

The sales rep informed me that I should receive it within a week at the latest.

Thirty minutes later I headed out to a computer store and picked up a large monitor that I planned to hook up to my portable computer. I figured that I would be on the system for as much as eight or ten hours a day, so I needed a big screen to avoid eye fatigue and headaches.

As it turned out that monitor was one of the best investments I made, because there were many fifteen hour marathon days that I eventually spent at the PC once my creative juices really started flowing.

By noon I was back at the apartment and had begun to sketch out some basic flow charts that would map out the backbone of my program. I was amazed by how organized and fluid my thought processes were, and I said a prayer of thanks to my Higher Power for giving me the confidence and ability to attempt this project.

≈≈≈

The rest of the day flew by, and soon it was 6:00 p.m., and time to choke down a sandwich, shower and head out to the Monday night meeting in Medfield.

When my head hit the pillow around midnight I took a brief personal inventory, and I was amazed by my progress over the past nine months of sobriety. I was full of hope and optimism, where less than a year previously I had been paralyzed by anger, fear and foreboding.

I was actually "doing," instead of just dreaming about doing, opening myself up to the immense opportunities that the world offered rather than running away in hopelessness and denial.

I now found myself reaching out to my fellow recovering alcoholics, rather than hiding away in shame and self-loathing in an apartment where the shades were permanently drawn shut.

The Lone Wolf wasn't quite so lonely anymore.

I knew that I had a long way to go, but I was on the path, so I just had to keep attending my meetings and counseling, and attempt to do the next right thing one day at a time, one hour at a time, one moment at a time, one heartbeat at a time.

I would have good days in the future, and without a doubt a few not so good ones, but I knew that if I remained sober all of my days would be far better than anything I had experienced over the prior twenty-five years.

And from where I was standing that was a deal I couldn't refuse.

≈≈≈

I received my application development software a week later, right on time and as promised. It was an easy load onto my PC, and the installation went flawlessly. I was up and running within an hour, so I spent the remainder of the day playing, exploring and training myself.

I felt like a little kid in a great big candy store, and for the first time in memory I found myself looking forward to getting up the next day to go to work. In fact, I began calling it "going to fun" after only one week on the computer.

It was a gem of a program, simple, logical and expandable, with good documentation, and I fell into a comfortable routine almost immediately. I rose at 7:00 a.m. every weekday morning, as usual, said my prayer and brewed up a large pot of coffee. By 8:00 a.m. I was at the dining room table plugging away on my programs. The time flew by, and many days I skipped lunch because I was too involved in solving this or that programming riddle to even bother to glance at the clock.

But there were two things that I never skipped – my AA meetings and my counseling sessions with Eileen. Nothing, no matter how important, could ever keep me away from them, because skipping even one meeting could potentially set up a pattern that would make it progressively easier and easier for me to start down the slippery slope of denial.

I didn't fully realize it at the time, but I was slowly learning discipline, punctuality and responsibility. These are attributes that most people learn as children and young adults, but like many other things in the development and rehabilitation of this recovering alcoholic I had a lot of catching up to do.

So I guess that I matured emotionally somewhere along the line, because even if I didn't see it in myself, others seemed to have noticed a difference in me.

I also made a rule that I would stop working at 5:00 p.m., at least for several hours, and I stuck to it. This was my time to shower, relax, fix a decent meal for myself, and get centered. Most nights were also meeting nights, so I always found myself looking forward to catching up with my friends. I'd arrive early, have a smoke outside the hall, and catch up on the latest news and gossip in AA.

I put together a great line-up of weekday meetings. First out of the gate was the Monday night Medfield Big Book meeting, then came the Tuesday night discussion meeting in Medfield, a Wednesday night Men's Step meeting in Norwood, a Thursday night open meeting in Millis, and my staple Friday night open meeting in Medfield.

I wasn't perfect, and I didn't get to all of them every week, but I always made at least four of the five, and I sometimes went on commitments to other area groups as well.

Oftentimes I would return home from a meeting and jump right back onto the computer for two or three hours to tweak and tune some of the day's work. I quickly learned that I was more relaxed after I had attended an evening meeting, and that my thought processes were more ordered and logical, and that I was able to be more open-minded and flexible in my thinking.

Those meetings, plus my Medfield weekend meetings, were the counter-balance to my work. They kept me grounded, stable, rational, at ease with myself and with the world. They told me that I was not alone, and they were the glue that held me together during those long programming sessions, and on those rare lonely nights when this drunk lay in bed and despite his best efforts took a head trip back to the bad times.

And so my journey along the "Road to Happy Destiny" proceeded for the next several months.

≈≈≈

I always looked forward to the weekends, because they were far less structured than my weekdays. Here was a time to relax, get to my Medfield meetings, catch up on my chores, fill the refrigerator and my stomach, and spend some time with friends in the Program.

The weekends also afforded me the opportunity to perform some back-testing of the previous week's work, as well as to map out the upcoming week's programming agenda.

I even managed to get to a Saturday night movie once in a while.

I went out on dates a few times, usually with women in the Program, but I was too busy rebuilding my life to get serious with anyone, so my romantic life always ended up on the back burner. And besides, they always hammered it into you to not get into a relationship during your first year of sobriety.

I had broken that golden rule once, and was fortunate to have remained sober, so I didn't have the time or the inclination to test my luck again.

And I guess, if I was to be honest with myself, I still missed Blue Eyes.

I was running up some big numbers at the time - on average I was attending seven meetings a week, sometimes more, rarely less, which put me right on goal for around 350 meetings in my first year of sobriety.

There was, however, one worrisome aspect of my life that I had been avoiding, but I knew that I'd have to overcome my denial, and tackle it before things went critical — that was the dreaded job search.

My monthly expenses weren't huge, but drip-drip-drip, they were slowly draining my bank account. I owned my car outright, which was a blessing, so my major expenses were rent, auto insurance, utilities, food, and the credit cards. I had four of the latter, and had managed to build up an uncomfortable level of unpaid balances on each one, because I was only paying off the interest.

The plastics financed computer equipment, software and related expenses, so they were necessities, but they tacked on an extra several grand to the debt totals, and I was getting nervous about keeping my head above water financially.

Finally, in mid-May, I admitted that I had no choice, so I surrendered to the inevitable.

It was time to find a part-time job - ouch!

≈≈≈

The job search turned out to be faster and easier than I had anticipated. I planned it out carefully, in the same manner that I planned my programming efforts, so before I picked up the phone or tried to cobble together a resume I set certain criteria that I would need to meet, such as the number of hours I could work, what days were best, and what types of jobs were non-starters.

It became immediately clear that it would be necessary to work two or three weeknights, plus weekends, and the non-starters were those in the bartender, restaurant wait staff, and liquor store clerk categories - in other words, every job where I might need to handle liquor.

I suppose this would be a good time to mention that I had taken a part-time job as a floor clerk at Boston's largest chain of liquor stores after I graduated from college, while waiting to go on active duty in the Army.

The best thing about that job was my daily trip down to the basement in the mid-afternoon, where I'd pull my list of stock to send up the conveyor belt in preparation for the evening rush hour traffic. That presented me with a perfect opportunity to sample the wares, which I did on a daily basis.

One day I guess that I'd sampled one too many, however, because I missed the conveyor's "up" button, and instead hit the silent alarm button that rang in the Boston Police station, which was located less than a mile up the street.

That would have been bad enough, but as luck would have it the store's Assistant Manager was walking out the front door to deliver two bags of the day's cash receipts to the bank, just as five or six Boston PD cruisers came screaming into the parking lot.

Needless to say, WesWorld was an unhappy place to inhabit for the next few weeks.

For that, and a hundred other reasons, I had no desire to work in any field remotely related to alcohol.

I also marked off retail sales work, because I didn't have any experience in the field, and wasn't sure whether I could get the hours I needed.

My choice was simple after that - I would become a hack, one of the noblest and most romantic jobs I could possibly imagine!

≈≈≈

Okay, so driving a cab wasn't exactly where a college grad with a magna cum laude degree ordinarily planned to end up at this stage of his career. But beggars can't be choosers, and this gig fit my schedule and basic needs better than most, so it was a no-brainer.

I had a couple of buddies who had driven cabs over the years, so I already had a working knowledge of the pros and cons of the job, and I knew that I could handle most of the problems that were likely to come along.

The pros were easy enough – the money was decent if you knew how to work your fares for tips, every day was different, and you could pretty much set your own schedule within some general guidelines.

On the flip side, however, I realized that not all of my fares were likely to be from the cream of society. Working nights and weekends meant that I'd have to take my fair share of the late night bar pickups, and those fares could always be potentially volatile.

I'd heard the horror stories from my friends, but I had been one of those drunk fares a few dozen times during my own drinking career, so I had a basic understanding of the dynamics, and figured that I could handle most of the problems.

What the drunk traffic all came down to was agreeing with everything they said, remaining patient, and knowing when it was time to boot them out the door - in a polite way, of course.

Or, as a last resort, perhaps in a not so polite way.

Weather and traffic conditions could also create difficulties. However, I had spent a lot of my sales career commuting along the infamous Route 128 highway, and in downtown Boston, so I'd already experienced a lot, including four hour traffic jams, blizzards and hurricanes, and even a maniac who took an ax to a few people one sunny Friday afternoon during rush hour.

But this was now May, the maniac was in a locked ward, there weren't likely to be any blizzards at this time of year, and I'd be working nights and weekends, so I figured why not, what could possibly go wrong?

As it turned out, not very much. I became a pretty fair hack, earned the cash that I needed to pay my bills, and by the grace of God and the fellowship of Alcoholics Anonymous I was able to juggle my AA meetings, software development project and cab job without undue difficulty.

I also received several rewards points, because I was afforded the opportunity to meet many interesting people, including a couple of Grade "A" nutjobs.

So I guess the moral of this little anecdote is that it's amazing what a recovering person is capable of accomplishing, once he or she tosses out that last bottle, and becomes an adult.

≈≈≈

It didn't take long to settle into my new routine.

My weekday morning schedule remained unchanged – I was out of bed at 7 a.m., the coffee brewing, and at the computer developing my programs by 8:00.

On those days when I would be driving the cab at night I programmed until noon, then headed out to one of the local "Loonie Noonie" meetings in the area. By 2 p.m. I'd be home, napping until 4:00, at which time I'd head over to the Broadway yard to clock in and grab my chariot for the evening.

Every night that I drove presented a different challenge, be it weather, or traffic, or a difficult fare, but I always managed to wrap up my last run around midnight, and was home in bed by 1 a.m.

I stuck to my regular programming routine on those days when I didn't drive, and made sure to hit all of my evening AA meetings.

On Friday and Saturday I slept an hour later than usual, hit daytime meetings, proofed my programs, sketched out my plans for the following week's programming effort, and was behind the wheel by 4 p.m. Those were the big money nights, so I generally drove until 2:00 a.m., and then collapsed into a deep, dreamless sleep an hour later.

Friday and Saturday nights were also the big drinking nights, particularly in the bars down in the Norwood Flats, where I caught a lot of my fares. My HP must have been looking out for me, however, because I never ran into a situation that I couldn't handle peacefully. I understood that it was always better to simply nod my head, and agree with the rambling and often incoherent dialogues that the more inebriated riders laid on me.

After all, I'd been a card-carrying member of the clan less than a year previously, so who was I to look down on them now that I had a few months of sobriety?

Cab driving being what it is, however, I also had to consider that not all of my fares might have Wes's self-interest at heart, especially where I was carrying a big wad of cash in my pocket every night. I'm grateful to note, however, that the 18 inch cut-off Louisville Slugger, which other hacks had urged me to place under the driver's seat for self-defense purposes, was never employed in anger.

And then, finally, Sunday rolled around. That was my day of rest, and my favorite day of the week. I slept in, rose around 9:00 a.m., ate a lot, programmed, napped, ate a lot, then programmed, napped, ate a lot and then headed over to the Sunday night Step meeting in Medfield.

Those were long and exhausting weeks, but they brought in much needed cash, and I soon discovered that sobriety had endowed me with a much greater physical and intellectual capacity than I would ever have thought possible back in my drinking days.

I wasn't Superman, but nevertheless I was able to balance many activities and responsibilities, while always maintaining my highest priorities – sobriety and sanity.

And so my journey continued on as I put one foot in front of the other and attempted to do the next right thing. My life wasn't perfect, by any means, but I had hope for a better tomorrow, and that was a gift from God that I will be eternally grateful for.

Dare I say it? There were times when Wes almost thought of himself as a healthy, contributing member of humanity.

≈≈≈

I lost another friend to the disease of addiction in the late spring, just before my first sober anniversary.

Devin was a few years younger than me, and had grown up in my hometown. I hadn't done any hard partying with him, but he was related to other friends of mine, so we ran into each other once in a while during our drinking days, and more recently at AA meetings.

It turns out that he had been bouncing in and out of the Program for at least as long as I had, so we had a lot in common in those days, including heavy doses of denial, and we were both charter members of the 'Skid Row' section of the Medfield Friday night meeting back then.

I hadn't seen him for quite a while, but I ran into him again at a Medfield meeting about a year before I got sober.

One of his parents had driven him there, because he was on crutches.

We got reacquainted at the smoke break, and he told me that he had been homeless, living in a tent in the woods the past winter, behind a shopping plaza that had a liquor store. It had been a cold, snowy winter, so he drank himself to sleep most nights.

He came down with frostbite in both feet that winter. The docs tried to save his right foot, but they lost the battle, so they amputated it, and that was the reason for the crutches.

I ran into Devin several times over the next few months, as I dropped in occasionally on Medfield AA while I played out the string on my denial game, and then I didn't see him for a couple of months.

When I finally did, in the summer of 1992, fresh back from my last trip to Beech Hill, squeaky clean, he was in a wheelchair, because they'd taken his other foot.

A few months later I found out that they had taken one leg to the knee, and when I ran into him about six months after that they had taken the other leg to the knee.

I suppose that a person can only take so much. They couldn't stop the massive infections, so when they began talking about taking one of his legs to the hip he took matters into his own hands, surrendered to his disease in the only way that he felt he had left, and OD'd on a fistful of pain meds that he had been squirreling away for months.

So, when they tell you that the disease of addiction just steals, and steals, and steals from us, I guess that Devin would agree.

Damn, I hate this fucking disease.

≈≈≈

Tick… tick…… tick……… The clock appeared to be slowing down appreciably as the calendar announced that it was June, 1993. The weather was warming, daylight was lengthening into the early evening, and the fragrant smell of blooming vegetation filled the air with its sweet, damp, sultry aroma.

Spring was transitioning into summer, and I was on the verge of entering my second year of sobriety, difficult as that was for me to comprehend. I'd be celebrating my one year anniversary on June 7th, but that damned clock always seemed frozen in place whenever I checked it, which was way too often.

I felt like a little kid who was waiting breathlessly for a Christmas morning that he feared would never arrive, which then led me to the inevitable but inane conclusion that I didn't deserve for it to arrive, because I hadn't worked hard enough to earn it.

Talk about "stinkin thinkin," I realized that I still had a lot of growing up to do, and that it wouldn't be a bad idea to go a little easier on myself, to "let go, and let God," as we say.

It turns out that I wasn't alone in downplaying my progress, however. Most people who come into the Program, including myself, do so on our knees. We're at the low point of our lives, feeling broken, hopeless and clueless, and rarely do we perceive much that's good about ourselves. Sadly, this pernicious disease has taken, taken and taken from us, and has conditioned us to concentrate so much on our faults and failures that we never seem to get around to acknowledging our good attributes.

Fortunately, several of the longer term members of the Medfield AA groups, including Eileen, had noticed my mood swings, and had suggested at various times over the past year that I write out a Gratitude List.

These lists were meant to give all AA members, particularly newcomers, the opportunity to acknowledge our progress over the course of our sobriety, and to express our gratitude for all of the good things in our lives that were occurring because we were sober.

In the first few days of June a couple of the people who had been around for a while suggested that this would be the perfect time for me to acknowledge my personal growth over the past year, and to count my blessings while I waited impatiently for the magical day to arrive.

I knew that it would be futile to object. Those kind people had a lot of past experience to draw upon, and they had laid down the footprints that I was now following in, so there was nothing to be gained by arguing, because the proof of their wisdom lay all around me.

≈≈≈

I wrote out my Gratitude List at the end of the first week of June, 1993.

I decided to keep it short, simple and straightforward, and I promised that I would go easy on myself by concentrating only on the positives. I was already working on my 4th Step, which was the housecleaning step where I was making a searching and fearless moral inventory of myself, so I was dredging up plenty of pain there.

My Gratitude List would be the perfect counterpoint to that, so on a warm Sunday morning I took a notebook, my beach chair and a thermos of coffee down to Duxbury Beach, staked out my claim on a secluded spot near the dunes, and went to work.

It must have been the environment - the warm sun and the gentle sound of the waves lapping up onto the sand. They lulled me into a peaceful state of mind, everything just flowed, and I completed my list within an hour. It was short, concise, and I stuck to the major points, just as I had promised myself.

First, last and always, I was grateful for my sobriety, for I understood that it was the true and only path to my survival, inner peace and fulfillment. My sobriety had gifted me with choices today, and that allowed me to have hope for a better future.

So yes, my heart was full, and this was the foundation upon which I would build my house one day at a time, one brick at a time, one heartbeat at a time.

Close behind, in second place, were my new AA friends. Through the grace of God and the Fellowship of Alcoholics Anonymous I had been introduced to hundreds of wonderful, courageous people who had laid down a path that I could follow to a future that might be beyond my wildest expectations. These were many of the friends who cared the most about Wes - the person and the recovering alcoholic - and I knew that they would be there for me on the bad days, not just the good.

Third, I was grateful for my health, such as it was. Overall I was in okay physical condition, but I had my share of aches and pains. I was also smoking two packs a day, and I was tired and run down from burning the candle at both ends. I wasn't eating healthy, and I had begun to notice some pesky lower lumbar twinges of pain that extended down the back of my right leg and into my foot, a result probably of spending seven or eight hours a night on dilapidated cab seats.

But what could I expect? Most of those conditions could be traced back to collateral damage from a lifetime of self-abuse, but none appeared to be all that serious, yet, and it was a miracle that I had survived where so many hadn't.

So in my mind these ailments were all just the cost of doing business, and Wes wasn't in that business anymore.

Fourth, I was grateful for my new career opportunity. My fledgling software project had been a gift out of the blue, and it had come along just when I was ready and capable of accepting it. It had arrived in God's time, not mine, and I was determined to make the most of it.

And last, but certainly not least, I was grateful for my family and lifetime friends. I had drifted away from most of them as my disease progressed, and I had pushed them away completely when things went out of control, but they had never given up on me, and were now expressing support for my recovery.

To this day I feel blessed to have them in my life.

So that was it, simple and straightforward. I would often look at that list as my sobriety progressed. It became my benchmark, my touchstone, my proof that I was recovering even if I didn't always see it in myself.

In time I would add to that list, and it became my Holy Grail.

≈≈≈

The magical day finally arrived – Monday, June 7, 1993, my one year anniversary without a drink or a drug!

Who'd have believed it? Certainly not that man who had crawled through the entrance to Beech Hill one year previously, a man who was broken, bereft and devoid of hope, a man who was simply running out the string as he awaited the inevitable.

Yet now, just one short year later, I had received the greatest of all gifts – hope, and a one day reprieve from the ravages of addiction.

On this day I decided to take a twenty-four hour vacation from life. I slept an hour later than usual, gave myself permission to stay away from the computer for a day, and went out for a jumbo breakfast of bacon, eggs, pancakes and English muffins, all of which I washed down with OJ and a pot of coffee.

I had gone into that last stint at Beech Hill weighing 165 pounds. For a guy who was six feet tall and broad-shouldered that wasn't very much, so I bore the resemblance more of a scarecrow than that of a human being, gaunt and emaciated, my cheeks hollowed out and my eyes sunk back into my skull.

Now, just one year later, I was pushing 190 pounds, I had developed something of a gut, and it was almost time to start thinking about going on a diet. But that certainly wasn't going to happen today - all in God's time, as they say.

I planned to hit the Medfield Big Book meeting that evening. I had decided, however, that I'd hold off my formal celebration until the Friday night Medfield open meeting that many of my closest friends and supporters attended. That was my go-to meeting, my home group, the meeting that fit me like a glove, so it was a natural that I would receive my medallion there.

Nonetheless, the Big Book meeting was just as important to my sobriety as any other, so for me it was just business as usual, anniversary or no anniversary. After all, a meeting is a meeting is a meeting, there are no bad meetings, just bad attitudes, and I understood that better than most.

I stopped at a shoe store after breakfast, and bought a pair of white high-top sneakers to celebrate the day. They were my gift to myself, and a reminder that sooner or later I would need to do some serious walking in order to lose a little of the jelly roll that I was carrying around my waist.

I headed back to the apartment, stretched out on the sofa, opened a paperback novel, and began to read. Ten minutes later I was fast asleep, and for the next several hours I progressed through the virtuous cycle of nap, read, snack, rinse and repeat, until it was time to head out to the movie theater to take in an afternoon matinee.

Moments after I returned to my apartment I was dead to the world again, and when I woke up at five o'clock I didn't have a single regret. Three, or was it four, naps in one day was a record for me, so I congratulated myself for being so slothful.

I jumped into the shower to rinse the sand out of my eyes, then headed out to a local restaurant, where I wolfed down a steak dinner with all the fixings.

When the waitress asked me what I wanted to drink I told her to bring me a glass of cold water, and to "keep 'em coming," like I was giving my drink order to a barmaid.

She looked at me curiously, but made sure that I had a full glass during the remainder of my meal.

Finally, I drove over to the Medfield meeting and, as usual, ran into some friends. We smoked outside for a while, where I received several hugs and congratulatory handshakes, and then we went in to the meeting room.

It was a small, intimate venue, and I paid attention to every word my fellow alcoholics spoke. I also made sure to do what the Oldtimers had suggested, so I put myself in each speaker's shoes and identified with them, rather than compared. By so doing I was able to understand that we're all different and have a right to our own opinions, but we're also similar in so many basic ways, so we must afford all of our members the freedom to express their own outlook on life if our society is to survive and grow.

Little by slow I was beginning to understand that AA is the great leveler, the equalizer, and that even if I strongly disagree with somebody about their politics, or religion, or the direction our society is heading in, I must nevertheless respect them, and accept the fact that we are all different but equal before the God of our own understanding.

I guess that in AA the short form would be expressed as, "I don't need to go to every war I'm invited to," just because I disagree with somebody who holds markedly different views than I do.

Hmmm, come to think of it, that's probably just as important in the halls of Congress, or the workplace, or a family gathering, as it is in the fellowship of Alcoholics Anonymous.

≈≈≈

It was mid-evening when I arrived back at my apartment. I was exhausted, but I had one final thing to do before I could place an exclamation point on my day, so I pulled out my telephone list and called the number for Beech Hill. I had contacted a staffer there a few days earlier, to make sure that one particular person would be working today, and after I got her to agree to keep it on the down low I was informed that a certain lady would be on tonight's shift.

A staffer at the front desk near the Fish Bowl picked up, and I asked for Donna.

A moment later I heard her gentle voice, "Yes, this is Donna, who's calling, please?"

"Hi Donna, its Wes, I hope you remember me. You greeted me exactly one year ago today, and took me out to the garden for a talk. I'm celebrating one year of sobriety today, so I just wanted to let you know, and to thank you. You'll never know how much that talk meant to me, and I'll never forget you. You were my Angel of Mercy, and you helped save my life."

There was silence on the other end, so I figured that she was struggling to remember who this guy was, but then she spoke, her voice cracking, and said, "Dear God, of course I remember you, Wes! I think about you often, and pray that you're doing well. I've been so anxious to hear from you!"

This time it was my voice cracking, "Well, I'm taking it one day at a time, one hour at a time, one moment at a time, and one heartbeat at a time, just like you told me to do. Despite the ups and downs, I'm getting to a meeting every day and I never thought that my life could be this great. You gave me hope, Donna, and I'll be forever grateful to you."

We talked for another ten minutes, then said our good-byes. We never spoke again, but her gentle words from that day in the peaceful garden still resonate with me, and I will never forget my Angel of mercy.

An hour later I hit my knees, thanked my Higher Power for keeping me sober for another day, crawled into bed and was out cold by midnight.

This had been one of the best days of my life.

≈≈≈

I awoke at seven o'clock the next morning, said my daily prayer and was back at the computer nursing a large mug of coffee by eight. It was business as usual, just another day in the life of a recovering alcoholic who had bills, responsibilities, and a dream to attend to.

The week continued to drag on in God's time, certainly not mine, but somehow I managed to remain focused on my work, and I made sure that I went to a meeting every day.

I also began to recite a mantra to myself over the course of that week. I had been working on it for a month or so, but now I redoubled my efforts in the hope that it would distract me from the case of the nerves I was experiencing, as the clock plodded along at a snail's pace toward my official sobriety celebration.

I had been introduced to hundreds of quotes and sayings over the past year. Alcoholics Anonymous is a hotbed of creative expression, so all it usually takes to come up with a nifty new saying is two drunks sitting around a coffee pot discussing their sobriety - it's better than even money that one of them will come up with a new witticism before the pot is empty.

I got a big kick out of the tradition. I'd been an avid reader for all of my life, and I enjoyed putting words together, so I was always experimenting to see whether I could come up with the next great AA quote. It was enjoyable, it kept me focused on my sobriety, and it had become something of a challenge for me.

Over the next several days I tweaked and tuned, polished and refined, and eventually came up with a saying that resonated with me. And, hopefully it would resonate with other newcomers, whose heads were also spinning, like mine, as we crawled up and out of our disease and into a brand new alien world that bore no resemblance to our past lives.

It was short, simple, and for me one of the most important lessons I could make use of at this stage of my recovery, because it became a catch-all for navigating through the uncertainties and chaos of modern life:

"Please, God, help me to remain present, centered and aware, and grounded and mindful."

By breaking the 'ism down into its integral parts the message was simple:

Present – I must remain anchored to this one unique, perfect moment in time. There is no past, nor future, there is only the "here and now" that I need to be concerned with.

Centered – I must remain balanced between my sobriety, my work, my relationships with others, and with my Higher Power.

Aware – I must always be cognizant of the world around me, and of my unique space in it.

Grounded – I must conduct my life by being based in reality, not fantasy and wishful thinking.

Mindful – I must always be respectful of others, and of their unique and inviolable space in the world.

That simple phrase, for me, represents everything I need to do on a daily basis to remain sober, rational and focused on my journey. It's my touchstone, the great equalizer, the roots that hold my sobriety steady and reliable no matter what chaos is circling around me.

It has become my security blanket over the years, and twenty-six years later I still pull it out of my pocket a half dozen times a day - it's my best friend.

But, because this is life, and because life can by its very nature be unpredictable, I don't always bat a thousand as I go careening madly through the Universe, and my ego will sometimes take me to places I am probably better off not visiting.

I'm also capable of lapsing into dis-ease mode when I'm tired, stressed, ill, or simply fighting life and my time machine. And I've even been a lucky man – I've won Powerball at least a hundred times, in my head, anyway, so just because I'm sober it doesn't mean that I can't project my own brand of nonsense far into the future, just like anybody else.

But here's the point – by getting lost in a daydream, or by making predictions about an unpredictable, unknowable and uncertain future, I rob myself of spontaneity, and of the joy and beauty that is all around me in the here and now, just begging to be celebrated in this one single, unique and perfect moment in time.

So once again I must remember to accept my life exactly as it is, one day at a time, one hour at a time, one moment at a time, and one heartbeat at a time. When I can do that I will indeed be present, centered and aware, and grounded and mindful, and I will be better prepared to withstand the inevitable storms of modern life that come along to test my serenity.

And if I can do that, then I will be at peace with the Universe, and with myself.

≈≈≈

Q: What's a drunk's favorite "wine?"

A: "Whaaaahh, I want it now!!!"

Okay, groan if you must, but that pretty much summed up my attitude on the morning of Friday, June 11, 1993.

The big day had finally arrived, with a whimper rather than a marching band, and that was fine by me.

If I'd had my druthers I would have preferred to skip the celebrity status altogether, but that's not how the game is played. Your sober anniversary is the one day out of the year when you can let your hair down just a little, pat yourself on the back for a job well done, and enjoy being the center of attention rather than just another one of the worker bees.

It's like your birthday, Christmas and the New Year are all being celebrated at the same time, and you get to be up on the stage all by your lonesome.

So now it was here, even though my official anniversary had been several days earlier, and I was champing at the bit… and perhaps just a little nervous at the same time.

One's anniversary can be an ego booster, and a confirmation that hard work pays off. However, it always helps to remember that overinflated egos were a major cause of our downfall in the first place, so an alcoholic's propensity for allowing his or her self-will to run riot doesn't necessarily go away just because we stopped drinking, or a page on the calendar turned, or we hit on a scratch ticket.

I knew that well enough from past experience, and I had no desire to play that game again, so I was grateful, but humbled, and anxious to make it through the day and into a brand new year of sobriety.

I kidded myself into thinking that I could stick to my regular workday routine, but that lasted about twenty minutes, so by 7:30 I had powered down the computer, was nursing my second cup of coffee, and was attempting to think up a little harmless mischief to get into.

I decided to go with my tried and true beach trip solution. I've been a beach freak all of my life, and it's been a source of great enjoyment over the years. There's just something about the warm sun, the feel of sand between my toes, and dozing off in a beach chair to the soft melody of water lapping onto the shore that sets my spirit at rest.

I'm also one of those hardboiled (some would say deranged) New Englanders who actually enjoy swimming in the cold, clear Atlantic waters, and at this time of year there was still plenty of cold in that water. I'd grown up swimming off the southern Maine beaches, and I could think of no better experience than to be floating in the water just as a harbor seal popped up five feet away to say hello, or to scold me for invading his turf.

I arrived at Duxbury Beach around 10:00 and staked out my claim up near the dunes. This was a weekday, and it was still late spring, so the beach was almost deserted – just what the doctor ordered.

I pulled an Elmore Leonard novel out of my duffel bag and began to read, but within minutes I was rolling in and out of consciousness, and five minutes later I was dead to the world.

And so my perfect beach day progressed. I sunned, I read, I napped, I walked, I napped, I swam, I read, I napped, I feasted on a large clam roll and a chocolate frappe at the refreshment stand, and I pretty much ignored the rest of the world for the next five hours. It was Nirvana, and I thanked my Higher Power a half dozen times for delivering me unto this most beautiful and serene place.

I walked back to my car in mid-afternoon, slightly burned but very much at peace with the world, and then made the forty-five minute ride home before the Friday afternoon rush hour traffic really got going.

Evidently all of my napping had exhausted me, so I grabbed another one when I got home – the therapeutic benefits of indolence can never be overestimated!

≈≈≈

I arrived at the Medfield meeting thirty minutes before the start, and it was already becoming crowded in the smoking area as I plowed through a gauntlet of outstretched hands on my way into the meeting hall.

I hadn't been advertising my upcoming anniversary, but in true AA fashion most people already knew that today was my celebration day, and so it began.

I spent ten minutes out in the kitchen, schmoozing with some of the regulars while I took down a couple of chocolate desserts that were lying around. I felt relaxed, at peace with myself, enjoying the conversation and the sensation of knowing that I was right where I needed and wanted to be at that one perfect moment in in my life.

I also ran into my Friendly's Saturday morning breakfast buddy, Patrick R., who had recently returned from the Auld Sod, where he spent several months a year tending to some real estate investments that he had been fortunate enough to make as a result of being sober.

We spoke for a moment, and made plans to grab breakfast and then hit the Saturday morning meeting in the little parish house under the elms.

Soon it was time to head into the Hall, so I grabbed a coffee and took a seat up near the front. I chuckled at the irony, as I recalled the disdain with which I had looked down on all of the regulars who sat up there while I was still an active and angry drunk hiding out near the back of the room on 'Denial Aisle.'

A group from Millis put on the commitment that evening, and. I tried to identify with each of the speakers, rather than to compare our stories.

Once again I was amazed by the similarity of recovering alcoholics wherever I attended meetings. The program's beauty lay in its simplicity, and it always boiled down to a common understanding that each of us shared one disease, that we could begin our journey to recovery only when we had surrendered and admitted complete defeat, and that we must rebuild our lives little by slow, one day at a time, on God's calendar, not our own, just as Bill Wilson and Doctor Bob had laid out sixty years previously.

≈≈≈

Finally my moment in the sun arrived, and my knees began to knock just a little.

Traditions vary from group to group, but virtually all groups, including the Medfield Friday Nighter, wrap up their meetings by reciting the *Lord's Prayer*. On this evening the chairperson of the visiting Millis group asked us to return to our seats after the prayer, because there would be a presentation.

With those words the butterflies began dancing in the pit of my stomach, my knees knocked a little harder, and I took a deep breath to calm myself.

We all stood and recited the prayer, and as we were sitting back down Donna, the chairperson of our home group, walked up to the podium and spoke, "Tonight I'm happy to say that we have an anniversary to celebrate. Wes has one year of sobriety, and I'm proud to present him with his one year medallion," she said, "he's worked very hard this year, so would you please give him a big welcome."

Instinct took over at that moment, and I felt as though I was walking through a slow dream. Rather than feeling anxious or out of place, however, a sense of calm overcame me as I made my way to the podium. I had the sensation of being in a bubble, safe and calm and floating on cool blue waters as I walked to the front of the Hall, accompanied by the sounds of clapping and a few loud shouts of support that resonated throughout the room.

For one perfect moment there was no past, nor future, there was only 'now,' and I knew that there was no place in the world I would rather be.

I'll never be a polished public speaker, but I had conducted several hundred computer presentations for business groups over the years, and had spoken at a half dozen commitments in the prior twelve months, so I knew the basics about grabbing peoples' attention and staying on message.

I also knew that a little humor never hurt when you were trying to loosen up a crowd.

"Hi, my name's Wes and I'm a grateful recovering alcoholic."

"Hi Wes," and "Welcome!" came the enthusiastic responses from the group.

I paused to order my thoughts, then got straight to the point, "I'm grateful to be here tonight, and I'm grateful to be sober. I never really thought that I'd find myself up here saying something like that. I drank and drugged for twenty-five years, and it nearly killed me. I was on my last legs when I crawled in here a year ago, and I doubt that I would have lasted more than another couple of years if I hadn't found the Halls."

"Keep coming, Wes," came a shout from the audience.

"I want to thank all of you for your help. I wasn't always the happiest camper in the early days, as most of you know."

I paused, allowing the hoots of laughter and shouts of "No, really?" to quiet down, then plowed on. "I'm grateful to each of you for helping me to get better. Every one of you has been a power of example to me at one time or another over the past year, and I wouldn't be here, sober, maybe not even alive, if it weren't for you."

There was some applause, but I didn't plan to overstay my welcome, so I wrapped things up, "I have hope for a better life today, and choices, and wonderful friends, and that means more to me than you could ever know. I'm grateful to all of you, so that's about it, because I see a lot of goodies with my name on them sitting on the refreshment table, so once again thank you all!"

A shiver run down my spine as the room filled with applause and shouts of "Way to go, Wes," and "Keep coming, Wes, " and on and on as people came up to the podium to shake my hand.

It was then that I finally understood that the Lone Wolf would never have to be alone again.

One heartbeat at a time.

≈≈≈

I was pleasantly surprised to see two faces emerge from the crowd just moments later, and I was grateful that they had come to celebrate my anniversary with me.

The first was Brad, my lifetime buddy. He and I had played high school hockey together, and we had partied hard during our younger years.

Brad was one of those people who had an "empty leg," which meant that he could consume huge amounts of alcohol without going out of control or passing out. You didn't want to get into a drinking contest with him back in those days, because you wouldn't stand a chance, as I learned to my dismay several times while praying on my knees to the porcelain throne.

Fortunately for Brad, however, he was blessed to have never crossed that invisible line between occasional drinking and becoming an out of control, down and out alcoholic. I don't know whether it was his genes, or upbringing, or the luck of the draw, but he never took that last fatal step into the abyss, and into a lifetime of insanity, and he always managed to stop when it was time to stop.

Brad graduated from college with a B.A. in Education, and he married his high school sweetheart, Karen, six months later. They raised three talented children, and he soon became a health sciences teacher and track coach. He taught in a couple of small school systems, and eventually moved up to Brockton High School, where he spent most of his career.

Brockton is a tough old mill town, with serious drug and gang problems, but Brad had a gift for communicating with those kids, and he turned many of their lives around. He established and ran a gang program at the high school that is still saving young people's lives to this day, and many of his toughest kids received college scholarships upon graduation.

Over time Brad became a long distance runner. He competed in many Boston Marathons, and he eventually moved up to doing triathlons later in life, at an age when most jocks hang up their running shoes.

He also took up hiking in the White Mountains of New Hampshire in his thirties, and at the ripe old age of fifty-nine he hiked the entire length of the Appalachian Trail from Springer Mountain, Georgia to Mount Katahdin, Maine.

He covered all twenty-one hundred brutal miles in five months.

Brad continues to hike the Whites to this day, and his son Tom accompanies him on many of those treks, as does his black Labrador retriever. They take it right to the edge, because they do a lot of winter hikes in that treacherous terrain, and those winter snowstorms can be life-threatening up there in the heart of those mountains.

Suffice to say he's one tough old dog, and I'm proud to call him my best friend to this day.

Two weeks previously I had mentioned to him that I'd be receiving my medallion tonight, but I never thought that he'd drive up to share in the celebration. Yet here he was, pumping my hand and slapping me on the back. He didn't mention it then, but I found out later that he had stopped dropping by the house to visit me several years previously, because he didn't want to be the one to find my body.

He had a valid point there, and it turns out that a lot of people had arrived at the same conclusion not so long ago.

So on this evening of gratitude Brad snuck into the Hall and was sitting alone in the back row, wiping the tears from his eyes, grateful that he was at my celebration rather than my funeral.

≈≈≈

The other surprise attendee that night was Lynn, my other best friend for life. We had known each other since junior high, she had eventually married one of my best friends from high school, and we had partied hard over the years.

But she too, like Brad, had walked away from the partying before it stole her soul, and was now in recovery.

Okay, so maybe I should back up and mention my coffee mug before I get into her story.

I do most of my writing at my computer, which sits on my dining room table. It's a comfortable workspace, and I have a special spot laid out for my mug right next to the monitor.

The mug bears a simple quote that is inscribed, "Miracles Happen," and I know a lot about miracles, because Lynn was one of my mine.

Lynn gave me that mug when she became aware of my desperate situation in 1991, while I was performing my final dance with Death by alcohol. Not surprisingly, she made it her mission to help me, and I think that most of us who knew her understood what would happen whenever Lynn made it her mission to accomplish something, so she went to work on me for one solid year while I stared straight into the eyes of the Grim Reaper. It wasn't pretty, and I know that I hurt her feelings a few times along the way, but she hung in there with me, and made me accountable for my actions.

She was one of the few people still in my life who made me take a long, hard look at the Man in the Mirror, and little by slow her hard work paid off.

Lynn cajoled me into attending some meetings, and she put the pressure on me to enter treatment centers a couple of times, and she never let up. She was tenacious, passionate, and she made it clear that she wasn't going to give up on me.

Lynn was my Angel of Mercy, and I know beyond the shadow of a doubt that I would not be alive today were it not for her unconditional love and compassion.

And, lest I forget, for her Yankee stubbornness.

She drove me nuts at times, but she helped save my life, and I will be eternally grateful to her, because perhaps in turn I have helped save somebody else's life, as the virtuous cycle of rebirth and redemption plays out in Alcoholics Anonymous on a daily basis.

By then there were others coming to my rescue, particularly that group of kind, courageous members of Medfield AA who were so instrumental in my early recovery - a few, then a dozen, ultimately a hundred.

But in those last desperate days of denial Lynn was the final driving force that made me keep coming back after every one of my failures, and she became the conscience that I never had.

Over the years I have tried to pass on the message of recovery to sick and suffering alcoholics and addicts from Vermont to Florida, as it was passed down to me, and every time I come to a moral or ethical crossroad in my life I need only remember her passion for helping others in order to understand intuitively the proper path that I must walk.

So now here was Lynn helping to celebrate my first year anniversary. She was one of the greatest cooks I have ever known, and on that evening of celebration and renewal she brought a cake, chocolate, of course, and was sharing in my happiness.

That alone was worth the price of admission I had paid to earn my seat in the Halls.

≈≈≈

There's more I want to tell you about Lynn, for she had been blessed with that most precious of all gifts – a passion for helping others. She was deeply religious, and belonged to a church that stressed action beyond the words, so she began doing some volunteer and missionary work in a few of the crime and drug-crippled inner cities of Massachusetts and New York.

She was born to do that work, so eventually she went farther afield, accompanying members of her congregation to Haiti in order to assist its citizens, who were suffering under a multi-decade humanitarian disaster.

As fate, or God's plan would have it, Lynn and her sister Jane were in Haiti, building schools and caring for orphans, when the earthquake hit in January, 2010.

They were at the epicenter, and they were surrounded by death, destruction, terror and despair beyond comprehension.

They went to work immediately, with no thought for their personal safety, comforting the terrified children, triaging the injured, extending their stay and helping any way they could until they were literally kicked off the island for their own safety.

But by the time Lynn was boarding the plane for her flight back home she was already getting her second wind, and making plans for her return trip to Haiti.

Lynn took part in a dozen missions to that island over the next five years. She often lived out in the fields for a month or more, amidst the mud, insects and tropical diseases, and she volunteered for every bit of "scut work" she could find in order to help "her" children.

And before she was finished she had left a legacy of hope and promise for a thousand little kids who would otherwise have had no future at all.

≈≈≈

Okay, so back to that mug that has accompanied me on my life's journey ever since 1991.

It's now 2019, late winter, and my mug still rests next to my computer, while here I sit, drinking my coffee and wiping away a tear. The tears come and go whenever I think of Lynn, for she passed from this world to sit at God's table three years ago, and I know that there were a thousand heartbroken children in Haiti who mourned her loss as deeply as I have.

But I also know that many of those children will grow up to pass along her teachings to others in need, and thus the virtuous cycle of hope, healing, service and unconditional love will remain unbroken in Haiti.

So I just did some quick math. I figure that I've polished off somewhere in the neighborhood of thirty-three thousand sober cups of coffee from that mug in the past twenty-seven years, so I'd have to say that the $3.95 investment my friend Lynn made in 1991 has turned out to be a pretty decent one.

Because, when you come right down to it, what is the value of a person's soul?

≈≈≈

We kidded about my mug when we spoke over the phone on Christmas day, 2015, and I told her one final time that I loved her. That was the last time we spoke, because she passed away two weeks later.

I still cry sometimes when I think about her, like now, but please don't worry, Lynn, they're sweet tears of joy for having been blessed to have known you as my friend those many years.

Oh, and by the way, I learned one other lesson about life from Lynn, namely that I don't need to know what plan my Higher Power has for me, or for anyone else. All I really need to know is that God has a plan, and it is my job to be grateful for what I have today, to accept life on life's terms, and to be the best person I can possibly be.

My friend Lynn taught me that, so yes, I do indeed know a lot about miracles.

≈≈≈

I woke up at 7:00 a.m. the next morning, and drank a cup of coffee from my mug while I mapped out some ideas for the following week's programming effort.

I arrived at Friendly's in Medfield at 10:00, had breakfast with Pat and a couple of other guys from the Program, and then drove over to the meeting, where I once again ran the gauntlet of congratulations, handshakes and hugs.

But for me it was just another day in the life of a recovering alcoholic, so by four o'clock I was sitting in my cab down at the Norwood Central train depot, having a smoke while I waited for my first fare.

I figured that it would be a busy Saturday evening, so I recited my mantra and attempted to get centered for the evening's fun and games:

"Thank you, God, for keeping me sober, and please help me to stay present, centered and aware, and grounded and mindful."

Yeah, it was just another day in the life of a guy who had finally come out into the sunshine.

≈≈≈

In early August I made my first software sale to an insurance agency that was located on the South Shore of Massachusetts Bay. It wasn't a big purchase, and I realized that after my expenses were factored in I would be lucky to break even, but for me it was a big deal, nonetheless, somewhere up there with winning the lottery.

This wasn't a sale as much as it was a validation that I could be creative, that I could take chances, that I could develop a work ethic, and that I could be a contributing member of society.

And all I had to do in order to reap the rewards of my efforts was to remain sober, grateful, humble, and on the Path.

≈≈≈

My life got busy after that first contract was signed, and I quickly learned that I would need to wear many hats in order to succeed in my fledgling business.

Taking first things first, I would need to order a copy of the software from the publisher, and then customize it to fit the unique requirements of my new client.

And that meant, in turn, that I'd have to spend a day at the client's office in order to learn everything I could about their business processes and work flow.

Fortunately, this was a typical Main Street small insurance agency, so I already knew a lot about their business.

Additionally, I had sold them a turnkey system, which meant that I'd also need to buy the computer and printer that they'd be using, configure the equipment to fit the unique layout of their office, and then load the software and test it at my apartment.

I also had to purchase a third-party standalone insurance quoting program, because the agency provided competitive price quotes for their auto and homeowners policies.

And, after all of this prep work was done, I had to set aside three days for staff training, which also meant that I'd have to create a manual for the staff to refer to, as well as make myself available for the support calls that a brand new technology client was likely to make.

I realized that I had my work cut out for me, but I also knew that I was sober, motivated, and for perhaps the first time in my life, organized.

I dug in my heels and went to work the next day, but only after reciting my simple prayer, "Please God, help me to accept the outcome of my efforts today."

That prayer became my mantra over the next few weeks as the system roll-out proceeded without any unexpected glitches, and it still holds a prime position in my 'God Bag' - hardly a day goes by that I don't use it.

≈≈≈

"The fog comes on little cat feet."

That's the starting line of a short poem by Carl Sandburg, and to a great extent it has as much to do with relapse and the disease of addiction as it does the weather.

One of the "Three Amigos" slipped away from the pack that summer, and disappeared.

Dave had been having a rough time of it. He was finding it difficult to balance meetings, work, and his family obligations, and by the end of July he had begun to follow a familiar pattern that generally leads to trouble, and it was a pattern that I knew all too well.

First came Stage One, the skipped meetings. He usually had a valid excuse for why he couldn't accompany us to a meeting – the kids' Little League games, babysitting while his wife had a Girls' Night out, or job pressures that forced him to work a lot of overtime.

But when all of those distractions start coming one after the other, a bad pattern of behavior can be established, as it becomes increasingly easier for the recovering person to justify taking a night off from their AA meetings.

And when those nights off start coming more frequently than the nights on, you'd better watch out, because it often means that your disease now has the upper hand.

In fact, you can pretty much bet on it, particularly if you're in early recovery.

And I surely knew that from my own experience.

Next comes Stage Two - the resentment. We become short-tempered, pressured by having to handle all of the distractions in our lives. And it just isn't fair, is it? "Why me? Why am I the one who always gets stuck handling all of this garbage? Why can't I ever just have some fun? I work hard to satisfy many masters, but what do I have to show for it?"

Yup, been there myself, said that more than once!

So now we slide into Stage Three without blinking an eye, "and, besides, what's the big deal about skipping one meeting, just that one meeting, one time, and after all it isn't the best meeting of the week, and I was getting tired of it anyway, and a couple of the know-it-alls were beginning to drive me nuts with their "suggestions" about how to run *my* life.

Oh yeah, I've been there alright, and don't forget, we can go to two meetings next week to catch up, right buddy?

Sure, absolutely!

But then a funny thing happens when "next week" arrives, and Stage Four slips innocuously through the door. We lie down after work to take a nap and get centered before heading out to our meeting, but just then the phone rings and it's one of our good 'ole drinking buddies.

We haven't spoken with him for a couple of months, so its catch-up time and we chitty-chat for an hour, and then it's too late to go to our meeting, but no big deal, because there's always that meeting next week to get us back on our routine, right?

Oh, yeah, and by the way, now that I really think about it, it wasn't that I was tired of that meeting, it's really that I just plain didn't like any of the people there. They were stuck up and know-it-alls who thought they had all the answers, and could dictate my life to me, so perhaps I should try to find a friendlier group, perhaps one where people understand me better, rather than bossing me around like I'm some kind of immature child.

"Yeah, that's the ticket, I'll look for another meeting next week! Screw the Tuesday Nighters, they were a snotty bunch to begin with, and I never identified with most of them in the first place!"

Ahhh, and so it goes, as we wrap up the next verse of the bittersweet song of denial, and I had been a virtuoso at it.

Dave's final stage of relapse came two weeks later. We had finally harassed him enough that he agreed to accompany us to the Millis Thursday night meeting, so he reluctantly met us at Friendly's for coffee beforehand.

He remained quiet, studying his coffee, almost morose, while we talked "Program."

I noticed that he didn't say a word on the ride out to Millis, either, that he fidgeted a lot at the meeting, and that he wasn't paying much attention to the speakers. He also stepped out twice to have a smoke, which was never a good sign.

He might have been there in body, but I knew that in spirit he was in a very dark, faraway place.

I was the designated driver that night, so after the meeting was over I headed back toward Medfield.

Dave was usually talkative, upbeat and joking around, but on that ride he didn't say a word.

Andy had also noticed his personality change, and he finally asked him whether he was doing okay.

Evidently he wasn't, because that simple question set him off and he went full tribal, pounding the glove box and screaming obscenities, shouting that we all needed to stick to our own flippin' problems and not start analyzing his. He was doing just fine, thank you very much, and besides, if you had his problems you'd know what he was going through, so just back the hell off!

It was a textbook response, and there was nothing more to be said, so we remained silent for the remainder of the ride.

Moments later Andy and I went into Friendly's, and Dave drove off for points unknown.

I never saw Dave again. I heard through the grapevine that he relapsed and eventually tried to get back into meetings, but then he relapsed once again, and after that there were no more Dave sightings in the local halls of AA.

So that's how a relapse "just happens," and I ought to know, because that was my pattern for the last five years of my drinking career.

I understand now that the price of my freedom is eternal vigilance, and that I must never let my guard down, or become complacent, because with the snap of my fingers it can be one, two, three easy steps and poof, Wes will be off and running again, and that will be my death sentence.

I pray that Dave finally made it back to the Halls one day.

But for the grace of God go I, one day at a time, one hour at a time, one heartbeat at a time, or whatever the hell it takes.

≈≈≈

I performed the system installation for my first client in late August.

I wised up early on and decided to bring in some outside help for the hardware set-up. I knew a talented systems guy by the name of Jim, who I had initially met when I participated in a couple of installations while working for a former employer, and he agreed to help me with some of the program integration, tweaking and tuning.

Jim was a highly certified professional, and just his presence on the installation created an additional level of confidence on my client's part.

It also made sense for me to hand over the hardware support agreement to him, including the related support fees, because that freed me up to spend more time on sales and programming, where my skills lay.

Yes, I could probably have handled things by myself, but I admired Jim's work ethic, his rates were reasonable, and I figured it wouldn't hurt to at least have the appearance of being more than a one-man dog and pony show.

I suppose that the appropriate saying in AA would be, "We did what I couldn't do," or in this case, "We did a whole lot better by teaming up than I could ever have done alone."

Little by slow the Lone Wolf was learning to curb his ego, to become humble, and to ask for help in *all* of his affairs.

And guess what? It didn't hurt, I didn't get the cooties, and I ended up with a satisfied client.

≈≈≈

I settled into a regular routine by mid-September. It was high intensity, and it kept me on my toes 24/7, because in addition to my programming and sales activities I was also driving the cab four or five days a week, and was still managing to get to six or seven weekly meetings.

But the meetings came before all else on my priority list, because I understood that without them there would be no business to worry about, or anything else for that matter – that was just as much a certainty as knowing that the sun would rise in the East the next morning.

In fact, my fear of relapse helped me to get creative, because it forced me to find new meetings that fit my busy schedule. As a result I met plenty of interesting people, and I was exposed to many fresh slants on addiction and recovery.

There was, however, one downside to my busy schedule – I had virtually no social life. I was running straight out each day, especially with the cab job, and that left no time for exercise, taking in a movie, or dating.

To some extent AA has a quasi-social environment that exists before and after meetings, but in some ways it's like hanging out with family members – interesting for a while, but it can get stale at times.

I also continued to bat zero as far as my love life went. I had dated another AA woman twice that summer, but for whatever reason I didn't feel any romantic connection with her, so I stopped calling. I figured that I just had different priorities, or that I was still stinging from the failure of my brief entanglement with Blue Eyes.

Or perhaps it was simply that I had a lot of work to do on Wes before I could become emotionally intimate with another person, and the chains that had bound me in my youth were still there, rusting, yet stubborn and all-powerful.

Whatever the case, my romantic score was a big fat zero, so I stuck to the AA basics, hit my meetings, hung out with my AA friends, and reminded myself that everything happens in God's time, not mine.

But geez, God, couldn't you at least make it just a little bit interesting?

God didn't reply, so I guess He must have been busy creating a few billion new lifeforms, or whatever, and I knew better than to push Him too hard, because He could get sorta touchy when you whined and nagged Him too much.

I suppose that I would too, if I were in His sneakers.

≈≈≈

"Road Trip!"

My AA buddy Dallas rang me up one afternoon in early October. He was a bright guy, an inventor, and he had strung together many years of sobriety. He was in his late fifties, but he had a youthful and inquisitive mind, which made his choice of professions a natural.

He was also an aviator, and he had his own plane that he kept at one of the small municipal airports that dotted the western suburbs of Boston.

You could always expect to learn something new about life, and the world, when you had a conversation with Dallas.

"Hey, Wes, it's Dallas, what are you doing tomorrow?"

That was one of the things I liked about him - he always got right to the point.

"Hi, Dallas, tomorrow? Well, pretty much the same as always, working on the software and trying to make a living. Why?"

"Cancel your plans, we're flying down to the Cape to have lunch with Jack."

"Huh?"

"Yes, you heard me, they're forecasting a great weather day tomorrow, perfect for flying, and I told Jack that I'd bring you along."

Jack, my first sponsor, had moved down to Cape Cod about six months previously. I hadn't heard much about him since then, so under circumstances like that its customary for relative newcomers such as myself to obtain a new sponsor.

One of the more important goals for a person in early recovery is to select somebody who attends a lot of the same meetings as you, or to be able to grab a quick cup of coffee together, because it's essential that you maintain the eye to eye contact on a regular basis.

So, after a quick search, I had located a new sponsor, who I was still getting acclimated to.

I liked Dallas's idea, a lot, but as usual I had plenty of work projects on the stove.

"Geez, Dallas, I don't know, I've got a lot of stuff going on these days..."

He laughed, then said, "Hmmm, I don't exactly recall making this optional, so you're going!"

"But," I began, and then he cut me off, "But no buts, meet me over at the main hangar at Norfolk Airport at 9:30 sharp tomorrow morning - you'll be glad you did!"

"But..."

He laughed again, then said "I told you, no buts, and isn't this one of the reasons why you got sober, to enjoy life just a little?"

He had me there. "Well, yeah, I guess so, yeah, I'll see you at 9:30," I said, but Dallas had already hung up by then.

His invitation couldn't have come at a better time. It was just the prescription that the "Big Pilot in the Sky" knew I needed, and I was reminded once again that God does listen, so we must always pay attention, hold on tight, and be grateful whenever He drops one of these precious little nuggets into our laps.

≈≈≈

I will never forget that day. It was well up on the top-ten list of fun things that Wes did in his life, and I will be forever grateful to Dallas and my Higher Power for giving me this special gift, compliments of sobriety.

I arrived at the small municipal airport around 9:15, and parked behind the single hangar. Dallas's car was already there, so I went around to the front of the building and located him just as he was finishing up a walk-around visual check of his single engine aircraft.

The first thing I noticed was that the plane was small, very small, but it had the appearance of having received plenty of the type of TLC that only a dedicated flyer would have taken the time to perform.

The plane was spotless, glistening in the mid-morning sun.

"Hey, you made it, right on time, is this a perfect day, or what?" Dallas greeted me.

"I'm already really, really glad that you talked me into this," I replied, "what a great day to play hooky."

"You ain't seen nothing yet," Dallas chuckled, "just wait 'til we're airborne, you won't believe it!"

"Oh, I already believe it, this weather is perfect," I said, and it was. The temperature had climbed into the low seventies, with low humidity, and the sky was cloudless, shining a deep azure blue that guaranteed the visibility would be virtually unlimited at cruising altitude.

"I'm just finishing up my check," Dallas said, snapping the engine cover shut, then fastening it, "so give me a hand pulling the chocks out."

I bent low and moved cautiously under the right wing, then tugged the wedged wooden chock out from beneath the wheel, and Dallas did the same with the left side chock.

Then he clambered up the left wing, pulled open the pilot-side door, and eased himself into the seat.

I moved a little more slowly along the right-side wing, then squeezed myself into the passenger seat, pulled the small door shut, and fastened it.

The first thing I noticed was the cramped size of the cabin – it provided about the same space as the front seat area of the Volkswagen bugs I had driven in college. We were crammed in tight, our elbows almost touching, my knees slightly bent against the map box, and I wondered momentarily how this little plane could possibly get us airborne.

I received my answer soon enough, however.

Dallas pushed the ignition button, the engine turned over once, twice, then sputtered as the single prop flared momentarily before almost stalling out, and then suddenly all systems were go as the engine shuddered and then exploded into life while the prop spun up to max rotation.

Dallas taxied slowly out to the grass runway, then revved the engine, and we began to accelerate down the field.

We moved slowly at first, gradually gaining speed, but then, just as I was beginning to wonder whether we'd run out of runway before we hit lift-off velocity, Dallas pulled back on the controls and we were airborne, angling up into a steep climb.

I had never been in a small plane before, had never taken off from a grass runway, and had never been a passenger in the front seat, watching as a pilot performed his magic. But, rather than feel any anxiety, I knew only joy, and the exhilaration that comes when one is untethered from the Earth, floating and bouncing gently upward on the air currents, free from the bonds of gravity in a way that I had never dreamed possible.

There was silence up there, save for the muted, hypnotizing drone of the engine.

I was speechless, awestruck, experiencing a high unlike any I had ever known, soaring as if on the wings of angels.

I knew infinite peace then, in that one perfect moment in time, and I have sought out that feeling every moment of my life since that day.

This was what I had gotten sober for, this was worth all of the pain and sorrow I had subjected myself to, and this was a gift from my Higher Power that I will forever cherish.

And it was then that I knew that after a lifetime of struggle I had finally let go of "IT."

≈≈≈

And then things got even better.

Shortly after we attained cruising altitude at four thousand feet I noticed movement several hundred yards off to our west. The clear, crystalline air provided virtually unlimited visibility up here, and off in the distance I detected a smudge of dark shapes that appeared to be moving parallel with us.

It only took me a few seconds to realize that I was watching a V-shaped squadron of perhaps fifty Canadian geese as they flew south on their autumn migration to the southern U.S. and

Mexico. They were disciplined, flying with military precision, each creature knowing its place in the formation, and they must have noticed us at the same time, because the wedge appeared to be veering slightly closer to us, no doubt curious to see what the strange, noisy contraption that was ruining their privacy was all about.

At that moment a sense of euphoria overcame me that was unlike any other I had ever experienced.

Here was Wes, sixteen months sober and grateful, sitting in a tiny little plane, floating along the air currents on a perfect autumn morning while I watched these beautiful creatures sail through the heavens on their annual sojourn to their winter feeding grounds.

I was close to breaking down into sweet tears of joy as I surrendered to the moment, and accepted it for the gift that it was. For perhaps the first time in my life I felt free from the bondage of self, centered in the moment, floating through the Heavens, accepting this gift of sobriety that had been handed to me in my darkest hour.

All I could do then was to murmur, "Thank you, God, for delivering me unto this place."

Dallas just chuckled in agreement.

Then I said, "Hey, Dallas, thanks for bringing me along, this doesn't suck!"

Dallas just chuckled again, then said, "Yeah, it sure doesn't, Wes."

≈≈≈

We played tag with several squadrons of southbound geese for the remainder of the forty-minute flight to Hyannis. They were as curious about us as we were about them, but it was dangerous to allow them to get too close to the aircraft, because a mid-air collision with even a single bird could have taken out the prop and sent us pin-wheeling into Cape Cod Bay.

So we respected their space, and they respected ours, and I marveled at the beauty and grace of these ungainly creatures that my Higher Power had been kind enough to introduce me to on this perfect autumn morning.

I was also spellbound by the limitless colors and hues of the foliage reflecting upward to us from the October coastline. The world looked like an entirely different place from our altitude, and for possibly the first time since I put down the drink I realized how differently life appears when viewed through the crystal clear prism of sobriety.

I had survived for the past twenty-five years by living in a monochromatic world of dull gray, lacking variety, creativity or inspiration. There were no gradations or degrees, I either existed under the dark influence of alcohol and drugs, or I was planning how to get my next high.

But now life was multicolored, intricately layered with shades and nuances, a brilliant tapestry of colors and creatures that was exhilarating, mystifying, and, some of the time overwhelming in its beauty, and it led me to wonder once again, why did I get sober, if not for this?

≈≈≈

Dallas nudged the plane into a half circle as we began our approach into Hyannis Airport, then lined us up so that we'd be coming in for the landing with the wind in our face.

He feathered the engine moments before we touched down, and we glided in for a perfect three point landing. Then we taxied off the runway and over to a parking area for small civilian aircraft.

Jack was standing there, waiting.

It was wonderful to see him again. He was a great human being, full of love and compassion for his fellow alcoholics, and his gruff, crusty exterior belied the kind and generous person who had made it his life's mission to help every sick and suffering individual who crossed paths with him.

He had helped save my life, and God only knows how many others had been likewise blessed by his unconditional love and compassion.

We shook hands, exchanged greetings, and then Jack led us over to the airport's combination main building and control tower. There was a small restaurant inside, and at this time of day it was practically empty, so we picked a table near a window that looked out over the runway.

I was famished, so I ordered up a bacon and cheese omelet, home fries and English muffins, and juice and coffee, and Dallas and Jack ordered coffee and toast.

We spent the next ninety minutes swapping updates about our activities, and naturally much of the conversation revolved around AA, and the comings and goings of its various members.

Jack was enjoying his meetings down on the Cape. He was making a lot of new friends, and true to form he had already started sponsoring a newcomer. He was dedicated to service, service, service, and I had no doubt that he was making a big impact on newcomers down on the Cape, just as he had in the Boston suburbs.

The morning flew by, and by 1:00 it was time to make the flight back to Norfolk.

We shook hands with Jack, and then he accompanied us out to the plane. It was all gassed up and ready to go, so we said our good-byes, pulled out the chocks and climbed back into the cockpit.

Dallas taxied out to the runway, checked his instruments one final time, then revved the engine, pointed us into the wind, and we accelerated down the asphalt.

We were airborne seconds later, and within a couple of minutes we were once again out over Cape Cod Bay, heading northwest into the prevailing autumn winds.

The formations of geese were still parading south, honking their greetings, the weather and visibility were still perfect, and a billion shades of red, yellow, orange and gold foliage sparkled below our cocoon as far as the eye could see.

We remained silent for most of the return flight to Norfolk After all, there really wasn't much left to be said when you've just witnessed perfection, and I wondered then for the briefest of moments whether I had just experienced transcendence.

I never saw Jack again, but I will never forget him.

≈≈≈

My one day vacation from responsibility had energized and inspired me, so I dove back into my programming efforts with a renewed sense of confidence and imagination. My thought processes were clear, linear and logical, and I soon began to experiment with some ideas that I had been timid about playing with previously.

In the beginning I had decided to concentrate my efforts exclusively on insurance prospects. That was a vertical market that I understood inside and out, and I was fortunate to still have a lot of connections there, despite my various burnouts. I felt comfortable in that segment, secure in my knowledge of the industry and its players, confident that I could carve out a small, profitable niche for my programs.

I acknowledged, however, that I would never be more than a small player in that market, and that sooner or later I would run out of prospects. The handwriting was already on the wall, and many of the smaller agencies were merging with each other in order to gain market share, and to compete more efficiently with the larger, established shops.

Much of that industry consolidation was being fueled by automation, and that meant I'd soon be competing with the big players in the large systems marketplace. Several of those outfits were my former employers, so we would all be gnawing on the same bones.

That wasn't a comfortable feeling, particularly when I looked back at my checkered history with several of those companies, who might have plenty to say about me if they chose to do some trench warfare.

The bottom line was that I needed to get proactive and have a "Plan B" in place before things got too crowded, rather than remain complacent until it was too late.

≈≈≈

I called a systems consultant one week after my adventure with Dallas. Her name was Nancy, and she was affiliated with Alpha, the software development company whose database programs I was using. She was writing her own programs on that platform, as well as consulting with third-party developers such as myself.

Nancy came over to my apartment several days later, and I ran through a demo of my insurance programs for her.

She was impressed.

"Wow, you've done a nice job here, Wes," she said. "I don't know much about insurance, but there's a lot of detail here, and I like the way you've integrated some of the third party programs into yours, and the menu structure and marketing orientation. It's one of the better programs I've seen an individual developer produce in any vertical market."

She paused, then asked, "Okay, you have a potential winner here, so what exactly are you concerned about?"

I explained that I was worried about becoming a one-trick pony, that the insurance marketplace was consolidating, and that I might get shut out of it sooner, rather than later.

"Well, that's the trend in a lot of verticals these days, and it's all due to the innovations that you and I and the big players are coming out with," she said.

"I know, so here's my question. You understand the big picture as far as Alpha goes, so with your background do you think that with some tweaking and tuning my programs could be adapted to lots of other verticals, the small Mom and Pop shops, the retailers and service industries?"

She smiled, then said, "Hmm, I'm not sure I should tell you this, because you could become my competitor, but what you've already developed could easily be modified for dozens of other verticals."

That was what I had been hoping for, and it was all I needed to hear.

"Dozens? Well, if that's the case, it sounds like we have a big pond to fish in, so I won't get in your way," I said, smiling, then added with a laugh, "but quid pro quo, you can't play in my little sandbox either."

Nancy just beamed at me and said, "Agreed, and remember, dozens and dozens and dozens of verticals, so who knows, maybe we'll become partners someday and corner the market – stranger things have happened!"

She left a few minutes later, and a big, wide grin crossed my face – Nancy had just handed me the keys to the kingdom.

≈≈≈

If I thought that I had been busy before I met with Nancy, then I hadn't seen anything yet. In the next few weeks my work took on a new urgency, as I salivated over the vast opportunities that lay ahead of me. I felt energized, motivated, and my creative juices were bubbling over as the full potential of my simple little software programs became apparent.

Thankfully, however, I was sober, and somewhat grounded, so I was able to pull back on the reins just a little before visions of sugar plum fairies started dancing in my head. I reminded myself that I was still an alcoholic, first, foremost and forever, and yes, I was in recovery, but the last thing I needed to do was let my ego take over. I had worked too hard, and endured too much pain, to simply throw everything to the wind and go full bore into the programming efforts without first thinking things through.

I realized that I would need to re-do my business plan in order to capitalize on the new opportunities that were staring me in the face, but first I had to take a look at my recovery plan, because without recovery I would have no use for a business plan.

I also understood that henceforth I would need to manage my life by maintaining a prudent balance between recovery, meetings, counseling with Eileen, building my business, driving the cab, and improving my relationships with others. I would have to work hard at each component of the plan, because they were all interwoven, and this was the only means by which I could maintain the virtuous cycle of healing that would keep me present, centered and aware, and grounded and mindful.

And, bottom line, sober.

In even simpler terms it meant planning the work, then working the plan by locating that elusive sweet spot that struck a balance between all of my responsibilities. That would stabilize me, and assist me in working more efficiently, and smarter.

Conversely, I believed that the same work ethic which I was utilizing to build my small business could also energize and motivate me to work my recovery program more effectively.

I called it my benevolent cycle of recovery, work, rest and recreation, and I understood that without every one of those elements supporting the others there was a high probability that the entire system could collapse under the load.

Recovery was my house, but it wasn't habitable unless the framing and masonry and plumbing and electricity all worked as one.

Sticking to my meeting schedule now took on a new urgency as I settled into the cycle, because meetings will always be the vital touchstones upon which my physical, mental and spiritual survival depends.

≈≈≈

It was around this time that I began to experience frequent stiffness and twinges of discomfort in my lower back and right leg, and some intermittent numbness in parts of my right foot. It wasn't too painful, yet, but on the other hand it was present and somewhat of an annoyance.

I attributed the discomfort to being a result of bad posture over the years, lifting and hauling heavy computer equipment in my car, and driving a lot of beat up old cabs that had various defects in their front bench seats.

Oh, and of course there was that time, perhaps a year before I surrendered, when I came out of a blackout experiencing the same mysterious numbness and discomfort, combined with occasional sharp pain - cause unknown for obvious reasons.

Nevertheless, there was no regular pain currently, and Mister Hard-Ass tough guy was busy and needed to keep the cab job in order to pay the bills, so I ignored the discomfort, figuring that it would go away of its own accord at some point, as it previously had.

Because, like, I mean, don't bad things always go away when we ignore them?

Looking back in the fullness of time it's easy to understand that denial takes many forms, and ignorance isn't necessarily the pathway to bliss.

≈≈≈

Hoorah!

I signed my first contract with a non-insurance prospect in November of 1993. My new client operated a small wholesaling business that warehoused and sold industrial and hardware products to retailers and jobbers. His requirements were simple enough – he wanted to track inventory and sales, bill customers and manage his receivables.

My software fit his needs easily, once I made the appropriate modifications to my database program, and the installation and training went off without a hitch.

In fact, training time was much shorter for this business than for the typical insurance agency, support calls were few and far between, and I was able to bill this client the same as for an insurance customer, for half the work.

I also installed my software on the client's computer, which meant that I didn't need to be in the hardware business where competition was fierce, margins were low, and hardware support expensive to perform.

I was quick to make note of all that because it could simplify my life immensely. This was the KISS formula in actual practice, so just think things through Wes, don't get greedy, and just stick to the basics.

Hmm, and wasn't that what Jack had been hammering into me since the first day I crawled into the Halls?

Bottom line, the client was pleased, and he even agreed to be a reference for other prospects if the need arose.

All in all, life seemed to be working out quite swimmingly for the Onion as the holidays approached.

≈≈≈

In early December I was reminded once again that God has a great sense of humor, and irony!

Cabbies in the Norwood area were sometimes dispatched to a couple of the local prisons for pickups of newly released inmates. There were two facilities – MCI Norfolk, which was a medium security facility, and right down the road from it was MCI Walpole, which was maximum security, the "Big House."

The routine was simple. The cabbies would park just outside the facility and wait for the released convict to come out to take his first breath of freedom, and then we'd drive him out into "the World."

Call it the luck of the draw, but for whatever reason most of my pick-ups originated at the "Big House," and it was ordinarily a straightforward process. The inmates always came out through a designated gate, and would walk over to the cab wearing civilian clothes and carrying their one duffel bag of possessions.

Virtually all of these guys were headed for Boston, so I would make the ten minute drive to the MBTA station in Walpole Center, where I dropped them off.

Sometimes the prisoner wanted to chat, so we'd talk, usually about sports, and other times we remained silent for the short ride to town.

I always left it up to them to start the conversation.

Things went differently right out of the gate on one of my pickups in early December. This guy wanted to talk – a lot! He had been in the joint for eight years on am armed robbery bid, and it was clear that he still had a few unresolved "issues" from his past life that he needed to work out. I didn't interrupt him, just listened intently, and counted the minutes until I could drop him off at the station.

All in all he was wrapped pretty tight, especially for a guy getting his first breath of freedom in eight years.

Just as we approached our destination he asked me to stop, mentioning that he had to pick up something.

"Aww, just great," I thought, as I pulled into the curb in front of a downtown liquor store.

He was out the door and into the packey in a flash, and back in the cab several minutes later, grasping a pint of vodka in a paper bag.

"Hey, buddy," he said, "could you make it a slow ride to the station? I've been looking forward to a pop for eight years now!"

Damn, just what I need, an alkie ax murderer in my cab who's planning to go on a drunken crime spree, with Wes kidnapped as his accomplice, I growled to myself.

Talk about jumping to conclusions – get to a freakin meeting, Wes!

But then again, knocking back a pint of cheap vodka just ten minutes after you've been released from an eight year gig in a maximum security prison probably wasn't the ideal set-up for beginning a brand new chapter of one's life.

"Well, okay, but make it quick, will ya?" I said, "the 4:45 inbound is gonna be here in five minutes, and it's the last one for an hour, and it's a cold wait at the station."

"Okay, buddy, you got it!"

I made one pass around downtown Walpole while the con took down a big chunk of his bottle. I was nervous, fidgety, and not looking forward to a confrontation if this guy decided that he wanted to make a change in his itinerary, like perhaps asking me to drive him to Boston.

That wasn't going to happen, but I wasn't looking forward to having that discussion.

But then I had a flashback – I remembered the day that I left Beech Hill eighteen months previously, and the concern in Bob the Cabbie's eyes when he picked me up just a mile from the Concord Reformatory. He had the same nervous expression on his face that I'm sure I was now projecting to this ex-con.

I couldn't help but smile then, as I put myself in the guy's place. I could have been him – in fact, in a strange way I had actually been a lot like him not too long ago, my life entirely owned by substances, my decisions made by a bottle or a line of coke, possessing no more free will as a prisoner of addiction than this inmate had known as a prisoner of society for the past eight years.

So maybe this was just God's way of reminding Wes to be humble, and to remember that He was looking out for me. And maybe He was telling me that there but for His grace go I, and that I needed to remain on the path, and to remain grateful for the life I had these days.

Or maybe He just wanted to suggest that I not judge others, as I would not have them judge me.

A moment later I announced, "Okay, pal, here ya go – this is your stop."

I saw the con smile in my rearview mirror as he reached out to hand me a fin and said, "Hey, buddy, thanks a lot, I needed that. I'll see you around!"

I doubted it, but I said, "Good luck pal, hope everything works out for you."

And then he was out the door and bounding up the steps to the platform and a new life.

"Yeah, there but for the grace of God go I," I mused, as a gentle snow began to drift through the frigid December air.

≈≈≈

The New England winter of 1993/1994 went into the record books. It was the snowiest season in modern Greater Boston history, with the city itself receiving nearly one hundred and twenty inches. The snowfall amounts were even higher in the western suburbs, where we were insulated from the relatively warm Atlantic waters.

I'd been a snow freak since I was a little kid. I'd always looked forward to being out in the most dangerous weather, be it snow or thunderstorms, heatwaves or hurricanes, or anything else that Nature could throw at us. I guess it probably had something to do with my addiction to chaos, because there was nothing more exhilarating than experiencing a big weather event at that certain moment when everything went out of control, and I realized that I was powerless, that my life was in danger as the storm exploded all around me.

Okay, so I guess that might also have been a reason why I drank and drugged to excess – they were just other vehicles for getting high while I flirted with death and mayhem.

But of all the weather events, I especially loved the big windy snowstorms that dumped a foot or two of the white stuff, the ones that shut down school for a day or two, the ones that gave a drunk a day off from work because the roads were closed.

I had even slept in my car when I was marooned out on the Route 128 commuter highway during the epic Blizzard of '78. I was hung over and strung out from an alcohol and cocaine binge weekend, running out of smokes, the blowing and drifting snow burying my company car to window level on all sides while it rocked violently in the hurricane-force winds.

Tragically, many people died out there that night, victims of exposure and suffocation.

But for me, the chaos addict, there was no place I would rather have been at that particular moment in time.

What is it they say about God watching over fools and drunks? Well, the Big Guy surely watched over me that terrible night, as He had a thousand nights previously, despite any death wishes that I might have been secretly harboring.

≈≈≈

One of the first tangible results that I had recognized in myself by virtue of sobriety was my improved work ethic. The life lessons that I was learning in AA had made me more responsible, reliable and teachable, and those attributes carried over into my work life. The weather might have been bad, but that didn't stop me from working on my software sales, driving hack, or, most importantly, getting to all of my meetings.

In fact, the more it snowed, the more it made for a fun, challenging game.

My mindset became, "Okay, God, so what are you planning to throw at me today? Whatever, it ain't gonna stop me from staying sober and doing what I need to do."

I'm sure that God got a big chuckle out of my arrogance, but He never threw me something I couldn't handle.

So every day I woke up at 7:00 a.m. sharp and hit my knees to pray that He would keep me sober for that one single day, and that He would help me to accept whatever life had in store for me.

And then I would plan my work for the day, and work that plan.

Snow? No big deal! The sniffles? No big deal! A support issue with one of my software clients? No big deal! Struggling to pay all of my bills at the end of the month? No big deal! That twinge of pain that ran down my leg with increasing regularity? No big deal! No time to have a woman in my life? "No woman, no cry," Marley's song played on the stereo in my head every day.

And so it went through that long, arduous winter of the big snows.

≈≈≈

I carved out my personal cabbie turf in mid-December, when it became apparent that we were destined to receive one big storm after another. I planned to remain close to home, under the radar, taking local fares whenever possible, and that meant I would need to stake out a spot in Norwood that had plenty of townie riders.

I settled on the 'Norwood Central' train station that was located near the busy downtown area, right behind Norwood Hospital. It was the perfect hideout, and it had hundreds of commuters passing through daily, with limited parking due to the large number of hospital employees and visitors who grabbed many of the parking spaces.

My logic was simple - if you couldn't park there, how would you get home when you stepped off the train?

I had their solution, so I'd arrive there around 4:00 p.m. three or four days a week, just as the commuter rush started, and mid-afternoon on Saturdays, and I'd take my spot right next to the terminal. It was a perfect set-up and I did well there – usually.

But there were those evenings, of course, where things didn't go exactly as planned. Sometimes it would be a three hour night run into Logan Airport to pick up a late arrival (it always seemed to be snowing when I took those fares), or somebody who stuck around the bar until last call, and then expected me to take them way out into the boonies.

And, of course, there were any number of other scenarios with some of the commuters that for some strange reason always seemed to have one common denominator – alcohol and/or drug abuse.

I'd shake my head in wonder at those bizarre occurrences, then sheepishly recall that I had experienced a few dozen of my own during my checkered career that were just as bad, or worse.

And sometimes late at night, in the silence of the cab, I would imagine that I heard a low, deep chuckle from somewhere very far away, and the only logical conclusion I could arrive at was that my Higher Power certainly had a warped sense of humor at times.

≈≈≈

People in the Program suggest that we not project our fears and doubts into the future, and I generally avoided doing so, but nonetheless I'd been dreading New Year's Eve for weeks. That was amateur night, when all the rookies had the opportunity to escape from their Walter Mitty existences and play in the Big Leagues, and I anticipated that this New Year's Eve for Wes the Friendly Cabbie would no doubt be a terrifying trip to the Land of Oz, a hallucinogenic flashback to my own legendary follies.

I swore that this was God's way of getting even with me for putting Him through all of the nonsense that I had laid on Him over the course of twenty-five pathetic, drunken New Year's Eves.

But forewarned is forearmed, so on this day I was as prepared as any military commander who was about to go into battle, and I was in my ride and posted up at Norwood Central just before noon. I had my strategic battle plan all mapped out, and it was very simple - pray a lot, and hide.

First, I said a prayer requesting that I be capable of accepting the outcome of whatever came down the pike at me on this most amateur of all nights.

Second, I reviewed my rules of engagement. I was keeping it simple, so I had two rules:

Rule # 1: I would maintain a stealth presence at the station, and not check in with the dispatcher to grab rides. I would only snag those people who were coming off the trains from Boston, because they were sure to be locals, so I could drop them off and be back at the station ten minutes later. I'd get a lot of rides that way, and the tips would be great as everybody went into party mode.

And, most importantly, I wouldn't get stuck somewhere way out in Indian Country.

Rule #2: If all else failed, and I was forced to take a call from Dispatch, I would use every trick in the book to stay local, including but not limited to lies, threats, deceit and blackmail.

Out of sight, out of mind, that was my motto and I was sticking to it, come Hell or high water! I had my peanut butter and jelly sandwiches, a thermos of hot coffee and two packs of Marlboros to get me through the next eighteen hours, so Wes hunkered down and went silent.

≈≈≈

Oh, by the way, did I ever mention that my Higher Power has a great sense of humor?

Yes?

And did you ever hear the military truism that all of the best laid plans of the generals go right down the crapper the moment the first shot is fired?

Yes?

Well, welcome once again to WesWorld! Twenty minutes after I arrived at Norwood Central I was hauling my first fare into one of Boston's Back Bay neighborhoods. The dispatcher had pushed that damned call button up on Vernon Street for ten solid minutes before I broke, and I had surrendered without firing a shot.

I was now at their mercy, and I feared that I might never see Norwood for the remainder of the night, or ever.

My guess was pretty close. I estimate that I traversed the streets of Norwood for perhaps thirty minutes over my "Shift from Hell," but I sure did a lot of sightseeing in and around Foxboro, Waltham, Braintree, the outskirts of Worcester, and I even got a fun run up to Lynn – Lynn, Lynn, city of sin - up on Boston's North Shore.

Oh, and naturally I was blessed to take several more fares into Boston, including one sweetheart of a rush-hour run into Logan Airport.

It was obvious that God was having a grand old time showing the Onion who would be 'King Cabbie' that night.

Much of the evening was just a blur, and for that I'm grateful, because as day progressed into night the blood alcohol level of my fares rocketed, as did my surly disposition.

I behaved and remained polite for the most part, however, and I was grateful to the Big Guy for convincing most of my guests to do the same.

I'd be remiss, however, if I failed to mention my last fare, because it pretty much put the exclamation mark on that magical night.

≈≈≈

I received the dispatch at 3:30 a.m. I had just dropped off a fare in Waltham, which is a small municipality in the northwest suburbs of Boston. Why I had been sent way up there I have no idea, but now I was being ordered to pick up three people at the Quincy Market.

About the last place that anybody with a functioning cortex would wish to be at 4:00 a.m. on New Years' day was the Quincy Market, which was situated near the Boston waterfront. It would be party central, with hundreds, perhaps thousands of inebriated revelers making their last stand for the night.

I actually whined, groveled and begged the dispatcher to cut me a break.

No such luck. The miserable sadist just laughed at me, and thus began my odyssey.

≈≈≈

Somehow, and God only knows how, I located the partyers outside one of the bars that was situated just around the corner form the Marketplace.

The group consisted of two young women who appeared to be in their late twenties, and a guy of about the same age.

They were ripped, staggering, slurring, laughing hysterically, and it was all I could do to pry out the address that they wanted to be dropped off at.

Unfortunately, the address that they gave me was bogus, just a figment of their eighty-proof imaginations. It was located on Commonwealth Avenue, which at the time was one of Boston's most sought after Yuppie breeding grounds. Tiny, ancient little studio apartments had been converted into tiny, nouveau little condos through the magic of one coat of paint, and voila, you were now the proud owner of a five hundred square foot castle that was priced beyond anything imaginable.

I understand that the real estate sales agents' description for the neighborhood was "gentrified."

Yeah, well whatever floats your boat, I suppose.

My fares stumbled out of the cab and staggered over to some steps that led down to a basement apartment, uh, excuse me – condominium. It had a breathtaking view of a window well and the sidewalk, so I'm certain that the owners paid an extra fifty grand for the location, location, location, because this sparkling little gem of a luxury home was conveniently located mere steps from transportation.

They tripped down the stairwell, laughing hysterically, and banged on the door.

Nothing.

So they banged harder, and then began to shout.

Still nothing.

Finally they staggered back up the steps and held a strategy meeting, and seconds later they stumbled over to the cab and informed me that I had misunderstood their directions, and that we were supposed to be one street over, on Marlborough Street, which was also a shining example of urban gentrification.

Really?

Whatever, I thought, not bothering to object to the rebuke, because at that point an extra ten minutes would calculate into an extra five bucks for Wes, the suave, world traveling cabbie who was there merely to serve at their pleasure.

Five minutes later we arrived at the same numbered address on Marlborough Street, and sixty seconds later the outcome was the same, right down to their not so good-natured appraisal of the Lone Wolf's geography skills.

That made two strikes, but I said nothing. By now the meter had gone into double figures, and I was in no mood to drive off into the sunrise without getting my hard-earned moolah.

So I grudgingly took the high road, again, and mentioned politely that it was getting late, and that we needed to wrap things up so I could report back to the Yard.

They huddled for a few moments, then informed me that they were positive we should be over on Beacon Street, claiming once again that I should have known that from the start.

By now I had recited four prayers of acceptance to God, but evidently He was still exhausted from His own New Year's Eve revelry, because He didn't get right back to me.

So once again it was hi–ho, hi-ho, and off we went skipping merrily to Beacon Street.

Same gentrification. Same miniscule basement dump. Same result.

My new best friends for life came staggering back to the cab, where I was leaning against the hood, smoking, but before they could say a word I calmly and politely expressed my humble opinion about the situation.

"Oookay, don't even start. Three strikes, you're out, so don't even go there. You are officially fired, I want nothing more to do with you, you owe me fifteen dollars, and a tip would be very much appreciated, so pay up and I'll be on my way. And please, have yourselves a really cool New Year! Are we clear?"

I never realized it over the years, but friends have mentioned more than once that I get a certain expression on my face at times like this. It's not intentional, but I've been informed that it's rather stern, and it generally leads to my getting the point across in a non-confrontational manner.

It must have something to do with my curly red hair.

These folks were a little slow on the uptake, however, so I added a bit of clarification to assist them in their decision-making processes.

"Let me repeat, you owe me fifteen dollars, and if you don't wish to pay me for my services, fine, you have three options."

They just stared blankly at me. I knew that my eyes were bugging out of my head by then, but I was beyond caring.

"Door Number One – reconsider your decision, pay me, and I'll be on my way."

They just stared at me, clueless.

"Door Number Two – the same as Door Number One. Pay me what you owe me, and I'll be on my way," I stated slowly, somewhat menacingly, as a sadistic smile spread across my face.

They stared and swayed, then began shuffling their feet.

And then it happened, because apparently God was back behind the wheel again, accepting fares - from out of nowhere a shiny yellow Boston taxi rolled around the corner, slowed, and stopped next to us.

This wasn't a development I was particularly thrilled about just then, because there was a long history of contention and turf warfare between locals like myself and the big city beef haulers.

The driver rolled down his window and said, "Good evening, folks, so what's happening here?" in a brusque voice, while he checked me out, checked out the three world travelers, and then stepped out of his cab.

He was big, and I could see that he was plenty pissed off that an out-of-towner was apparently trying to hijack a local fare. Ordinarily that wouldn't have phased me in the least, because those guys had short memories, and were notorious for pulling the same stunts when they were out on the suburban turf.

But now something clicked, as I saw the perfect opportunity to wiggle out of this mess, so I played mister nice guy, prayed that the three lost sheep would remain quiet, grabbed the cabbie by the elbow and maneuvered him away from the cabs.

Once we were out of earshot of the others I said, "Hey, perfect timing, buddy, I was just telling these folks that they should be taking a city cab rather than an out-of-towner, because I sure don't want to pirate one of your fares."

That took the wind out of his sails for a moment, and he knew enough to not look a gift horse in the mouth, so he said, "Oh, okay, if that's the case I'd be happy to take this run, and thanks for the hand-off, pal."

"Hey, it's my pleasure, buddy, I know you'd do the same for me, so have a great New Year!"

"Yeah, you too."

I was in my ride in two seconds flat, beating feet, and the last thing I saw before they disappeared from my rearview mirror were the three lost sheep swaying and stumbling and giving directions to who I knew would soon be one angry individual.

That was the best fifteen bucks that I never earned, and one more reason for why I was grateful to be sober.

Moments later I began chuckling, and it soon grew into a full-throated roar of laughter.

"Okay, God, I get it, there but for your grace go I, because I could have been them, so thanks for the reminder!"

God didn't respond immediately, which led me to worry momentarily whether He had partied too hard Himself, because I'd heard it on the grapevine that He had acquired a big taste for the Schnapps during the holidays.

≈≈≈

I had an inspiration fifteen minutes later, just as I approached the intersection of the VFW Parkway and Route 109 in Dedham, right near the VA Hospital and an open-air MDC hockey arena where I'd frozen my ass off in scrimmages back in my high school hockey days.

It was already 4:45 a.m.., but for some reason I had received my second, or was it third, wind.

That might have been due to the ten cups of strong black coffee I had swilled down over the past eighteen hours, or perhaps it was just another gift that arrived out of the blue from my Higher Power when I was most in need of a boost.

Whatever the reason, it dawned on me that there was an overnight New Year's Alcathon scheduled to be held at the Dedham Congregational Church, which was the same church that had sponsored the 4th of July Alcathon that I attended the day after my return from my last visit to Beech Hill.

I'd always been curious to see what the crowd was like in the wee hours of one of those celebrations, and now I had the opportunity to find out, so I took a one mile detour, arriving at the church moments before 5:00 a.m.

The pre-dawn air was cold and clear, invigorating, and the waning moon was still visible as it slid toward the eastern horizon.

It was easy to find a parking space close to the church - in fact, there was only one other vehicle parked anywhere nearby, so I locked the cab, then limped slowly, painfully through the cold, bracing air, my bad leg dragging behind me, and entered the church.

≈≈≈

The layout was the same as it had been on July 4th, so I found myself standing in a large function room, where approximately one hundred folding chairs were lined up in two sections facing the speaker's rostrum and a podium.

At first blush the building appeared to be uninhabited.

On the left side of the room I spied a couple of tables that my eyes locked onto. They were stocked with the remnants of cakes, pies, cookies, donuts, fruits, juices, jugs of soda and a large coffee urn.

Bingo, Wes had been magically transported to Alkie Heaven, and all of the stress, aggravation and exhaustion of the prior eighteen hours melted away in a millisecond.

I stood motionless for a moment, and said a quick, silent prayer of thanks to my Higher Power for delivering me to this place, and for reminding me once again that I was still just a recovering alcoholic – nothing more, nothing less.

Then I made a beeline for the tables, grabbed a paper plate and piled it to overflowing with a large assortment of goodies, including a few chocolate-based delicacies. I filled a large plastic cup with cranberry juice, walked over to the stage, hopped up onto the edge and dug into my feast.

A guy who appeared to be about my age walked into the room from the kitchen area several minutes later. I didn't recognize him, but it was clear that he was on the sponsoring AA group's late night shift, and his eyes lit up when he saw me.

It dawned on me then that he probably hadn't had much company for the past couple of hours.

He walked over, introduced himself as Jim, and we shook hands.

"So, Wes, what brings you here at this hour?" he asked.

I gave him a quick three minute recap of my fun adventures, and he got a big kick out of my story about the three poor lost souls who had nearly taken a swim in the Charles River, and the Boston cabbie who had probably issued an all-points bulletin for me.

"Wish I'd been there to see that," he chuckled, "although that could have been me not so long ago."

"I hear you, brother, me too, but it was a great 'remember when,' despite the aggravation."

"Amen to that," he said.

"Yeah, amen to that for sure!"

We met the requirements for an official AA meeting by being two drunks with a coffee pot, so we spent the next thirty minutes telling our stories and shooting the breeze.

It was one of the best AA meetings I have ever attended, and I'll always cherish the memory, but I was exhausted, so I finally shook hands with Jim, wished him well and hit the road.

≈≈≈

Ten minutes later I dropped off my cab in the yard at the Broadway depot in Norwood, handed over a big pile of cash to the dispatcher, pocketed slightly over two hundred bucks in tips, then made the short run back to my apartment.

I hit my knees, thanked my Higher Power for keeping me sober for another day, and then hit the sack. I didn't even bother to undress, just surrendered to the Sleep of the Dead for ten hours, never dreaming once.

One day at a time, one hour at a time, one moment at a time, and one heartbeat at a time I had survived Amateur Hour, and this had been my best New Year's Eve ever.

Well, so far, anyway, but that's in God's hands, because He's the 'Big Cabbie,' and I'm just along for the ride.

≈≈≈

It snowed and it snowed and it snowed that winter, as a conga line of storms rolled up the eastern seaboard and slammed into New England.

Driving conditions were treacherous. I never actually slid off the road, or had an accident, but nonetheless I had to crawl along at a snail's pace in order to react to unseen cars backing out of driveways, or to avoid the ones that were sliding through stop signs at intersections where the snow was piled ten feet high on all sides.

So all I could do was keep it simple. I would rise at seven in the morning, as always, hit my knees to say my prayer, drink my coffee, work on my software and call prospective clients.

On some days I hit the loonie-noonie meetings in the area, or had an appointment with Eileen, but by midafternoon I always prepared my peanut butter and jelly sandwich, changed into my grubby cabbie attire, drove over to the Yard, selected the most comfortable pile of junk I could find, then rolled over to Norwood Central, where I would claim my spot for the night.

Then I'd leave the engine running, jack up the heat, crack the window slightly, light up a smoke, and wait patiently for the first Boston commuter trains to arrive, while the snow drifted silently through the dark, frigid air, and the smoke from the hospital's power plant swirled up into the winter gloom.

After all, it was just another day in the life of a recovering alcoholic, so first things first, little by slow, one snowflake at a time, one heartbeat at a time, or whatever it took.

And then I would thank my Higher Power for keeping me sober, and for delivering me unto this place and time of healing.

Part Four: Tough Love

"The best laid schemes o' mice an' men gang aft a-gley."

From the poem, "To a Mouse"
by Robert Burns

"What's that you say? Your wife left you for your best friend, and now they're living off the alimony checks that you send them every month?" they asked.

"Tough shit, Joe – just don't drink," they said.

"What's that? You didn't get that big promotion at work, instead it went to that wimpy little office butt kisser?" they asked.

"Tough shit, Mary – just don't drink," they said.

"Run that by me again? You lost your job, they repossessed your car, and now they're coming for the furniture?" they asked.

"Tough shit, Bob – just don't drink," they said.

"Oh, how sad! Your beautiful little dog that you loved like it was your child got run over and killed?" they asked.

"Well, I feel your pain, Fred, and it's happened to me," they said, "but tough shit, because we just can't drink over it!"

"So what are you whining about now, Buttercup? You blew your back out, you lost your software business, you're twenty grand in the hole and the banks have cut off all your maxed-out credit cards, you're sleeping on a filthy mattress on the floor of a crowded sober house, you have no health insurance, you walk like the hunchback of Notre Dame dragging your leg behind you because of that damned ruptured disc, and you're in so much physical pain that you're thinking about taking a one way trip down to the railroad tracks with those pills that you know you can score at midnight from that skanky drug house across town? That's it, that's all you have to worry about?" he asked, scowling.

"Tough shit, Wes, stop the whining, just don't drink, and get your sorry ass to a meeting," Ulysses growled, as his eyes burned a hole through the final remnants of my self-centered pride.

≈≈≈

It's a painful fact of life that tragedy, death, disease, financial loss, betrayal and all manner of other distress invades our lives, and the lives of our loved ones, whether we're sober or not. Life can be hard, perverse, heart breaking, and it damned sure doesn't seem to be very fair at times.

But there's a saying in AA, short and simple, that reminds us that God doesn't give us more than we can handle at any one moment in time. Recovering alcoholics certainly aren't immune to tragedy and loss, but it's how we react to misfortune that will determine whether we can remain sober or not, and by so doing perhaps become a symbol of hope and promise to others who are suffering as well:

"I don't need to drink or drug over it, no matter what!"

So simple, yet not always so easy, but when the hammer comes down, and life turns us inside out, it can be a time of disaster and relapse, or it can be an opportunity to buckle down, stick close to the program of Alcoholics Anonymous, walk our talk, and let go and let God, as difficult as that may be when we're in the center of that raging storm.

The choice is ours alone, so do we give up, and go, or do we fight with our last breath, and grow?

And, perhaps most difficult of all; can we remain grateful for our sobriety when the walls are crashing down all around us?

≈≈≈

I realized by the end of "The Winter of the Eternal Snows" that I was in beaucoup trouble. It wasn't a single event that awakened me to the peril, but rather a process, a gathering storm that started slowly, innocuously, creeping in little by slow while it whispered sweet nothings and denial in my ear.

The occasional pain and numbness that radiated down my right leg and into my foot had become constant, around the clock, and it was probably pushing up toward eight on a scale of one to ten on the pain meter. It was interfering with my ability to work, walk, sleep, drive a car or perform manual chores on a daily basis and, worst of all, it was affecting my attitude in a big way.

By late April I had to admit that it was time to make some difficult decisions that I'd been avoiding, while I went through the final stages of denial about my situation.

The first thing I had to look at was my fledgling software business. I had been fortunate to make a few sales to some small insurance agencies and wholesalers during the winter, but I was learning that the market was very competitive, which meant that margins had to remain lean, and that I had to be aggressive in my pricing.

And that meant lower profits, and less cash flow to survive on.

To make matters worse, I had borrowed against four credit cards to finance equipment, software and some of my living expenses, and now I was finding it difficult to make even the minimum payments on those cards that averaged twelve percent interest. The total balance that I was in the hole for ran around twenty thousand dollars, and I was making zero headway in knocking it down even a little – strike one!

Hand in hand with the business uncertainty was my cab job. The vehicles I was driving were old, poorly maintained, and the broken-down bench seats were uncomfortable for somebody with no back issues – for me, they were agony, and they put extra stress on my blown-out lumbar disc.

Additionally, I could only get assigned about a dozen hours a week now that the good weather had returned, but owing to the deterioration in my back that was a moot point.

I had no good choices here, there were just dead-ends, so I quit hacking in mid-April, which cut off the remainder of my income.

By then I had no sensation in most of my right foot, and it felt like a burning sword had been shoved down my butt and right leg. The pain was excruciating, around-the-clock, never subsiding for even a moment, hammering me night and day, messing with my head and hampering my ability to work my program of recovery.

And, to make matters worse, I had no health insurance, and I couldn't have afforded it even if some company was foolish enough to offer it to a person with a full-blown disc rupture - strike two!

Strike three? That hadn't arrived quite yet, but it would be the killer, penniless, crippled, and living on the streets, unless I could come up with a plan, and fast!

So it finally came down to one thing - fight or flight. I was at the crossroads of my sobriety, and perhaps my very existence on this planet, because I knew that if I didn't get proactive, and fast, I could wind up dead.

In the end, I chose to fight.

≈≈≈

Chronic pain is like water torture, drip, drip, drip, it's with you constantly, always in your face and quick to remind you that it's not going away, ever. It gets up inside your head and it just picks away at all of your defense mechanisms, one after the other, day after day after day, and then one day it owns you lock, stock and barrel, and you're its whore.

The one thing that I still had any control over, however, was my sobriety, so regardless of the pain I hit all of my meetings, where I talked, raged, and swore at God, and when I finished all they said was, "Thanks for sharing, Wes, and just keep coming."

So I did, come Hell or high water.

I'll never understand how those kind people put up with me back then, but I will be forever grateful for their acceptance and unconditional love.

≈≈≈

There's another one of those simple sayings in the Program that we hear a lot, "Let go, and let God," and so I finally did.

On a warm, sunny day in early May, 1994, I let go of the steering wheel, surrendered to life, asked God for help, and the next day He sent me some guy named Frank.

Geesh, who'd have known it could be that simple?

≈≈≈

Frank was the general manager of the South Middlesex Opportunity Council, or "SMOC," for short.

SMOC was a well-regarded social services organization that had a significant presence in the Framingham area. It provided jobs training programs, shelters for battered women and their children, alcohol and drug detox facilities, and sober houses.

In hundreds of cases a year SMOC provided that last critical wall of defense that saved individuals and families from ending up on the streets.

I had heard about the organization over the previous year, but had no reason to pay much attention to it.

I was aware, however, that there was a guy named Frank who occasionally hit meetings in the Millis area, and he was reputed to be a big honcho at SMOC. For whatever reason, I had stored that little nugget away in my "what if it all hits the fan someday" folder for safekeeping.

And now, on the morning after I surrendered to life, like magic, Frank's name popped into my head.

I thought about it for a couple of hours, debating whether I really needed to take such a drastic step, but I finally admitted that I was in deep trouble, that my options were limited, and that if I stood around for too long procrastinating then it might be too late.

So I got humble, again, swallowed my pride, called Directory Assistance, and the operator gave me the general number for SMOC.

Then I took a deep breath, said a prayer that I be willing to accept the outcome of my call, and dialed him up.

God must have told Frank to expect my call, because he picked up on the second ring after the switchboard operator patched me through.

≈≈≈

"Hi Frank, my name is Wes H., and I'm calling to get some information."

"Sure, Wes, how can I help you?" he replied, his voice deep and confident.

"Well, I'm in recovery from alcohol and drugs, coming up on two years sober, and I'm currently living in Norwood. Things aren't going so hot for me right now, and I heard that you might have sober housing in Framingham for people like me, so I'm hoping to get some information."

"Yes, we do have sober housing. Can you fill me in on what's going on with you these days?"

"Sure," I said, and then I gave him a quick summary of my predicament.

"How many meetings are you attending in an average week?" he asked.

"I usually hit six or seven, and I go to one-on-one counseling every two weeks."

"That's good… so, where you're living, are you tied up with a lease or rental agreement?"

"No, I'm pretty sure that I can get out of it."

I was fortunate, because just by chance my lease was running out at the end of the month, and I didn't want to forfeit my security deposit by breaking the lease.

"When would you be looking to make the move?"

"I have a lot of loose ends to tie up, but maybe for June 1st, if something's available."

"Well, you're in luck, because there's less demand for sober housing during the warm weather months, so we should have some open rooms."

"This would be in Framingham?"

"Yes, right off the downtown area, near shopping, the train, and plenty of meetings. It's not the Ritz, but you'll have your own room, and you'll share the bathrooms with everyone else, plus there's a common kitchen and dining area, and off-street parking."

"Okay, so what do you need from me?"

"We'll need you to come over for a one-on-one interview with me, and if all goes well we can take a run by the building so you can check it out. You pay by the month, in advance, sixty dollars a week, utilities included, with a two hundred dollar cash deposit up front."

"Okay, when could I come over to meet you?"

"How's tomorrow, late morning?" he asked.

"Okay, I'll see you at 11:00?"

"Sounds good," Frank said, and then he gave me directions to his office, and that was that.

Surrender takes many forms, and I had to wonder whether I'd ever make it to the Promised Land. But regardless, just for today, it appeared that I would have a roof over my head, and I was sober, so that was enough to give me hope, and just a little bit of gratitude.

Because at the end of the day it always comes down to first things first, being grateful, and being humble enough to ask for help.

≈≈≈

The next morning's interview went well. We recognized each other from the Millis meetings, so Frank knew that I was active in AA, and that was the big hurdle that had to be overcome. That alone gave me street cred, and it turned out that we had a lot of other things in common as well, so I passed with flying colors.

"Do you have twenty minutes to run by the house and check it out?" he asked.

"Sure, I'd like to see it."

I followed him over to a turn-of-the-century three story Victorian home that was located on Union Avenue, near the hospital and the Museum of Art. It was situated in a middle class neighborhood close to the downtown shopping area, appeared to be well maintained, and had ample off-street parking out back for about a dozen cars.

So far, so good.

We entered through the back door, which opened into a combination kitchen and dining area. The room was clean and well maintained, and there were a couple of guys in their mid- to late thirties seated at the dining room table, smoking, talking and drinking coffee.

Frank made introductions all around, and then explained that I was there for a walk-through. We spoke briefly, and I got the impression that these guys were serious about their sobriety. You can usually tell pretty quickly whether one's walking his or her talk, and these guys appeared to be on the up and up.

Then we made a quick survey of the first floor. In addition to the kitchen and dining area there were five single bedrooms, a bathroom, and a payphone in the hallway, and everything appeared to be neat and orderly.

We slowly climbed the stairs to the second floor, my right leg dragging one step behind me, and it was more of the same, eight or nine single rooms and a couple of bathrooms, and all were well maintained.

We met two more residents upstairs, a man and a woman, and spoke briefly with them. They had the appearance of sober people who were working a good program of recovery, and I got good vibes from them.

You can tell a lot about a person just by whether they look you in the eye when speaking, and all of these residents had passed that test.

I had seen enough. Like Frank had warned, it wasn't the Ritz, but it wasn't a dump, and it met my simple needs, so Frank and I went back downstairs and exited to the parking area.

"So, what do you think?" he asked.

"I like it. Nothing fancy, but the residents seem to be serious about their sobriety, so I think it will fit my needs. You said there'd be a room available by the end of the month?"

"Yes, it's a full house now, but we have a few people leaving over the next couple of weeks. I'll make sure that we get you into a first floor room, because you won't want to be maneuvering those stairs every day."

"Thanks, that would be a big help," I said, then added "Okay, I'm gonna go with my gut and take it. What do you need from me?"

"Well, I've got your address and number, so I'll send you a lease that you can look over and sign. Please get it back to me by the 20th, with the $200 deposit, and call me if you have any questions. Sound good?"

"Yeah," I said, "it's a deal."

So that was that, and we shook hands. The Lone Wolf was slowly learning how to live life on life's terms, and whereas it might have been a step down in lifestyle, it was nonetheless a big step up in humility.

And that trade-off probably saved my life.

≈≈≈

I had a lot to accomplish in order to prepare for the big move. This was in the days before the Internet, so I couldn't make use of email, search engines, or online bulletin boards to assist me in selling off my furniture and other unnecessary toys and trinkets.

In fact, there weren't even cellphones, either, so all of the tools that we use today to make our lives more manageable didn't exist back then.

Nonetheless, there were a few publications that would fit my needs, so I placed some "Furniture for Sale" ads in a couple of the weekly rags, and the bargain hunters bit the hook quickly.

Divesting oneself of all the material toys can be a humbling experience, and for me it was necessary, but painful. This process was, however, very similar to what I had been doing on an ongoing basis with regard to my addictions, so I knew that it wouldn't be any more difficult to surrender some over-priced pieces of wood and leather than it had been to walk away from the alcohol, the drugs and all of the nonsense that accompanied them.

Bob Dylan's lyrics came to mind once again, "When you ain't got nothing, you've got nothing to lose." He had hit the nail on the head, and then I thought of Gandhi, and Mother Teresa, and they both seemed to have been fairly content living in poverty, although I couldn't say much for their choice of wardrobes, so who was I to complain about the loss of a few overpriced toys?

And, besides, maybe by losing I could win. After all, it had worked once before, just two years previously - two very short years that might just as well have been a lifetime.

I guess at some point God took over the show, because the divestiture of most of my physical possessions went off without a hitch, and He even made sure that I was paid in cash rather than ducats.

And, since cash is king, the Scandinavian Design teak dining room set and leather sofa and recliner went first, then all of the area rugs, then some trendy wall art, and finally the stereo.

I walked away with a few grand from the sales, all cash, which I calculated to be about twenty cents on the dollar from what I originally paid, and nearly all of it went straight into my meager bank account. After paying minimum interest on the credit cards this translated into approximately six months of rent at the sober house, if it came down to that, plus some food and gas, so I was grateful for every penny of it.

I retained my teak platform bed, however, because it had a firm King mattress, and I knew that it would provide much better support for my back than any lumpy, smelly, twin-sized piece of cloth that had been used and abused by a couple dozen sober house residents of various shapes, sizes and hygienic practices over the past ten years.

≈≈≈

It was at this point that something peculiar occurred. Rather than experiencing depression over the sacrifice of my most cherished worldly possessions, I felt a sense of freedom that grew in direct proportion to the disposal of those very same objects. The more I cast off, the better my mood became, the less I found to worry about, and the more a sense of hope and opportunity snuck into my thoughts.

Keeping things simple, I realized, meant fewer complications and more freedom from worry at a time in my life when I had plenty of other things to concentrate on.

The student was learning once again that 'letting go' is an enabling experience, whether it's in the casting off of the chains of addiction, or the material trinkets that we think we can never survive without.

Letting go, and letting God, so simple, yet so hard won, and now the gift of freedom from worry grew as my worldly goods drove away in U-Hauls.

I didn't even wave good-bye to them as the buyers drove off with their newfound treasures.

Then the hunchback turned and hobbled slowly, painfully, back into his apartment, dragging his right leg behind him.

≈≈≈

I awoke from a fitful sleep a week later, lying on a beaten-up, foul smelling mattress that was laid out on the floor of a closet-sized room in the sober house.

I was in agony, my back cramped and in spasms, with bolts of pain radiating down my right leg to my numb foot.

This was my third day in Framingham, and the move had occurred, but it hadn't gone off without a hitch. A couple of the residents had decided to extend their leases at the house, and one other had been delayed in moving out for a few days when his friend's truck broke down.

So that left a crowded house, and because I was last in the pecking order I got the closet-sized room until the guy's truck was fixed and they could get his furniture cleared out.

Fortunately, I was able to find storage for my bed in a short-term facility in Framingham, but it was doing my back no good for the time being.

I was down in the dumps, juggling, trying to get acclimated to a new residence that was full to overflowing with complete strangers. My only furniture was that filthy mattress, and I was stressing out on financial uncertainty, a business going down the toilet, and a case of crippling pain that I doubted would ever end.

Life seemed intent upon ganging up on me, and I was having a tough time coping with it all.

I will admit that I hadn't gone easy on God during those first few days at the sober house. I ranted and raved at Him in the privacy of my room, swore, threatened, whined, and basically acted like a petulant child who couldn't get his way.

To make matters worse, I was a few weeks shy of completing my second year of sobriety, so I guess that I also had a case of the "Terrible Two's" to deal with. I mean, I went through the hell of getting sober, so shouldn't my life have been all fun and games by now, or at least somewhat fair? Why me, God, why would this happen to a college grad, a former Army officer, a business professional?

Well, what I should have asked was "why shouldn't it happen to me?" because when you get right down to it there was nothing special about Wes – I was just another bozo on the bus.

God pretty much took it all in stride, however. I could almost hear Him chuckling at times, *or* maybe He simply understood that it was time for Wes to walk his talk, be a big boy, and take his next steps to emancipation.

Looking back now, in the fullness of time, I realize that my Higher Power had been preparing me for the ultimate test of my sobriety, and even of my very will to live. I guess He thought that I was capable of standing on my own two feet after almost two relatively plain vanilla years of sobriety, so now it was time to give the pupil his mid-term exam.

In all honesty I would come to wish that He had been busy elsewhere that day, week and year, but on the other hand He gave me what I needed, not what I wanted, and I'm a better person for it.

≈≈≈

Yippee! God hadn't forgotten about me after all! On the fifth day He handed me a room of my own. It was on the first floor, larger than most, and it had a double window that looked out over a tree-lined yard and a quiet side street. It was well away from the noise and traffic in the kitchen and dining area, and it even had an ample closet that would hold all of my meager wardrobe and sparse belongings.

I felt like a king that day, like I had won the lottery, like I finally belonged.

And on the fifth night I slept in my platform bed, and for a couple of hours I even managed to get some deep REM sleep.

Little by slow the transition was working for me. I was getting what I needed, and whereas it wasn't Nirvana it was nonetheless a safe harbor, and a big improvement, so I will tell you this - if it could work for me, than it can work for you, if you stay straight and just try to do the next right thing.

≈≈≈

I became acclimated to sober house life fairly quickly after that, considering the circumstances.

However, I had roomed by myself for the previous dozen years, so it was natural that I would be somewhat concerned about adapting to life in a cramped space with a dozen complete strangers, all of whom were in various stages of recovery, or in one or two cases, non-recovery.

But once again the Big Guy set me straight on that fear-based misconception, by reminding me that I had lived for four years in noisy college dorms, and had served in the Army during the Vietnam War years. If you've ever had to bunk in a dilapidated barracks, and shared a latrine with forty other guys for three or four months, then you can pretty much survive anywhere, so my integration into sober house living proceeded without undue difficulty.

≈≈≈

I stuck to the basics in the early days, asking my HP to grant me acceptance to get through the back pain and the self-centered fear that was always lurking in the background, and I made a big effort to introduce myself to every resident in the house.

It was an eclectic group, comprised of eleven men and two women, plus myself. Our ages ranged from the early twenties to the mid-forties, which made me one of the senior members at that time. We came from all walks of life, backgrounds and races, and there were deeply religious people, occasional worshippers, and even a couple of atheists thrown in for good measure.

It became clear to me once again that the disease of addiction was an equal opportunity destroyer that didn't particularly care what your background was, so just come on down and join the party!

I began to attend meetings in the local Framingham area right from the night I moved in, not only because they were crucial to my sobriety, but so that I would have local support if things went south in a big way.

I also kept to a regular schedule of my three go-to Medfield meetings, however, because that was where my major support group for the past two years met, and I wanted to remain close to it while I was in crisis mode. Those kind and giving people knew me better than anyone, so for the time being they were my lifeline, at least until I could find a couple of similar meetings in Framingham.

It was also time to make a sad, but necessary decision. My move placed me twenty-five miles away from Eileen, my wonderful counselor who had taught me so much over the past two years, and who I had come to rely on for advice in so many areas of my life. But I could hardly drive five miles without lapsing into a severe pain episode, so twenty-five each way was out of the question.

I had forewarned her that I would be moving, but now I needed to make the formal call. There was a phone jack in my room, so I was able to have a private line installed a week after I moved into the house.

I called her the same day that my phone was activated.

"Hi Eileen, its Wes. I just wanted to let you know that I made the move to Framingham. I'm in a sober house down on Union Avenue, and, like I mentioned, your office is just too far away to get to, what with my back situation and all."

I hesitated, then said, "I want to thank you for everything you did for me. You helped save my life, and I'll be eternally grateful to you."

"I know, Wes, I'll miss you too, but hopefully we'll still see each other once in a while at the Medfield meetings. I think you're doing the right thing, and I'm glad you're in a safe place."

She paused, then added, "I knew that this would be coming, so I want to give you a number, and I suggest that you call this man immediately. His name is Pat R., he's a counselor in the Framingham and Natick area, and he has lots of good sobriety under his belt. He'd be perfect for you, and now that I think of it, you may even have seen him at the Medfield Step meeting occasionally."

Bingo, she hit a homerun with that one! I knew Pat – he had been the clinical coordinator at the Framingham Detox facility that I had rolled into during my six month crash and burn that eventually ended me up at Beech Hill and, yes, I had noticed him at a few of the Medfield Step meetings.

He struck me at the time as a stand-up guy, with a good sense of humor and a firm grasp of the recovery process.

"Oh, yeah," I laughed, "I know him. You're right, he'd be perfect, so I'll call him today."

Eileen gave me Pat's number, we said our good-byes, and then I rang him up.

≈≈≈

I met up with Pat for my first appointment one week later. His office was on the second floor of the administrative wing of Leonard Morse Hospital in Natick, just five or six miles from the sober house, so it was a relatively easy drive, even for me and my deteriorating back.

I knew that I had made a good decision within five minutes after making the painful climb up the stairs to his office. Pat was a bright guy, a couple of years older than me, and it turned out that we had a lot of similar life experiences, so we hit it off right from the start.

The fact that he was an avid, scratch golfer didn't hurt, either, although I feared that I might never get the opportunity to play a round with him unless I had a miracle recovery from my back situation.

He was easy to talk to, and he had a good sense of humor, although some of his jokes were on the corny side, some even bordering on pathetic - sorry to be the one to tell you that, Pat, but it's an honest program you know!

Then again, I wasn't exactly a stand-up comic in those days either, and comic relief wasn't what I was paying him for anyway.

So I endured Pat's humor, lobbed back some of my own, and it was a good session. It turns out that he was a real professional, and just what the doctor ordered, because like the saying goes, "When the student is ready, the teacher will appear."

And I was as ready as they come.

Early on in that meeting Pat said, "I don't know if you recall, but we met two years ago when I was the clinical coordinator over at Framingham Detox. I did your out-take interview," he said, laughing, then added, "and I hope this doesn't hurt your feelings, but I had a sense that your drinking career wasn't quite finished back then."

I just stared at him with a droll expression on my face, then replied, "A deaf and dumb blind mute could probably have figured that out, Pat, so welcome to the club."

The hour went by quickly after that, and we settled on a schedule of bi-weekly meetings, and a fee structure that was fair, to the point of being generous on his part.

We shook hands, and then I maneuvered down the stairs and out to the parking lot. It was a bright, sunny day in early June, and I was a few days shy of my second sober anniversary.

The pain was still just as debilitating, but for the first time in months I felt a certain sense of calm and hopefulness settle over me, and damned if that didn't lower my pain level just a smidge. I had taken the necessary steps to adapt to my condition, I was sober, and I held out hope for a better tomorrow, if only I could remain on the Path, continue to ask for help from my Higher Power and my friends in AA, and be grateful for what I had.

I understood then, for perhaps the first time in my recovery, that sobriety was 99% an inside job, and that little by slow I was healing in God's time, not mine.

"Okay, God," I mused, "it looks like we're on a roll, so let's keep this party going."

≈≈≈

It didn't take long to settle into a routine at the sober house. The adaptation wasn't nearly as difficult as I had feared it would be – it's funny how that fear thing works. I slipped into a rhythm within a week or two, and soon made some fledgling friendships with a few of the other residents.

I'd been around the Halls long enough by then to have a good read on who was working an honest and committed program of recovery, and who was simply gaming the system, so like the Oldtimers always suggest, I stuck with the winners.

I had only been at the house for about ten days before they kicked out a heroin addict who had been living on the third floor. I had hardly ever seen him around, and he never hung out down in the dining room during the daytime. He was secretive, non-talkative, and he usually remained in his room all day, went out in the late afternoon, and then crept up the squeaky staircase outside my door in the wee hours of the night.

The staff figured out his game pretty quickly, so they hit him with a surprise urine test one day, and bingo, we have a winner!

He was back on the streets that night.

He wasn't the first, and he wouldn't be the last, for such is the nature of addiction, and I knew that well enough.

But for the grace of God go I.

~≈~

Days turned into weeks, and before I knew it I had been a resident at Union Avenue for a month. My integration into sober house life was progressing without too many hiccups, and I was quick to thank my Higher Power for that.

My second AA anniversary came and went. I celebrated it at my Medfield Friday night meeting, where I spoke briefly from the podium, but it didn't have the pomp and circumstance that was usually reserved for first anniversaries.

That was fine by me, because my back was deteriorating, so I was content to keep things short and simple.

My friends understood, and I had twenty phone numbers of people who told me that I could call, day or night, if I needed someone to talk to, or to just rant and rave at.

I took advantage of those numbers several times, and each person said basically the same thing:

"I'm glad you called, so thanks, Wes. This probably helps me as much as it helps you, so call me anytime, day or night."

So I did.

~≈~

We had two more departures at Union Avenue in late June, and then a new resident arrived on July 1st.

His name was Ulysses, and he was a tough, rugged black guy, originally from New York City. He was built like a linebacker, and he usually had a no-nonsense expression plastered on his face. He was about my age, and he had been clean and sober for two years as well.

It turned out that we had a lot in common, and over time we became good friends. Ulysses worked a disciplined program of recovery, but underneath the tough guy image there was a lot of compassion, unconditional love, and respect for his fellow alcoholics and addicts.

He was driven, in fact, to help those who were suffering under the lash of addiction, and the lower on the ladder they had sunk the more he tried to help.

Ulysses also had an extra strike going against him, and that only increased my respect for him, because during his using years he had a cocaine arm, and he had a heroin arm, and one day one of those arms got hit with a dirty needle and he caught the virus.

That was a death sentence in those days.

A lot of people don't take a diagnosis like that very well, especially if they're an alcoholic or addict. Many make a simple decision – they have a terrible disease, it's very controversial, it will eventually kill them, so why bother going through the pain and angst of withdrawal and recovery?

For what, being thought of as a leper, for being discriminated against, for ending up dead anyway?

No, just party on, do what you need to do to get by, and when the end comes, it comes, so tough shit.

Well, you sure didn't want to put Ulysses in that category, and you can trust me on that, because no disease, no matter how gruesome, could ever stop him from attending his meetings, helping other alcoholics and addicts, and living his life to the fullest.

Ulysses walked his talk, he expected others to do the same, and he had no problem with calling you out if you tried to lay a line of bullshit on him. He was the real deal, and the number of alcoholics and addicts that he eventually helped and inspired was in the hundreds, and that put him at the top of my Hall of Fame.

≈≈≈

There is, perversely, something very enabling about hitting financial rock bottom, because it makes life predictable and manageable. There are no country club and Porsche bills to pay, which is good, because you have no money to pay them with.

There's no alarm clock jarring you awake at 6:00 a.m., because you don't have a job to go to anymore, and you needn't worry about your social or romantic lives, because you don't have any social or romantic lives, nor money to support them with.

So when we strip away all of the facades and walls and false icons that we construct around ourselves in order to show the Smiths and the Joneses how important we are, we're left with the only things that matter at the end of the day – our sobriety, our blood and guts, a couple of hopes and dreams that haven't yet washed down the crapper, and one other thing – our fighting spirit.

That spirit and determination to remain sober, and alive, kept me going during the summer and fall of 1994.

The pain had now ratcheted up to a constant Level 9 on the meter. I no longer walked with a limp - rather, I stumbled along dragging my right leg behind me. I could pull myself along that way for about fifty feet before I had to crouch down onto my haunches, like a baseball catcher, which temporarily took some of the pressure off the sciatic nerve that was being crushed by my blown-out L5-S1 disc.

Ironically, there was some great AA humor attached to that act, because when I attended my Medfield meetings I'd stoop down into the crouch position, and the people I was talking to would do likewise. It became an ongoing joke, and we received some weird stares from passersby, especially when a group of four or five of us did our pow-wow thing on the sidewalks in front of nearby stores and offices.

Those were about the only laughs that I had in those long, agonizing days, and my love for the alcoholics and addicts who kept my spirits up grew exponentially, especially three wonderful women named Paula, Chris and Lynn, who could always coax a smile out of me.

≈≈≈

I wasn't having any success in obtaining health insurance. It was one of those pesky things that I had considered to be a nonessential when I was building my software business, and at the time I had managed to convince myself that the cash could be better allocated elsewhere.

Insurance is funny, though, because when you don't need it, you can get it, but when you do need it, you can't get it. That's just what's known in the trade as "the law of adverse selection." Insurance companies want to bring in the premiums to pay their overhead, and to make a profit, but they don't want to pay out claims, especially to new insureds who haven't been paying into the pot for very long.

I had paid out many thousands of dollars into a half-dozen employee-sponsored health insurers over the years, and rarely made claims, so when I went into business on my own I got cocky and took a gamble by going naked, naively believing that I would never get "too sick" or "too injured."

That didn't turn out to be the brightest decision I ever made.

So now, with no insurance, there would be no doctors or surgery for Wes, and that meant I was facing a wall of agony 24/7 for as far into the future as I could see. There was no good prognosis, and as the pain built my thoughts grew blacker, and my options fewer.

There were even those rare moments, usually in the dead of night, when it would have been so easy to say "If you had my problems, you'd think about drinking also."

But then I'd remember Ulysses, and a couple of dozen other AA'ers I had known over the years who had endured far more pain, fear and uncertainty than I was going through, and I remembered what they would always say:

"Sorry, but we've had your problems. We've experienced the accidents, fatal diseases, deaths of loved ones, loss of our homes and jobs and bank accounts, the emptiness and yearning of lost love, we have experienced the horrors of war firsthand, and we just don't drink or drug, period!"

Well if they could do it, then I was damned sure going to do it, so I did the only thing that seemed to work for me – I doubled up on my meetings, dragged my sorry ass up the stairs to my counseling sessions with Pat, where I ranted and raged for a solid hour, and I prayed to my Higher Power for the ability to accept my life exactly as it was.

And somehow, despite the fear and chaos that filled my life, I persevered, remained sober, and made it through my vacation in Hell for just one more twenty-four hours.

≈≈≈

Not long after Ulysses moved into the house he mentioned a new AA meeting that he had been attending.

He said it was 'kick-ass," and something he thought I should be hitting as well.

I thought that I knew about all the good meetings in the area, but this one wasn't in the Meeting List book, nor had any of my other AA friends ever mentioned it.

My curiosity finally won out one day in early August, so I asked him about it.

"It goes by 'TSDD'", he said, "and that stands for 'Tough Shit, Don't Drink.' It's a new men's meeting, and we get together in a big hall out by the turnpike, up on the "Mountain."

I knew the area, but had never heard of the meeting. The "Mountain" was a business park comprised of mixed industrial companies and general offices. I had worked for a while as a financial software salesman for a company that was located up there several years previously, but had been canned six months later for... guess what?

"So how come I don't know about it?"

"Well, we've been having trouble getting Central Service to add it to the approved meeting list because of its name - they don't think it fits the AA image. So now we're trying to get them to approve just the initials – 'TSDD' – but so far no luck."

"So what's the big deal about it?"

"It's for every guy who's serious about his sobriety. We have members that run the gamut from doctors and lawyers to construction workers, businessmen, unemployed guys, and even a couple of cons who just came off the chow line at Walpole State the day before."

"Interesting, how many members do you have?"

"We've got about sixty already, and word is spreading fast. We put on a lot of commitments, usually four or five a week, with as many as seven or eight guys hitting each one, so they're starting to hear about us out there."

"A week? I know whole groups that don't do that many in a year!"

"Yeah, well tough shit for them," Ulysses growled, "because they're missing out on a lot of good recovery. We're not exactly a meeting that attracts the quiche eaters, and we don't pretend to be. The only thing you need to do is keep your street shit outside, where it belongs, and check all the whining and ragtime stuff at the door."

I chuckled and said, "Gotcha, just what the doctor ordered, so what night do you meet?"

"Monday nights at 7:30. I know that it's tough driving for you, so I'll take you over next week."

And, just like that, I was a new charter member of 'TSDD.'

≈≈≈

Ulysses, myself, and Eddie, who was another seriously sober guy from the house, made the short ride over to the "Mountain" the following Monday evening.

Ninety minutes later I limped away from that building a changed man. My physical pain might not have been any better, but my attitude certainly was, because what you got from the 'TSDD' group was tough love, support, and a size 12 boot in the ass whenever you started in with the "poor me, poor me, pour me a drink" song and dance.

And that was just what the doctor ordered for this Onion.

There was an energy, a machismo, and an unconditional love for your fellow alcoholic and addict circulating through that hall that I had never experienced before, and it helped me through some trying times over the next year.

I mean, really, how could I sit around and whine about my predicament when I heard a dozen stories a night from guys who really had it tough?

So thank you, God, and Ulysses, because you woke me up, and I will be forever grateful for your compassion, and for laying a little 'TSDD' love on me when I needed it the most.

≈≈≈

I was facing some significant financial headwinds by late summer. I had some residual income arriving periodically from my software clients, which financed their maintenance and support calls, but it was barely enough to cover my meager rent and food costs at the house, and I had no physical capacity for selling, installing or training potential new clients.

I had other expenses, such as the phone, car insurance and Pat's counseling fees, and the cupboard was bare because I had maxed out all of my credit cards, and none of the banks intended to double down on Wes at that point in his thriving career.

In fact, all they wanted was the interest on my balances, call it the 'vig,' because they were hoping to string me along forever, like the loan sharks they are, and I was finding it difficult to even meet those minimum payments.

I did have a stash that I was reserving for some indeterminate rainy day in the future, however, when all the walls had finally collapsed - it was my "get out of Dodge" cash. I had taken a grand from the last of my credit card limits, and a grand from my furniture sales, and I had sewed that cash into the lining of a business suit that was hanging in my closet. I doubted that I'd have any need to wear that suit for a very long time, if ever, but it made for a great hiding place.

That stash aside, however, I was going dead-broke fast, so I began a 'smiling and dialing' campaign in late August, seeking part-time inside sales and telemarketing positions with some of the local businesses. I concentrated exclusively on the insurance, finance and technology markets, because they were where my background and strengths lay.

As luck would have it I got a bite within a week. The owner of a small insurance publication was looking for an advertising sales rep to pitch ad space to retail and wholesale insurance companies. His office was situated in one of the refurbished warehouses along the train line in Framingham, just a mile from the house, so it was an interesting opportunity.

I knew that market well, so this was right up my alley. I called the owner, gave him my background, and he invited me in for an interview the same week.

I passed with flying colors, and started the following Monday.

The job was part-time, the pay wasn't great, there were no benefits, but it was a job, and it would allow me to cover most of my expenses while I tried to figure out some way to obtain insurance for surgery that I reluctantly admitted I would need. The pain was worsening daily, and I knew that I was facing an existential threat if I couldn't find relief soon. I had begun to visit some very dark places in my head that summer, and I feared that my life was in danger if I couldn't find relief from the pain that was hammering me 24/7/365.

And it turns out that I wasn't alone. It was only much later that I learned I had been placed on suicide watch at the house, and in retrospect I can't say I was surprised. I think it might have had something to do with the little temper tantrum I threw one day when things looked particularly gruesome, when I finally hit ten on the pain meter.

I got a little loud, and "rearranged" some of the dining room furniture that afternoon, and sent most of the residents scurrying for the safety of their rooms.

So this job came just when I needed it the most, as if from above, because it gave me a sense of purpose, and it helped me to remain somewhat stable both financially and emotionally, at least for a short while.

And, if nothing else was working, there was always Ulysses doling out his tough love for a down and out alcoholic, ragging on me, calling me Buttercup, knowing full well that I was as stubborn as they come, so I'd take anything he could throw at me and just get mad, like that long-ago day in Little League when I struck out the side.

So I did indeed get mad, and I ranted and raged, but I also remained stubborn, and at the end of the day I realized that God gives you what you need, not necessarily what you want, which in my world was probably just as well because suicide is, after all, a horrifically permanent solution to a temporary problem.

≈≈≈

Thank you, God, for my counseling sessions with Pat!

We were only a couple of years apart age-wise, we had many similar life experiences, and we both had what I will politely call "twisted" senses of humor. He was easy to talk to and a good dumping ground for my pain and anger, so little by slow I was getting comfortable opening up to another human being, which with the exception of Eileen, Ulysses, and one or two other people in the Program was a rarity for me.

He was also cunning and devious, and early on he ran a great con that kept me motivated and locked into my recovery. It was his way of giving me some hope for the future, and that was a rare commodity in WesWorld those days.

Pat was a scratch golfer. He had won some state amateur championships over the years, so some might say that golf came second only to his sobriety, and he mentioned more than once that his two ex-wives would probably concur.

In fact, he was such a student of the game that he even made golf clubs, and sold them at cost to friends in recovery.

My father had introduced me to golf when I was about seven years old. I loved the sport from day one, caddied at a country club and played the public courses mostly, and slowly, steadily improved my game, at least until I reached my mid-teens and was introduced to alcohol and drugs.

After that I was a hacker, so golf became just another excuse to drink, rather than a fun, healthy recreational activity, just one of dozens of sacrifices I made over the years to Demon Rum.

Now, however, Pat was making it his mission to get me back on a golf course someday. I could barely walk, and the idea of torqueing my back to swing a club sent chills down my spine, but nonetheless he dangled the lure in front of me and told me to keep my eye on the prize, no matter what, and that was powerful motivation.

Finally, I bit the hook, so we agreed that when I was finished with the back nightmare he'd build a set of clubs for me at cost, and we'd start playing golf.

For a guy who was thinking some very black thoughts, a guy who was out on the edge, hopeless and helpless, that was all the motivation I needed to get me through some of the darkest days of my life.

So I would crawl painfully up the stairs to his office every two weeks, and he would work on my head, and he would yank a little harder on the hook, and after an hour I would crawl back down the stairs, sober, feeling just the slightest bit of hope, and I didn't drink, and I didn't drug, and I didn't pop a cap in my head.

≈≈≈

It didn't take long for me to realize that I had made a deal with the devil.

My part-time job at the insurance publication started off well enough, at least as far as my ability to bring in the bacon was concerned, but the salary was low, and the scheduled paydays were "fluid," which meant that my pay was sketchy and didn't always arrive on time.

It turns out that the owner was holding on by his fingertips. Insurance companies are notoriously slow payers, because they derive a significant part of their income by playing the interest rate spread between the time they receive their payments from the premiums they bill, and the time they fulfill their obligations to their insureds and vendors.

And, as it turned out, that included their advertising vendors, as was eventually revealed to me.

That meant the companies paid my boss when they had worked the spread as hard as they could, and then he paid me when he got around to it.

Needless to say, that put me in a rough spot, because I was barely squeaking by financially, so every late paycheck created a great deal of angst for me.

Was I going to get paid in full today, or would it be a week late, or only half of what I had earned? And how long could the boss hold on financially, because I was answering the phones most of the time, and there were as many angry vendors calling about late payments as there were insurance companies ordering ads.

I had some sympathy for the boss, but I also had obligations to meet, so I was caught in the middle. I couldn't afford to dip into my hidden stash, I was tired of chasing him for each of my paychecks, and things became contentious at times.

≈≈≈

You hear a lot of anecdotes at meetings about how this or that person had solved a vexing problem, and sometimes you can relate their experience to one of your own, so I picked up a few ideas and decided to try a new approach with my boss.

Rather than get into a confrontation that would be fueled by resentment and testosterone, like the old Wes would have done, I decided to approach him in the manner I had learned at my AA meetings - sober, polite and considerate, albeit firm. I didn't have any plans to become a United Nations peacekeeper, or a crisis management specialist, but it stood to reason that I could attempt to meet him half-way without moving the needle toward DEFCON Three.

After all, its progress, not perfection, right?

Apparently not.

Some people interpret sober, polite and considerate as an open invitation to abuse a relationship, and before long my boss took that route, so rather than receiving my pay a few days in arrears I was getting it even later than usual.

I finally reached my limit in late October. My paycheck was two weeks past due, with no relief in sight, so I resigned.

He wasn't exactly overjoyed by that, and he became even less happy when I limped over to my personal notebook computer and started unhooking the connections. I had been utilizing it to manage the advertising sales process, and I'd even written a nifty little ad management, tracking and billing program specifically suited to his operation, and which had been written with my own software and resided on my own computer.

I provided this program free of charge, while I worked there, so that we could both receive the benefits of a system that would sell on the street for two thousand dollars, or more, at no cost to him.

And now he didn't want me to take custody of it, our voices were getting loud, and I sensed that we were getting dangerously close to throwing punches.

But for one of the first times in my life I behaved like a good little boy. I didn't rise to his threats, and I didn't buy in to the negative electricity that was passing between us. Instead I stood back, took a deep, cleansing breath, and said a simple prayer to my Higher Power, "Please God, help me to remain present, centered and aware, and grounded and mindful, and please keep me from reacting in anger - thank you, God."

And I'll be damned – it worked!

Within seconds my blood pressure backed off, my breathing returned nearer to normal, and that exhilarating but treacherous adrenaline rush began to recede.

We both stepped back from the abyss, and worked out a deal after that.

He agreed that the computer and software programs were my property, and I agreed that the data on those programs was his property.

Then we agreed that I would run a report over the weekend to dump all of the necessary data onto paper, and deliver it to the office on Monday morning.

What he did with the freaking data after that was his business, although I admit I had a few unspoken opinions about where he could stick it.

He agreed, in turn, that he would pay me all of the arrears that were due me, date and time non-specified, but "as soon as possible, as soon as I get paid by the companies."

I was skeptical about that "date and time" thing, having witnessed his business ethics for the past couple of months, but beggars can't be choosers, and this solution extricated me from an unhealthy relationship that was working on my head.

That night I said a prayer of thanks to my Higher Power for having granted me the wisdom and humility to walk away from a losing game.

And then I remembered Mick's lyrics to one of my favorite Stones songs, "You can't always get what you want, but if you try sometimes you just might find you get what you need."

Damn, that sounded like a deal to me – thanks, Mick!

≈≈≈

Surprise, surprise, six months later I sued the miserable turd in small claims court for the entire balance of the amount he had screwed me out of. I received half of what was due me through a negotiated settlement, and used most of the cash to pay off a portion of my mounting debt.

I was so over it by then that I scarcely cared anymore, but nonetheless I said a prayer to give credit where credit was due:

"Thank you, God, for another life lesson, and for watching over me in my darkest hours. Oh, and by the way, are we just about done with my education, because I don't know how much more of this nonsense I can handle!"

Then I asked Him for a new job, a new back, a new car and a girlfriend.

I guess He must have been straight-out busy creating another constellation somewhere out near Alpha Centauri, where the big new housing projects were going up, because He never got back to me on what I considered to be a very reasonable request.

≈≈≈

I related the story of my fun adventure in advertising to Pat at my next appointment, and he got a big kick out of it, chuckled, and said, "You're learning, Grasshopper."

Then he complimented me on my restraint, and launched into a long dissertation about adrenaline, neurotransmitters and the "fight or flight" response that's been built into our DNA since the day we crawled out of the swamps.

It was all starting to make sense to me now, this whole puzzle about why I was an alcoholic and why I had lived the life I lived. It didn't necessarily make things any easier for me, however, because it was, and would always be, "life on life's terms," take it or leave it, no matter how bad things got.

But, like they say, "From pain comes wisdom," so I figured that I just needed to keep trudging that damned road to Happy Destiny, try to avoid the worst of the potholes, and hopefully I would find my much sought after peace of mind someday.

The only question was when, and God was holding His cards close to the vest on that one.

I've got to hand it to Him, however, because I always had the feeling that I wouldn't want to be on the other side of the Texas Hold 'em table when He was running one of His bluffs.

≈≈≈

In late November I heard about a chiropractor who operated a small practice one town over from Framingham. She was reputed to be adept at manipulating broken bodies, and an AA friend who was her client hooked me up for a free visit with her.

I had heard the pros and cons about chiropractors over the years. Some people raved about the results, but there was also a significant group that wrote them off as quacks and pitchmen.

Beggars can't be choosers, however, and the price was right, so I figured nothing ventured, nothing gained. At that point in my life I would have taken a freebie from P.T. Barnum if I thought it would help reduce my pain level by just one measly point on the scale.

The Doc turned out to be an exuberant, athletic woman in her early forties who was working hard to build a practice. She was closely allied with the local healers and therapists who practiced the underground alternative modalities, including the various massage techniques such as Swedish and the Asian practices, as well as Reiki and acupuncture.

We had some shared interests, so we hit it off right from the start. Her manipulations relaxed me, and knocked my pain levels down by a point or two for a day or so after my visits, so I began going over to her office every two weeks for an adjustment.

She soon introduced me to other practitioners in the area who were also clients of hers, and it wasn't long before I discovered that alternative medicine has many advantages over traditional Western medical practices. It isn't that American practices are necessarily bad, but rather that the alternatives added a whole new dimension to healing, and can fill some of the gaps that conventional medicine doesn't address.

It soon became clear to me that there was ample room for both the traditional and the alternative, and I have utilized both modalities over the years, depending on my needs.

After a few weeks the Doc began giving me free adjustments in exchange for working her desk, answering the phones, and booking new client appointments a couple of afternoons a week. This was somewhat helpful financially, but more so for my spirit, because it kept me active and engaging the world, rather than hiding away at the sober house, a prisoner in my pain shell.

I didn't fully recognize it at the time, but all of the forces that would eventually contribute to my healing were coming into alignment, little by slow, and the Universe was setting me up for salvation and a life that would be second to none.

But like the man sang, "You've got to go through Hell before you get to Heaven," and my journey still had a long way to go.

≈≈≈

One day the Doc told me about a friend of hers who was a Reiki practitioner. Reiki has been around for thousands of years, and it's an Asian modality that involves the gentle movement of the hands to manipulate the body's chakras and energy fields, and by so doing restore and re-align the body, and spirit, to a healthy balance.

The Doc had spoken to her friend, Lisa, about me, and she had offered to give me a Reiki session at the Doc's office for no charge, with the understanding that if I found some relief I could continue the treatments for a reasonable fee.

I said sure, why not, because the chiropractic adjustments were giving me some temporary relief, but they weren't knocking down the pain level to anywhere near a tolerable number.

≈≈≈

I drove over to the Doc's office two evenings later, and she introduced me to Lisa, who led me into the examining area and instructed me to lie down on a massage table, fully dressed and face-up.

Then she dimmed the lights, switched on some meditation music, and told me to close my eyes and try to clear away all of my thoughts.

I complied, and then I waited.

And then I waited some more.

Lisa never touched me, so after ten minutes I peeked through my eyelids to see whether she was still in the room.

She was still there, silent, hovering, eyes closed, her face serene, her hands wandering slowly just inches above my body, floating, never making any actual physical contact with me, maneuvering over every square inch of me.

"Okay," I thought, "this is interesting, but how can she help me if she won't even touch me?"

I closed my eyes again, and then little by slow I received my answer as the pain began to recede, just a speck at first, then more, and more, and then I slipped off into a dream.

In my vision I had been transported back to the year 1969, and I was in a park on the island of Martha's Vineyard. There were seven or eight of us there, all in our late teens or early twenties, all from the same town in the Boston suburbs. It was a beautiful, warm Saturday afternoon in July, it was the Age of Aquarius, and we were about to go on a trip. One of my friends told me to close my eyes and stick out my tongue, so I did, and then she placed a little tab of purple blotter acid on it and I let it dissolve in my mouth.

Moments later the Universe exploded before my eyes, as billions upon trillions of stars went through their birth spasms, flashing and burning in a hallucinogenic dreamscape.

And now, twenty-five years later, the curtain shifted and I found myself in the Badlands of the Dakotas. I was a Lakota Sioux warrior, proud and pure and strong, fighting for my land, my people and my heritage. It was 1876 and the battle had been joined, and the Great Spirit was at my back as I charged into the fray. I fought well, and proudly, and after the battle had been won I took the blood of my enemy and drank of its power, and took that power for my own.

And then the tears began, and I wept as the pain drained out of my body.

≈≈≈

Eventually Lisa smiled gently and whispered, "This is all part of your healing, Wes, you're letting go of the past, and it's the end of the war you've been waging against the world, and against yourself. It will happen slowly, in your Spirit's time, not your own, but it will happen if you remain on your Path."

That night I prayed that she was correct, and I'll be darned but she was.

≈≈≈

I remained virtually pain-free for two blissful days. That might not seem like much, but for me it was probably the best vacation I have ever had. My mood improved, I was able to catch up on some chores that I had been ignoring, and I made it to three AA meetings, where I spoke optimistically about life and sobriety, rather than dishing up my usual helping of grunts and scowls.

314

I realized that this time-out was probably a lull in the storm, a temporary stop-gap measure, and that I would need surgery as soon as I could finagle it, but nonetheless my vacation from pain restored a degree of hope in me that had been absent from my life for almost a year.

It was Christmas week, 1994, and it reminded me that life can be good, and fun, and productive, so I basked in the sunlight for those two entire days, and thanked God for the reprieve.

≈≈≈

"To be, or not to be, that is the question."

Shakespeare's grand existential riddle was beginning to rent space in my head.

My short-lived optimism began to drain off right after the New Year was rung in, and by the middle of January, 1995, the pain train was back full throttle, hammering me day and night, playing with my head, knocking down one by one all of the defenses that I had so carefully built up over the past several months.

The chiropractic sessions stopped working.

The Reiki session was a thing of the distant past.

Even my daily AA meetings and sessions with Pat took a back seat to the pain, as I slipped little by slow into a spiraling funk that was with me 24/7.

It was relentless, insidious, all-encompassing, playing smash-mouth with me, and I knew that it wanted to kill me.

And then one day I began to think that wouldn't be such a bad solution after all.

≈≈≈

All of my days were the same.

I would crawl out of bed just after dawn, contorted, sleep-deprived, my back and neck muscles cramped and on fire from my broken posture, then hobble out to the kitchen, dragging my right leg behind me. I would carry a bath-sized towel with me, and soak it at the kitchen faucet. Then I'd drag myself over to the microwave oven and cook the towel for two minutes, until it was steaming hot, and then I'd wrap it tight around my neck, ignoring the scorching pain, and hold it in place for several minutes until my neck muscles, rigid and screaming, finally loosened up enough for me to rotate them ten or twenty degrees in either direction.

Then I would light a smoke and drink my coffee, and wonder whether today would be the day.

≈≈≈

Somehow I forced myself to get out to a meeting every day, if only so I could get some fresh air and pretend that things weren't as bad as I knew they were, and I continued to attend my bi-weekly sessions with Pat. They helped, at least as far as my head was concerned, but the constant wall of pain just kept hammering away at me, and soon I knew only hopelessness and despair.

Finally I took a short detour on my way home from a meeting one evening in early February. I drove through the south side of town, searching for one particular nondescript ranch house that was located in a cookie-cutter neighborhood of a dozen other nondescript ranch houses.

This was a very special ranch, however, a place where you could get anything your heart desired, so come on in! Drugs? Sure, step right up, what are you looking for, buddy? Something to grant you blessed release, a permanent vacation from all of life's pain and sorrow and fear? Sure, come on in!

And then I would drive up and down the street a half dozen times a night, trying to get up the nerve to take one last walk into the darkness, to secure my one way ticket on the train that was waiting for me down on the railroad tracks near the sober house, the tracks where I would find eternal rest.

But then every night something would stop me, and that nagging question that I had asked myself in the days before I surrendered to my disease in 1992 would return, and I would ask, "What if?"

"What if I can make it through one more day?"

"What if I can find some help for my back?"

"What if I am meant for something more than what I have today?"

"What if there's a drunk somewhere out there, suffering, who is depending on me?"

"What if?"

And then every night for one solid week I would tell myself, "All you need to do is take it for just one more day, one hour, one moment, one heartbeat. That's all you've gotta do Wes, so please God, help me to get thru this night just one more time!"

And somehow He would, and I did, and then I'd drive back to the sober house, lie in my bed in fitful agony and rise just after dawn to begin the routine all over again.

And I didn't drink, and I didn't drug, and I didn't lie down on the tracks and go to sleep.

≈≈≈

I guess that God had been paying attention to me after all, because He gave me the strength and willingness to get humble, and to ask for help one more time.

I finally surrendered to the inevitable in mid-February, 1995, swallowed my pride, and admitted that there was only one way out of my predicament besides taking that crosstown ride to score the pills that would give me a permanent release from all of the pain and terror.

But the solution was anathema to me. It embarrassed me, shamed me, and when I look back on it now it was probably the lowest, most depressing point in my sober life.

I fought it for a day, then a week, then two weeks, and then after one dark, sleepless night I surrendered to life one more time, took a deep breath and made the call.

I did not fully recognize it at the time, but this would mark my physical, mental and emotional bottom, and it came almost three years after I first began the lifelong process of surrendering to my disease.

≈≈≈

317

I had been an Army officer in the early '70's, so I knew from experience that government agencies aren't always a lot of fun to deal with. They're notorious for being stacked layer upon layer with bureaucrats, whose job skills appear to consist primarily of creating red tape, redundancy, and suspicion toward all who come seeking help.

But my experiences back then had taught me that yes, the wheels of progress in American government run slowly, but nonetheless they run, if one is open minded, honest, respectful, and just a little but stubborn.

At least I hoped that this was still the case.

And, as it turned out, the biggest hurdle had been in my own head, not in the workings of the United States government.

The bottom line was that I was ashamed to be seeking public assistance, no matter how much I needed it. The very act of humbling myself, of seeking government help, ran against all of the rules I had once upon a time believed a man was meant to live by.

You were supposed to get a job, work that job as hard as you could, keep your mouth shut, take the good with the bad and just keep on trucking, no matter what, because a blown out back was just an excuse, not a reason, to fail.

I don't know who the boy genius was who thought up that gem of a theory, but it had stopped working for me.

My only choices now were bad, very bad, or final, so I decided to treat this enterprise like it was just one more job application, and having lived the life that I had lived I had plenty of experience in applying for jobs, because I had plenty of experience in losing jobs.

So that's what I did – I pretended that I was applying for employment. This was in the era before the Internet had gained acceptance by most governmental agencies, so I called around and got the information I needed, then requested that they send me all of the necessary forms for submitting an application for health benefits.

When I had gathered up all the documentation that I thought I would need, and had filled out all the forms, and dotted all the i's, and crossed all the t's, I drove over to the Post Office and sent my application off.

Then I sat in my car in the parking lot and said my simple go-to prayer, "Please God, help me to remain humble today, and to accept the outcome of my decisions, and please keep me away from a drink and a drug just for this one freakin' minute... thank you, God."

And that was that, now it's your turn, Big Guy, so do your thing!

≈≈≈

I guess that God took a couple of hours off after He wrapped up all the galactic construction projects He had been running, because it took Him a while to get back to me, although I doubt that even God can always navigate the internal workings of the U.S. government paper mill.

But it is what it is, just your typical yin and yang thing, so I was used to it by now. When life is good, time just seems to fly, but when it's bad, and you're waiting for the largest bureaucracy in the history of mankind to respond to your plea for help, it's like the clock is frozen in place.

So I waited, hit a meeting every day, and crawled up the stairs to Pat's office every two weeks, where I ranted and raged, and prayed for acceptance.

And I even left the dining room furniture alone.

≈≈≈

The call came in early March, 1995. It was from a staffer at the local Social Security office.

"Hello, is this Mr. Hollis?" a lady's voice inquired.

"Yes, that's me."

"Good... well, Mr. Hollis, my name is Miss Jones, and I'm calling to let you know that we've received your application for assistance, and it appears to be complete. If you wish to go forward we will need you to come down to the office for an interview, and we can describe the process for obtaining your benefits in detail. Would you be able to do that?"

"Yes, certainly, Miss Jones, I'm in a world of hurt, so the sooner the better."

"Okay, well we're understaffed, but perhaps I can squeeze you in next week, maybe on Wednesday, in the morning?"

"If that's the earliest you have, then that would be fine."

"Okay, I have you scheduled for 10:00 a.m.," she said, and then she rattled off a list of things that I would need to bring with me.

I scribbled down some notes, thanked her, hung up, let out a deep sigh of relief, then said, "Thank you God, from the bottom of my heart, I had just about run out of hope."

I looked outside and noticed that the sun was shining, then wondered when the last time had been since I even bothered to pay attention to whether it was day or night.

≈≈≈

Wes was a busy little beaver for the next week.

I had forms to fill out, doctor's notes to locate, and a plethora of irritating little details to take care of as I prepared for my meeting with the Feds.

But first and foremost I had a lot of AA meetings to attend, because without AA I knew that nothing else would matter, so my priorities had to be sobriety first, last, and everything in between.

I was almost giddy as I considered the possibility that there might finally be blessed relief from my torture. Whereas I didn't want to get too far ahead of myself (in the program we call it "projecting"), I nonetheless felt a hint of the most important commodity on Earth – hope - because without hope is there really any reason to get out of bed in the morning, or to take that next breath?

I had merely to look back over the prior three years of my life to find the answer to that riddle, so I built up my paper pile of information for the interview. Then I prayed a lot, thanked

God a lot, hit a lot of meetings, had a great counseling session with Pat, and recited my simple mantra a dozen times a day, "One day at a time, one moment at a time, one detail at a time, one heartbeat at a time, hang in there, Wes, and just don't drink, no matter what."

So I didn't, and little by slow the steps of progress proceeded inexorably toward the following Wednesday.

≈≈≈

"Good morning, Mr. Hollis," Miss Jones said, giving me the once-over, "I'll be handling your case from here on in. I see that you're having some back problems, and you're inquiring about assistance and possible surgery?" she asked, cool, toneless, all "government" with a dour expression on her face.

"Yes, that's correct. I blew it out about a year ago and it's just gotten worse and worse. I'm in agony 24/7, I can hardly walk, or sleep, or drive, and I'm at the end of the line."

She stared at me for a moment, expressionless, then said, "You don't look very comfortable now."

"I'm never comfortable, it never stops, it just gets worse and worse, and I've run out of options."

"Have you been seeing a doctor?"

"No, it's been a couple of years, and I'm pretty much broke and living day to day off what's left of my money, which isn't much, and most of that goes to renting a cheap room in a sober house, and to food."

She stared into my eyes once again, searching for something, but I didn't have a clue as to what she expected to find there.

"Well, let's see if we can give you a hand," she finally said, and then spent the next ten minutes explaining the program and what actions I would need to take in order to qualify for medical benefits.

I was grateful that I had been treating the process like a job application, because it was very detailed, complex and time consuming. There were a host of forms to fill out, more doctor's reports to gather, even work history and a summary of my current income and outgo, of which there was little of the first, and plenty of the latter.

Finally she asked, "Have you had an MRI recently?"

I just stared at her, and said, "No, I don't have any free cash for stuff like that, and I maxed out my credit cards just trying to pay my living expenses, so now they're coming after me for late pays."

"Well, that's the first thing we need to obtain. We have an orthopedic surgeon on call, who diagnoses back cases in order to determine whether an applicant qualifies for medical benefits, which would include surgery. We need to make an appointment for you to get a full physical and back exam, and he'll also schedule an MRI if he sees the need for one."

"Okay, so what do I need to do now?"

"Nothing. We'll call his office and make the arrangements, and let you know. It typically takes two weeks to get everything booked. What's your availability, are you free most weekdays?"

"Yes, any time, any day."

"We should be in touch by early next week," she said, and then the cool, dour expression softened just a little as she added, almost under her breath, "Hang in there, Mr. Hollis, despite what you hear about the government, we really are here to help."

≈≈≈

"Tick, tick, tick," went the clock, and "damn, damn, damn!" went my head as Monday morning slid into Monday afternoon.

Being the typical alcoholic who needs everything "right NOW!" I figured that Monday morning at zero eight hundred would be a reasonable time to expect to hear from the nice lady. After all, she said, "We should be in touch by early next week," and wasn't Monday at zero eight hundred "early next week?"

In this drunk's mind it certainly was, so what was the delay? Were they ignoring me, or had they turned down my application already, without even an MRI?

"What what what? Why why why hadn't they called me? Whaah, whaah, whaah!"

Okay, so perhaps I still hadn't learned all of the angles for remaining present, centered, and aware, and grounded and mindful. But I was still a rookie, and at least I had the good sense to stay away from the phone, pray for acceptance, get to my Monday AA meeting, and somehow I made it through the day without any meltdowns.

And then Miss Jones called me early Tuesday morning, which was well within the parameters of "early next week," and just as she had promised.

I knew that I'd be receiving another scolding call from God pretty soon, another one of those "I'm over in Orion's Belt, repairing a few thousand stars that fell into a black hole, so I can't just drop everything to take care of your every whim, Skippy! I have my own responsibilities you know, it's not all just about you, and I haven't had a day off in several eons, so when they say in God's time, they mean in MY time!"

Duly noted, and how could I blame Him - the dude had some humongous responsibilities in those days.

≈≈≈

"Hello, Mr. Hollis," Miss Jones greeted me, "I'm calling just to let you know that things are moving along, and that we've scheduled an appointment for you to visit with our orthopedic surgeon. He'll give you a complete exam, and then, depending on what he finds, he'll schedule an MRI for you."

"Good, that's great, the sooner the better, and thanks so much Miss Jones! I was pretty much running out of hope, and there's no place else to turn. "

"Now, now, don't think like that, there's always hope, it's just that sometimes when we're stuck in the middle of the storm it's difficult to find it, but it's always there!"

"Hmmm," I wondered, "now where have I heard that line before… could she be one of us?"

Miss Jones then gave me the date for my appointment, which was scheduled for the following Wednesday at 11:00 a.m., and directions to the doc's office, and that was that.

I thanked her, and we hung up.

I was trying to keep my emotions in check, but nonetheless I felt a thrill of optimism for the first time in months, so I allowed myself to surrender to it for one brief moment.

Then I took a long, hot shower, letting the steaming hot water beat on my neck and lower back for ten minutes, and headed downtown to a looney-nooney meeting.

≈≈≈

Tick, tick, tick went the clock, again, and Wes worried that Wednesday would never arrive, but I hit my regular meetings, had a good session with Pat, and prayed a lot.

I stuck to my standard "go-to" prayer that I used when I was facing fear, doubt and insecurity. It was simple, and to the point:

"Please God, help me to accept the outcome of this doctor's appointment."

It was generic, short and easy, and it allowed me to change a word or two to fit the particular challenge I was facing at the time. It could just as easily have been:

"Please God, help me to accept the results of this job search," or,

"Please God, help me to accept the outcome of this meeting, or this traffic jam, or this Category 4 hurricane," or whatever the temporary problem of the moment might be.

Little by slow I was discovering that life was becoming much less intimidating when I reduced all of its challenges into simple concepts.

It was KISS formula 101, "Keep it Simple, Stupid," remain focused on the here and now, and just do the next right thing.

Geesh, and it had taken me forty-four years to figure out that little gem?

≈≈≈

Wednesday finally arrived, and at precisely 11:00 a.m. I found myself seated in the doctor's waiting room in Watertown, fidgety and uncomfortable. I had brought along a large envelope that contained all of my doctors' records for the past several years, although there were just a couple of records, because doctor's visits had been a luxury that hadn't fitted into my financial priorities for the most part.

A nurse walked up to me ten minutes later and led me down the hallway to the doc's office. We entered the room, and I dragged myself over to his desk where we shook hands, and then I collapsed into a seat facing him.

I was nervous, because I considered this to be a life or death meeting, and if I didn't pass muster here I had no other viable plan to fall back on, so in a way I felt like I was having a talk with 'The Hangman.'

Nevertheless, I had gotten this far, which in and of itself was a miracle, so I silently thanked my Higher Power for that, and asked for the ability to accept the outcome of this meeting, whatever it might be.

The introductions were brief, and then the doc began to question me in detail about how the injury occurred, what the pain level was, whether it was occasional or all the time, and how did it affect my mobility, my ability to perform daily chores, physical work, drive, sleep, cook, wipe my ass, etc. etc. etc.

At times I felt as though I was in a job interview, rather than a medical consult, but I remained patient and answered all of his questions completely and truthfully.

Then the doc asked me to stand and walk across the room and back, which I did, hunched over and dragging my leg behind me. He then gave me a couple of simple exercises to perform, which I failed, and which sent my pain number up a few more notches.

Finally, he examined my lower back, and all the way down my right leg to my foot, then told me to sit down.

I collapsed into my seat, sweating, in pain, and he stared intently at me for a moment before he spoke. I felt like a prisoner in the dock, about to receive my sentence.

"Okay, Wes, it appears that you have a serious injury here. Frankly, I'm surprised it took you this long to get help for it, because you must have been in a great deal of pain for quite a while."

"Yeah, but I didn't have any choice, it's like I've been circling down the drain, going from one disaster to another. I'm broke, unable to work, and that doesn't give me too many medical options."

"Well, I see your point, so let's get started, and the first thing we need to do is get you scheduled for an MRI. That will give us the full picture of the injury, and if it's what I think we'll see, it should open up the path to getting you medical coverage and surgery."

"What do you think it is?" I asked, relieved but worried at the same time.

"Well, until we get the results of the MRI I can't say for certain, but it appears that you have a ruptured L5-S1 spinal disc, and that's serious, and it's the reason why the pain is running down your leg and into your foot. I noticed some dead spots along your leg, and obviously your heel and lateral foot are affected as well."

"Yeah, I don't have any sensation in those areas."

He paused, then said, "I wish you could have seen a doctor sooner, because you have some permanent damage, and even with surgery it won't return the sensation to those dead spots."

"If I get surgery will I be able to at least walk, and be relatively free of this pain that I'm in 24/7?"

"I believe so," he said, "you should be able to return to pretty much a normal life, but there will be some ongoing pain, and perhaps a slight limp, and you'll definitely know when there's a change in the weather coming along," he said, trying to lighten the tone a little bit.

"Anything's better than what I have now, so what's next?"

"What's next is your MRI. I want you to get it ASAP, so I'll have the staff get that arranged, and we'll call as soon as we have a time slot for you. Okay?"

"Yeah, the sooner the better."

"I think we can get you in next week," he said, then gave me instructions on how to prepare for the procedure, and sent me on my way.

≈≈≈

Hope's a strange thing, because when we lack it we lose all of our motivation for change, growth, optimism, and for fulfilling our dreams. We inhabit a barren wasteland that's dull, gray, monochromatic, without a future to fight for, or to bleed for.

But when that tiniest sliver of hope comes creeping up from the void, like the first spring mountain wildflower, life becomes special, a gift, a moment for optimism and joy and change, a kaleidoscope of colors and hues and shades and gradations, a virtual wonderland of opportunity and beauty.

I wasn't all the way there, yet, but when I walked out of that doctor's office in March, 1995, I finally had hope, and that fueled my fire to survive.

≈≈≈

"MRI" is the acronym for 'magnetic resonance imaging.'

In technical terms, it's relatively simple - the patient is placed in an object that has the dimensions of a torpedo tube, or coffin, and then a strong magnetic field is created within the tube, and that energy field is bombarded by high-frequency radio waves that image the structures of atomic nuclei in various organs.

The result is a highly defined representation of various bodily components, including spinal tissue, and this "picture" reveals any anomalies that are present in those target organs.

That's the techie description, but in layman's terms I would just be getting my picture taken by a really cool camera.

The call from the imaging company came on Friday morning. The nice lady asked if I could come in the following Thursday for my MRI, that it was scheduled for 10.00 a.m. at a facility in Waltham.

I told her that wild horses couldn't keep me away, so she gave me my instructions for prepping for the procedure, and that was that.

I hit my meetings every day for the next week, prayed for the ability to accept the results of the imaging, whatever they might be, then pretty much counted down the seconds until I would be rolled into the torpedo tube.

I didn't sleep very well for the next week, but this time it was due to hope, rather than despair.

It was a funny thing, but it almost seemed like my pain level went down a notch or two, which I could only attribute to the possibility that my stress levels were unwinding just a spec as the cavalry came riding into town.

≈≈≈

Once upon a time I had traded stocks for a living, and I had learned through many years of hard-won experience that success in that endeavor came only one way, that after all the research and charting and testing of different models, and taking chances, and getting my clock cleaned, it all came down to the mo-mo – the momentum. When you caught that perfect trade, and it started to break out to the upside, and the volume came flooding in, you piled on with everything you had, and then you held on for dear life and rode it as hard as you possibly could, until the wave crested, the mo-mo train left for greener pastures, and you cashed in your chips.

Stock trading took discipline, confidence, and above all faith in my ability and desire to succeed, and I believe that these are some of the same attributes that we, as recovering people, must utilize every day of our sober lives.

So when I limped into the MRI facility that morning in late March, 1995, I sensed that the mo-mo train was pulling in to the station. Finally, after more than a year of pain, doubt and fear, I had hope, and that gave me the momentum I needed to take the next step to my emancipation.

I didn't come skipping merrily through the door, but I swear I was standing more upright than I had for months.

Such is the power and promise of hope, and mo-mo.

≈≈≈

It only took fifteen minutes to complete the paperwork, place my valuables in a secure locker, and step into a sexy little paper johnny.

I had to leave my lucky sobriety neck chain in the locker as well, because there was a possibility that if it broke off in the chaos created by the electromagnetic fields and high frequency radio waves it could do severe damage to the machine, or to me.

To tell you the truth, I think they were more worried about the machine than they were about the Onion.

Then an assistant led me into the imaging room and told me to lie down on a cold, hard, plastic table that reminded me of those autopsy tables you see in the television crime shows. And, yes, the johnny didn't cover me completely, so I had a very cold butt for a few minutes.

She tied my arms to the sides of the table to prevent me from moving around too much, then rolled me into the tube and left the room.

I felt a bit like a fish that was about to be fileted.

One moment later a male voice came over the intercom and said, "Okay, Wes, we're just about ready to start the procedure. There will be some noise in the tube, and you may experience some nervousness at being in a small enclosed environment, but we'll be monitoring you for the entire procedure, so just give a shout if you're experiencing any difficulties."

"Okay," I said, "let's get to it. I'm ready."

"Fine… oh, and one more thing, would you like some music piped in?"

Music?

"Uh, sure, what do you have, any 'Stones?" I asked, laughing.

"Oh yeah," came the reply, "it just so happens that we have the Beggars Banquet album, would that work?"

"Dude, you made my day… rock on, and make it loud!"

"You got it, Buddy, that's the only way we roll," he said, and moments later "Sympathy for the Devil" was reverberating throughout the torpedo tube.

≈≈≈

Thirty minutes later, just as "Prodigal Son" was wrapping up, the nice lady wheeled me out of the machine and said, "You're all set, Wes, you can go into the changing room and get dressed, and we'll forward the results to your doctor and the case worker in the next day or two."

And that was that - now I just had to wait, again.

I walked out of that building just a little more upright than when I walked in, then recited a new mantra, "Don't drink, Wes, don't drug, don't get ahead of yourself, just get to your meetings, ask for help and do the next right thing."

≈≈≈

God called me a few days later, just to let me know that He had been the one to request that the Beggars Banquet album was on the rack.

He wasn't particularly thrilled by my choice of songs, but He let it slide.

Man, you gotta hand it to that guy, He's on top of everything!

≈≈≈

Miss Jones, my case worker, called me the following Monday afternoon.

She got right to the point.

"Mr. Hollis," she began, "the results of your MRI are back, and unfortunately I need to inform that you have a significant spinal injury. We'd like you to come in to see our doctor again, as soon as possible, and he can explain the results in detail. He indicated that surgery is recommended, so he can run through that as well."

"Thank you, Miss Jones, but I'm not surprised by the results. I'm just grateful that I finally have a diagnosis. I was beginning to think that I was a goner, and if it hadn't been for your help, I don't know what I would have done, because I had some pretty black thoughts."

"I know," she said, "but please understand that there are still some additional things we need to accomplish in order to get you your medical benefits, so bear with us for now, and we'll move things along as quickly as we can."

"Sure, what can I do?"

"Well, you may want to locate a good orthopedic surgeon who specializes in spinal injuries, and meanwhile we'll take care of the processing of your application. Okay?"

"Okay, I'll wait to hear from you, and thank you again for all the help you've given me, Miss Jones."

≈≈≈

I went to a meeting that evening, and when I hit my knees that night I said my thanks to God, and then for the first time in memory I drifted off into a deep and restful slumber for two or three hours.

≈≈≈

Things began to happen fast after that, but I concentrated on keeping to my daily routine, and on remaining focused on the next step in my march to surgery.

I stuck to the tried and true concept of "first things first," so I hit all of my AA meetings, went to my counseling sessions with Pat, and prayed for acceptance – a lot!

For most of my life I would have been terrified by the prospect of lying on an operating table while a strange surgeon cut me open and played with my spine. I was a control freak, like some of us, and the thought of surrendering my body to the whims of a surgeon was inconceivable. My mind would have automatically jumped to the doom and gloom side – the Doc would cut a nerve and leave me paralyzed for life in a decrepit nursing home.

But that wasn't where my head was going this time. No, because instead of fear I was exhilarated, and I was actually looking forward to the day that they'd be rolling me into the operating room, because I was prepared to endure anything that might ease my pain.

I guess the student was finally beginning to understand that the ability to practice acceptance in all areas of his life was a gift from his Higher Power, and that it is through His grace that I survive and prosper.

~≈~

I began smiling and dialing the morning after I received the good news, only this time it was for back surgeons rather than software sales.

After making more than a dozen calls, however, I was batting zero. Many of the docs weren't accepting new patients, several had retired or were out of the country, and the rest didn't bother to get back to me.

I suppose that in retrospect I was pretty naïve to be looking for a spine surgeon in the Yellow Pages, because it wasn't like I was looking for a plumber to fix the toilet.

I took a break, then, and hobbled out to the kitchen, where I treated myself to a cup of strong, black coffee. That was one of the 'bennies" about living in a sober house – the java would put hair on your chest for sure. Then I went back into my room, closed my eyes, and said my simple prayer:

"Please God, help me to accept the outcome of my efforts to find a doc, and please help me to accept my life exactly as it is today."

I guess God had taken his own coffee break that morning, but evidently He was now back at work, because on my next call it was Bingo – we have a winner!

The doc's name was Joe Barr, and he was a Harvard Medical School grad and back cutter at Mass General, as well as at the Faulkner Hospital in Jamaica Plain, where I had been born.

And best of all he was a member of the consortium at my general practitioner's group, so I called my own doc to get the lowdown on him, and he informed me that Joe was a big time guy with a spotless record, and that he would be first on his own call list if he needed back surgery.

That was all I wanted to hear, so I took a deep breath, prayed to accept the outcome of my call, and rang the man up.

~≈~

The doc's receptionist took my call and informed me that he was in surgery that day, but that I could speak with Debbie, his administrative assistant.

"Yes, Mr. Hollis, the doctor is accepting new patients from Dedham Medical."

Yeehaaaa!!!

"Yes, I can set up an appointment for you to come in next week for a consult."

Oh, sweet!!

"He has surgeries scheduled most mornings next week, but would Tuesday afternoon at 3:00 work for you?"

Wild horses couldn't keep me away!!!

"Okay, we'll see you then, and we'll contact the imaging center to have your MRI results transferred over to us."

"Thank you, Debbie," I said, and hung up.

"And thank you, God," I murmured to the heavens.

The mo-mo train was gathering speed, and all my chips were finally in the pot.

≈≈≈

Joe Barr was a piece of work, and a no-nonsense type of guy. He was the son of a surgeon, cocky, hard-charging, and he had brass balls. He reminded me of a bantam rooster, a fighter, and that's exactly what I was looking for.

I got right to the point after we shook hands.

"You've seen my MRI. It's obvious that I need surgery, but a couple of doc's told me that they didn't think they could help. I'm at my wits' end, I need help, and I need it soon."

The doc just stared at me for a moment, stone-faced, then said, "Well, I really don't pay much attention to what other docs say – I have a lot more confidence in my own abilities."

Oh sweet Jesus, that's all I needed to hear!

"So when can you cut me?"

Joe was like an infantry commander preparing for battle, and in two minutes flat he knocked off a laundry list of things we would need to accomplish in order to get me under the knife.

"First, I need you to come in for another MRI, because that will give us a more definitive picture of that disc. We'll set up the appointment at the mobile lab at Faulkner for next week. What days are you available?"

"Are you kidding? Seven days a week."

"Okay, good. Now one big problem is the area around the rupture, because there's a lot of inflammation and swelling in there. It's obviously causing a lot of the pain, and it's the reason why you're dragging your leg behind you."

He paused to let that sink in, then continued, "It's also a problem for me, because it makes things more difficult for me to cut when there's all that swelling hampering my view of the rupture.

"So what do we do about it?"

"Well, once we get your surgery scheduled, I'll want you to come in to the office two days a week to receive physical therapy and a massage for your lower back. That will loosen things up, knock down the swelling and inflammation, and it should give us better access and a clearer view of the disc when we go in."

I liked this guy – the Marines were on the way.

"Okay, so what do I do next?"

"We'll call you in a day or two with the date for the MRI. In the meantime I want you to try some simple stretching exercises that will knock down the pain a little. Do you have time to see our physical therapist now?"

You better believe I had time.

And that was that. I finally had my cutter, and I had perhaps the most important commodity that anybody could rent – hope!

≈≈≈

Ulysses dropped me off at the Faulkner late in the morning of Friday, May 26, 1995, which was the first day of the Memorial Day weekend.

I walked through the entrance of that hospital with my pain meter down three notches, almost upright from the physical therapy, full of equal parts hope and acceptance.

We dapped, he wished me well, and then I checked in at the registration desk.

I had been born there forty-four years previously, so I said a silent prayer to my Higher Power that it would be there that I would be reborn.

I was as prepared as I would ever be, physically, mentally and spiritually. I'd been hitting every one of my AA meetings for the prior three weeks, had attended all of my physical therapy and massage appointments, had performed my stretching exercises twice a day on the floor of my room, and was praying like crazy for acceptance.

I travelled light, carrying just a small duffel bag with me, which contained one change of clothes, toiletries, my Big Book, a Frederick Forsyth spy novel, a few well disguised packs of Marlboro's, and a two pound bag of M&M's.

Okay, so maybe I'm still a chocaholic in denial, but after all its progress, not perfection.

≈≈≈

Fortunately, things happened fast after I checked in, so I had no time for thinking or worrying, and that was a good thing – if the cavalry's charging, then I'll charge also.

My room wasn't available yet, so a nurse walked me over to a changing area, where I stripped and put on a johnny, then placed my duffel bag and clothes in a storage locker.

Moments later I was in a wheelchair, being rolled down the hallway to a surgical prep room, where a nurse checked my vitals.

The stats all read "go," and moments later they wheeled me into the operating room and helped me climb onto the operating table.

It was a greenish, cool, antiseptic room, brightly lit, and there were a couple of nurses in operating gowns standing nearby.

Joe Barr walked in a few minutes later, spoke to a nurse, then came over to me and said, "Hi, Wes, you all set?"

"Go for it, Joe, I'm as ready as I'll ever be, so just get this show on the road, I've got a hot date tonight."

He chuckled, then said, "Okay, we're going to administer the anesthesia now."

Seconds later a nurse fitted a mask over my nose and mouth, and Joe said, "Okay, Wes, start counting backwards from 100."

I made it to 94, and that was all I remember, as I slipped into a dream, "Thaaaannkk youuuu Go…"

≈≈≈

I regained consciousness gradually, in stages, feeling similar to what I had experienced on that morning in June, 1992, when I came clawing up and out of my final blackout on the day that I surrendered to my disease.

I was told later that I had asked one of the nurses in post-op to marry me, but I don't remember a moment of it, so I figure she said no.

Oh well, that's been the story of my life – no woman, no cry.

≈≈≈

I was awake and shaking off the last of my stupor around six o'clock that evening.

Nurses came and went, checking my vitals, feeding me meds, and chatting me up to be certain that I was alert and cognizant of my surroundings.

I asked for some water, and a nurse handed me a paper cup and told me to just take a sip for now.

I did so, and then another nurse asked how I was feeling.

"I feel good, just tired, and my back is a little sore."

Actually it was a lot sore, but I had to keep up my tough guy image.

She saw through it, of course, and told me it was nearly time for my pain shot, "so just hang on for a few more minutes."

The doc and I had discussed pain meds back when we were scheduling surgery. I told him that I was an alcoholic and addict in recovery, and that I was okay with taking them for post-op pain relief, as needed, but that I didn't want to use the morphine pump. To me that would be like shooting myself up, and that wasn't a comfortable feeling. I had never taken that final step, hitting the needle, so the thought of self-medicating myself made me nervous.

In my head it was okay for a nurse to inject me, but I just couldn't do it to myself - it crossed a boundary that I didn't want to cross.

So ten minutes later a nice lady came in, had me roll over onto my side, stuck a needle in my hip, and ohhh, geeeeeewhizz, the pain slipped away as I floated off into another technicolor dreamscape.

≈≈≈

Another nice lady brought in a big dish of ice cream and some ginger ale around ten that evening, and it was one of the best meals I have ever had. In fact, it was just as good as the meal I had on that first night I arrived for my last stay at Beech Hill, in 1992, except this time the French fries were missing.

That night had been the start of a new life for me, and now this night was turning out to be a new chapter as well.

Thirty minutes later I asked a nurse whether they had brought my belongings up to the room, and she replied, "Yes, they're on the chair right next to your bed."

That's what I wanted to hear. I had my illegal stash in there, my M&M's and my Marlboro reds, but before I could roll over and try to get at them I slipped off into another dream.

≈≈≈

Doc Barr checked up on me a couple of times that afternoon, while I was coming out of my dream state downstairs in post-op.

Then, satisfied that everything had gone perfectly, he drove up to the coast of down-east Maine, and was soon tacking ahead of a warm southwest wind as he took a well-deserved sailing weekend on his 40 foot schooner.

For each of the next two years I would bring in a big box of chocolates for his staff on the anniversary date of my surgery – it was just this drunk's way of showing my gratitude.

≈≈≈

I descended out of another fuzzy dream around eight o'clock the next morning, and several moments later a nurse came in to administer another pain shot, and ask me what I wanted for breakfast.

I ordered toast, cereal and coffee, then she jabbed me and went on her way.

For the first time since they wheeled me upstairs I now had the opportunity to study my surroundings. I was situated in a semi-private room that was set up to hold two patients, but there hadn't been anyone in the other bed since I came out of the anesthesia the prior evening, and that was fine by me.

My bed was situated about five feet from the lavatory door, so I began to scope out my first stealth visit to the loo. You'd think I was prepping for a trip to Europe, but my head and my body weren't coordinating all that well yet, and the pain shot was adding an extra layer of confusion to my already garbled thought processes.

Nevertheless, I was on a mission, and I was determined to complete it before my breakfast arrived.

I took a deep breath, then pushed myself up and off the side of the bed, and cautiously inched my way over to the lavatory door. I pushed it open, crept inside, then shut and locked the door behind me.

Victory! Now it was time for my reward, so I turned on the shower, hoping that the hot, steaming water would obscure the cigarette smoke. Then I pulled out my pack of Marlboro's and my Zippo, extracted a cigarette, and in seconds I was in nicotine Heaven.

That may have been the best cigarette I ever tasted, although that's not really saying very much when you consider all of the swell health benefits that nicotine provides.

Five minutes later I was back in bed, and moments later a nice nurse came in with my breakfast. I noticed that she seemed to sniff the air once or twice, but made no comment, so I figured that my ruse had worked.

I played my stealth smoking game for the next two days, and it was only on Monday morning that a nurse told me that the staff had been on to my game since the beginning.

"Did you really think we're so gullible, or that you're the first smoker who's tried to put one over on us?" she chided. "To tell the truth, we wanted you to get up, and to start moving around as soon as possible, because it helps to get your bodily functions returning to normal," she laughed.

Swell, you live and you learn.

Four months later I stopped smoking, embarked upon an aggressive exercise regimen, and never looked back.

It was the second best thing I ever did for myself, so thank you, God.

≈≈≈

I got busy over that weekend. There were doctors' check-ups, a conga line of nurses tending to my every need, poking and prodding and pushing me to get out of bed, a dozen visitors to entertain, one unauthorized trip downstairs to smell some fresh spring air, and three fifteen minute walks a day up and down the corridor dragging my IV tree alongside me.

If you've ever seen a photo of a doped up middle-aged guy staggering down a hallway in a poorly-fitted hospital johnny, leaning on the tree with his bare butt hanging out, that was probably me, but thanks to the lingering effects of my morphine shots I didn't feel self-conscious at all.

I'm sure that God was getting a big kick out of that pathetic scene, although I'm not so sure that anyone who encountered me in the corridor did.

≈≈≈

On Monday morning, Memorial Day, 1995, my AA buddy Bryan W. picked me up at the hospital and drove me out to the sober house, where the first resident to greet me said:

"Hey, cool, Wes, welcome back - it looks like we won't need to build a handicap ramp for you after all!"

Man, you've just gotta love that sick sober house humor!

I walked out the front door of the Faulkner standing straight and tall that day, free of all but a slight residue of pain, full of equal parts hope and confidence.

I was a survivor, I was sober, and I may have been the most grateful person on Earth that morning.

I went to a meeting in Framingham that night, and I hit one a day for the next week, and spoke at each.

My topic? Gratitude.

≈≈≈

It took a while for me to adjust to the reality that I was free from that debilitating pain. After all, my existence had revolved around it 24/7 for eighteen months, and then suddenly one day a strange void took its place, like it had never existed. That had also been the case with my alcoholism and addiction, because I felt like a stranger in a strange land for several months after I returned home from my last trip to the Alps.

But I suppose that people can adapt to almost anything, given enough time. I mean, that's how we've survived for forty or fifty thousand years, isn't it, by adapting, accepting, even nurturing change?

So doesn't it always just come back to TIME, "Things I Must Earn?"

≈≈≈

Slowly but surely I returned to the world of the living. There was some post-op discomfort related to the actual cutting that the doc did, but it dispersed within several days, and the horrific pain that ran down my leg into my foot had been absent almost since the moment I came out of the anesthesia.

Except for a few days of residual "pain memory" my body had received the all-clear signal, and even my head and my heart were coming around to this new state of awareness.

With healing comes hope, confidence, and a healthy outlook on life, and I was suddenly blessed with an abundance of these attributes, so I attacked every new day like the precious gift that it was.

I didn't intend to waste any time, so I took a short, cautious walk around the block on the afternoon that I returned home from the hospital. I kept it simple, basic, nothing fancy, nothing aggressive, just a nice relaxing stroll, no stress, no adrenaline, and no competition with myself.

I took long, slow, relaxing breaths, celebrated the beauty of the spring foliage, exchanged greetings with passersby, and just enjoyed being out in the warm spring sunshine for ten minutes.

The next day I walked a few hundred yards down to the center of town to pick up a newspaper, and the following day I did the same thing, and soon I was up to a half-mile a day, then a mile, little by slow, no stress, no worry.

There's been some occasional pain that's remained with me over the years, but it's generally manageable, just enough to release some endorphins and catch a free high from life.

Whatever the walking did for my body, I quickly discovered that it did more for my head, and soon I was hooked. To this day I continue to take a daily walk, or hit the gym, and exercise has become my go-to remedy for combatting the stress and occasional chaos of life on Planet Earth.

≈≈≈

I celebrated my third year of sobriety a couple of weeks after my surgery, and then I went a little crazy – premeditated crazy, perhaps, but some would say crazy nonetheless.

Or maybe I was just coming down off the PTSD, the post-traumatic stress disorder, but whatever the case I went on a fun little adventure.

On Wednesday, June 21, the first day of summer, 1995, I drove up to Laconia, New Hampshire. It was a warm, sunny day, a perfect start to the season, but I wasn't there for a tan. No, I had a mission that I had been planning ever since my operation, so instead of a nice nap on the beach I spent two and one-half hours in a tattoo artist's chair.

The inker's name was Rock, and he carved a magnificent mythical creature into my shoulder.

That wasn't my first tat, but nevertheless you never get used to the pain, and that day was no exception. But this was summer, a new season, and all the hounds in Hell weren't going to stop me. I was a new man, free, sober, full of hope and confidence for the first time in years, so I celebrated in style.

Yes, it hurt, but now I knew the game, so for me pain was just another brick in the wall, and proof positive that I was still sucking air.

I walked across the street to a local restaurant after I left the ink shop, and ordered a jumbo bacon cheeseburger with fries. It hit the spot, but I was still famished, so I ordered up a hot fudge sundae with all the extras, then demolished it in five minutes flat.

Mission accomplished, I drove back to Framingham in time to hit a meeting, then slept like a baby that night.

≈≈≈

And so it went as my perfect summer continued to roll along, and I was amazed at the speed by which I regained my physical strength as a result of my daily walks, and the stretching exercises that Doc Barr's massage therapist had given me.

Even then there was still a small amount of residual pain, but it was manageable as long as I didn't try to be a hero, kept to a moderate exercise regimen, stretched my back muscles a couple of times a day, and kept the excess weight off.

Oh, and I always had a good supply of Ibuprofen on hand, and I thanked God several times a day for delivering me to the unique place that I inhabit in the world. I've never been able to figure out the why or the wherefore, but gratitude always seems to reduce my pain levels in direct proportion to the amount of that gratitude.

I also made it down to Duxbury Beach a few times, where I enjoyed the warm sunshine, read my books, and swam in the cold Atlantic waters. I soon discovered that floating took all of the pressure off my back, while gently restoring my natural posture, and everything seemed to automatically realign itself without any effort on my part.

I guess you'd call it going with the flow, rather than fighting it, and that seems to be a practice that works in most areas of my life these days.

So I did my physical rehabilitation program that summer, hit a lot of AA meetings, attended my counseling sessions with Pat, and enjoyed my new life while God prepared the next phase of His plan for me.

And that phase was a doozy, because God had decided that Wes would be taking up residence in a nuns' retirement home.

Because, like, why not?

≈≈≈

I received the call from Frank, the SMOC general manager, during the last week in August.

He was brief and to the point:

"Wes, I hear good things about you, and I'm glad to hear that your rehab is going well, so I need to discuss something with you!"

Hmm, what was this all about? I was attempting to maintain a stealth existence at the sober house, and just stick to my rehab program while I tried to figure out what direction to take my life in, so friendly calls from out of the blue by general managers weren't the norm in WesWorld, not unless I was in trouble of some sort.

"Hi, Frank," I said cautiously, "Yeah, things are a lot better, that's for sure. How're things over at SMOC?"

"Well, that's what I wanted to talk to you about."

Uh-oh. Now what?

"Ok, sure, did you get my last rent check?"

He chuckled, then said, "Yes, you're in good shape with us, I'm just calling because I want to make a proposition to you."

Double uh-oh. Behind his friendly demeanor lurked that one ominous word that still scared the bejesus out me – CHANGE!

"A proposition?"

"Yeah. You've been through a lot, but you stayed sober and you handled it well, except for that furniture stuff," he chuckled, "so I'm wondering whether you might want to take on a position within the organization."

Hmm, that was the last thing I expected to hear that day, and who ratted me out about the furniture?

"A position, you mean a job? Doing what? I still have a lot of rehab to do, and heavy physical work is out of the question from here on in."

"I understand, but this is an entirely different situation, and it shouldn't involve much physical activity."

"Okay, I'm all ears."

"Are you familiar with our 'New Beginnings' program?"

"Well, I've heard of it, but I don't know anything else about it, except that it's where James T. works, right?"

James T. was a friend of mine who had been a resident in one of the other SMOC sober houses in town. He had dropped in frequently at Union Avenue, and I had run into him at many of the Framingham area meetings, but come to think of it, I hadn't seen him for quite a while.

"Yes, he's the night manager over there, and he lives on the floor. What else do you know about the program?"

"Nothing much."

"Okay, well 'New Beginnings' is a residential program for recovering alcoholics and drug addicts who have contracted the HIV virus. Jim's been the night manager there for about a year, but now he's moving on to other responsibilities within the organization, so we're looking for a person with some maturity and good longer term sobriety who might want to take over his position."

He paused, then asked, "Would you be interested in talking about it?"

Wow, that was a bolt out of the blue!

I had heard about the program, but I didn't know any of the details. This was the mid- '90's, so the AIDS epidemic was just beginning to explode in the United States, and in addition to Ulysses I knew a half dozen other men and women in recovery who had contracted the virus. I had a lot of respect for them, because going through all of the pain and hard work of getting sober while you fought another lethal disease like HIV/AIDS must have been about the most daunting challenge a person could ever face.

I realized that Ulysses and the rest of those friends took that hard, lonely walk every minute of every day to remain clean and sober while they fought their own disease issues, and then I realized that I had a lot to be grateful for. Early on in my using life I recognized that the needle was the one thing that would surely kill me, and through luck and circumstance I had never ended up at the wrong place at the wrong time when it would have seemed oh so cool to slip a needle into my arm just to see what all the mystery was about.

My Higher Power had been looking over me during all of those insane years, and as I felt a rush of gratitude sweep through me I recalled a saying that I had heard many times in the Halls, "Faith without works is dead."

I got the message loud and clear - it always seemed to come around to "walking my talk," so I did.

"Sure, I'd be interested in talking. What's the deal?"

Frank gave me the details, and ten minutes later we hung up. Then I made the call to Sister Betsy, who ran the program across town, and we set up a time for me to drop by for a talk the next day.

≈≈≈

I had a long conversation with God that night. He was very enthusiastic about my new opportunity, as I knew He would be, because after all He had been the one pulling the strings in the first place.

"So you think I should take it, if she offers it?"

"Yes, my son, in a heartbeat - it will do you good."

And with that He was off to create a few million new planets somewhere out in the Pleiades neighborhood.

Geez, I could never have handled that dude's travel itinerary.

≈≈≈

Sister Betsy was one of those extraordinary individuals who, if we're fortunate, we may meet once or twice in a lifetime.

She was much younger than I had expected, in her early thirties, and she operated from a selfless, guileless love for her residents, and for mankind, that bordered on fierceness.

But hers was a fierceness borne of unconditional love, and of an unwavering passion to help the ill, the suffering, and the innocents, and on their behalf she was uncompromising, a force for good such as I have rarely encountered in my life.

She was also a woman who was very hard to say "no" to, as I discovered ten minutes into our meeting - it was just about impossible not to buy into her passion and world view.

The job description was straightforward. Sister Betsy was looking for a sober person to live onsite with the residents of the program, and to act as the night and weekend supervisor. I wouldn't receive a salary, but I would have my own rent-free room, which included a private bath and kitchenette, and my primary function would be to watch over the residents during the nighttime hours and weekends, when Betsy and her assistant were usually off.

The program was located in a six floor residential building that also housed battered women and children, as well as retired nuns. There were approximately one dozen residents in the New Beginnings program at the time, with one or two occupants to a room.

This was a sober-only program, so I would be responsible for helping Betsy and Jane, her assistant, keep it that way.

The key requisite would be to maintain an environment that was quiet and respectful of others, and which would allow the residents to feel safe at all times. I would maintain an inventory of their medications, to be distributed nightly and on weekends, and I also kept a supply of urine sample kits that would be used to obtain samples if I suspected that a resident was using illegal drugs or alcohol.

I was also on call nights and weekends for driving ill residents to the ER at the downtown hospital.

And that was about it. This was a "job" unlike any I had ever expected to take on, but for some strange reason it seemed to be a natural for where I was at that particular point in my life, and in my recovery.

So if I thought that I had walked my talk over the past three years, I had now been presented with the perfect opportunity to walk, talk and live it 24/7.

I rented a small U-Haul that Saturday, and Ulysses and one of the other residents at Union Avenue gave me a hand moving my small inventory of furniture and personal belongings over to the facility, and that was that – Wes was now living in a nun's retirement home.

But, once again, why not? Somehow it made perfect sense to me, because after all it was just another brick in the wall, another step on the road to redemption for this grateful alcoholic.

≈≈≈

I settled into my new life on the residential floor at New Beginnings rather quickly, and without any disruption to my own recovery program.

It turned out that I was familiar with several of the residents, at least by sight, because they attended some of the same local AA meetings that I went to.

It was encouraging to see those familiar faces, and it was good to know that there was already a well-established culture of recovery within the community.

I quickly developed a great respect for the residents, because they exhibited exceptional courage in the face of a devastating illness, they hit their meetings regularly, and they stayed clean and sober, no matter what. Some of them also held part time jobs, which kept them engaged in the outside world, and which endowed them with a sense of purpose and responsibility. These people lived their lives to the fullest, and no disease, be it from a virus, or a bottle, or a syringe, was ever going to prevent them from putting one foot in front of the other and doing the next right thing for themselves, and for their loved ones.

I thought then of John F. Kennedy's book, *Profiles in Courage*, and I believe that he could have devoted an entire chapter to some of those beautiful people.

≈≈≈

Days turned into weeks, then months. I continued to attend my AA meetings, went to bi-weekly counseling with Pat, and performed my duties on the floor. The group of residents remained relatively stable – one would leave now and then to live in the local community, usually with their children, and then another would arrive and I'd assist Betsy and her assistant with acclimating that person to his or her new environment.

I also continued to work gratis a dozen or so hours a week at the chiropractor's office, and several months after I moved into Bethany I slapped a nicotine patch on my arm and finally let go of a twenty-five year addiction to smoking. That disease had killed my mother at the age of fifty-eight, so I had witnessed firsthand the damage that nicotine could do to a human being – it was hideous. So now was the time, while my life was relatively stable, to let go of my last major addiction.

Two hours after I slapped the patch on, I stepped into a new pair of running shoes and ran a half mile in the cool, clear autumn air. It's true what they say about getting a runner's high, and this was better than anything I ever experienced during twenty-five years of drinking and drugging.

So, being the addict that I was, I got hooked on running, and was soon doing twenty-five miles a week. My back wasn't thrilled at times, so I had to take plenty of time-outs, but I jogged until my runner's knees gave out on me fifteen years later.

By then, however, I was living in the mountains of Vermont, so I took up hiking and snowshoeing, and was soon spending several hours a day exploring the pristine wilderness of the Mad River Valley.

≈≈≈

Not surprisingly, it was the occasional resident who wasn't in a recovery program, or who wasn't working his or her program diligently, who turned out to be the most difficult to oversee at Bethany. That was a very small minority, but it accounted for much of the drama on the floor, because these individuals didn't have the requisite structure and discipline in their lives that accompanies sobriety, or the willingness to change.

I walked residents down to the office lavatory twice during my year's residency on the floor, then stood outside while they produced samples that were sent out for testing for the presence of alcohol or drugs.

On one occasion the results came back positive, and the resident was removed from the program.

In another case a resident's disease had progressed to the extent that he was experiencing dementia. It was heartbreaking to have to remove him from the program, but he had become unmanageable, and was causing a lot of distractions for other residents who were working hard on their own recovery issues.

Fortunately, he was admitted to another facility for people whose disease had progressed to where they weren't capable of functioning on their own.

As a little kid I had heard my share of stories about nuns being strict disciplinarians, but I held a nun in my arms while she cried her heart out when that resident was transferred out of the program - enough said.

≈≈≈

The moment finally arrived when I knew that it was time to take another step on my life's journey.

My stay at Bethany Hill had been a wonderful experience. I had learned a lot about people, about the courage to stare down one's fears, to remain calm in the face of life's storms, and more about myself, but now it was time to move on. I had a strong base of sobriety, my body was healing from all of the damage I had caused it, and little by slow I was learning to become a responsible citizen of the world.

I'd had more than my fair share of baby steps, detours and dead-ends along the journey, but now I felt a renewed sense of purpose, and of confidence in my ability to participate in life, to show up and try to make a difference, and so I moved on.

In the late spring of 1996, four years sober, I moved into a small bungalow two towns away, in Millis, Massachusetts. It was located about five miles from my Medfield meetings, so this was a homecoming of sorts. My AA buddy Andy gave me a hand with the move, and it was a great feeling to repatriate what was left of my overpriced Scandinavian furniture from the storage facility where it had gathered dust for several years.

The furniture may have looked a little out of place in its new surroundings, but I was living on my own again, independent and free, so I wouldn't have cared if I was living in a building full of wooden crates.

I had selected a residence that was adjacent to a large tract of private farms and town conservation lands, with scenic country roads and sparse traffic. It was the perfect spot for indulging in my new addiction – jogging. I was never destined to be a long distance runner, and my fidgety back wasn't going to tolerate high mileage training, but I could do four or five miles, four or five days a week, and that kept me in great shape physically, mentally and emotionally. I ran in the sun, the rain, and the snow, and the combination of that placid country scenery, the wildlife, and the sense of peace that lifted my spirits every time I ventured out for a run was medicine for my soul.

≈≈≈

I remained in Millis for six years. It was a time of personal growth, introspection and healing, a period in my life where I immersed myself in Alcoholics Anonymous, explored, tested my limits, peered inwardly and took chances.

I had become fascinated by the explosive growth of the technology industry, and over the few short years since I had been selling and developing application software there had been momentous developments in the field.

Hardware capacity was doubling every eighteen months, as predicted in the 1960's by Intel CEO Gordon Moore's famous Law, and these new high-powered chips and drives were fueling an explosion of software programs that benefitted not only corporate America, but even Main Street USA and the consumer market.

And, now that I had a clear head and some self-discipline, I decided to ride the wave.

My back would never be capable of standing for long periods of time, or for crawling around behind banks of computers, plugging wires and swapping out boards. But I could work a phone as well as the best of them, so I took on a series of gigs pitching hardware and software services to various verticals, particularly in the banking and healthcare industries.

I also went back to school for some software certifications that I needed, and I helped perform the Year 2000 bank testing certifications for a dozen small savings banks and credit unions in Massachusetts.

Frank, the guy I was doing the Y2K testing for, had been my boss about eight years previously. He had been the sales manager at a banking software development company, and after I had been on the job for six months it was his duty to fire me for nonperformance.

Well, that was the polite term for it anyway – alcoholism, incompetence, chronic hangover-related absenteeism and a few other terms would have been more appropriate descriptions of my job performance back then.

But for whatever reason we had stayed in touch afterwards, and now, eight years later, he asked me to come on board to help out on his Y2K and bank telemarketing efforts.

Frank gave me a chance, where most probably wouldn't have, and I worked hard for him. They say payback is a bummer, but I say it's a gift from above, and in my case the greatest example of redemption that I could ever have dreamed possible.

So thanks for that, Buddy, I owe you one.

≈≈≈

One of my fellow students at the network engineering course that I attended in the late '90's was a likeable young kid named Peter. He was twenty years old, seriously intelligent, and he had a gift for solving complex computer problems.

About a month into school he disappeared for a week, then showed up at class one night on crutches.

At the break I inquired as to what had happened, and he told me that he rolled his car over on the way home from a job selling beer at a rock concert at Foxboro Stadium. It seems that he had been sampling his own wares just a wee bit too much, and he ended up with a broken foot and some cuts and bruises, but miraculously he survived what could have been a fatal accident.

Then he asked, "My parents and sister have been driving me around until I get the cast off, but I was wondering if you might be able to give me a ride home from school in the meantime. I can get over here okay, but it's getting home that's a problem."

I knew that he lived one town away from me, and that it wouldn't be much out of my way, so I said, "Sure."

I got to know Peter well over the next several months. He was a sharp kid, and during the twenty minute drive to his house we had some great conversations about life, goals, and the search for happiness. I mentioned early on that I was a recovering alcoholic, but I never put the rush on him to examine his own drinking. I told him bits and pieces about my own story when it seemed appropriate, and a couple of anecdotes about the great crew of guys at the TSDD meetings, but I left it at that.

I knew that the last thing on my mind when I was twenty years old would have been trying to face up to the fact that I didn't drink like "ordinary" people, so I just planted the seed, and I figured that he would know who to call if the time ever came when he needed help.

Computer school wrapped up in the late spring of 1999, so Peter and I went our separate ways. I was heavily involved in the Y2K preparations by then, plus hitting many of the Medfield meetings, and pursuing my jogging program, so I didn't call to inquire how he was doing. I just figured that if I was him I'd be partying on, and not very interested in hearing from a boring old sober fart.

Little did I know…

≈≈≈

The call came a couple of days after New Year's.

It was Peter, and in a somber voice he said, "Hi, Wes, I was wondering if you have a moment, I need to talk to you."

"Sure," I said, smiling to myself, because his tone had already ratted him out. I heard the unmistakable sound of defeat and surrender in his voice, so I asked, "How's life treating you these days, Peter?"

"Uh, not so great," he said, barely audible, "I had a jackpot on New Year's Eve, the police stopped me and took me into protective custody. I guess you were right when you said that some of us just can't drink like ordinary people."

"Well, I'm awful sorry to hear that, but maybe this is a good thing, a message that it's time to throw away some of the toys. You're a good man, Peter, and young and smart, so you can have a great life ahead of you if you stay sober."

"Would you be able to take me to an AA meeting?"

"Sure, in fact it just so happens that I'm going to one in Medfield tonight, so why don't you come over here, and we'll drive over together. Can you make it by seven?"

"Sure, I'll see you then."

And that was that. It was early January, 2000, and for Peter it was the start of a new century, and a new life.

He now has nineteen years of continuous sobriety, a wife and five children, a great job in the technology industry, and the greatest gift of all — the peace of mind that comes when we surrender to life, and do the next right thing for ourselves and the people we love.

And so the message of recovery rolls on, as the virtuous cycle of surrender, healing and redemption remains unbroken one alcoholic at a time, one day at a time, one moment at a time, and one heartbeat at a time.

≈≈≈

Okay, so one day in 2003 I decided on pretty much the spur of the moment that I'd move back to Florida.

Florida? Seriously?

Yes, I know what you're thinking, and you have every right to, is this guy crazy, and did he not learn anything from his disastrous moves down there in the '80's?

Well, perhaps not exactly crazy, although being sober doesn't necessarily rule that out.

But this time, at least, I had the good judgement to move to the Left Coast, rather than to the Right, which kept me safely away from Miami, and by virtue of being sober for eleven years I had been granted the clarity of mind to think through the pros and cons of an important life decision like this.

Bottom line, I had developed wanderlust, a desire to explore, and to seek out new adventures and opportunities, and I had the confidence in myself, and in my recovery, to take a calculated risk, so why not now?

And, besides, the snows were approaching rapidly, and I was damned if I was going to tolerate another New England winter.

≈≈≈

In early October, 2003, the Onion moved in with a sober friend, his wife and their five cats. They had a nice home right across the street from the beach in Fort Myers, so it was just what the doctor had ordered.

I went to an AA meeting my first night in town, picked up a meeting list, and began making the rounds. I soon found a sales job in technology, moved into my own place, and all of a sudden I had a brand new sober life in a nice part of the world.

And never once did the thought of picking up a drink enter my mind.

Geewhiz, gratitude's a wonderful thing!

≈≈≈

I remained in touch with Pat R., my counselor and friend, after the move to Florida. He had been a major contributor to my sobriety, and had always been there for me whenever it appeared that my life was going seriously off the rails.

And, yes, he was a great golfer who had helped this hacker put together a decent game on occasion.

So one day in March, 2006, I called him, and we cooked up a scam to get him down to Florida for a few rounds of golf and some good eating over the Easter holiday.

The plan was simple enough – he'd tell his wife that Wes was having a major personal crisis, so he felt it was his professional responsibility to come down to help me weather the storm.

To which his not so naïve wife asked, "And that would be why you're taking your golf clubs with you?"

What can I say, it's an honest program – usually.

≈≈≈

I would remain in Florida for three years before my new pal, Mr. Wanderlust, convinced me that those hot, steamy Florida summers were screaming out that it was time for Wes to make another change of address.

For the first time in years I was in great financial shape. Thanks to sobriety, and the clarity of mind and self-confidence that accompanied it, I had been successfully day-trading stocks, and had built up a nice nest egg.

I figured that I could live pretty much anywhere my heart desired if I had an internet connection for trading, so the search began in the winter of 2005/2006.

Not coincidentally, the state of Florida had experienced five direct hurricane hits the previous summer, which put a serious dent in my optimism about living year-round in the "Sunshine State," so I intended to relocate to a hurricane-free zone.

The search didn't take long. I had attended college in central Vermont in the early seventies, and I had always thought that I would like to take up residence there someday. Its mountains, scenic beauty, laid-back lifestyles and low population base had beckoned to me over the years, and now I knew that the time was right.

I performed a quick search on the internet, and discovered that Warren, Vermont, fit all of my needs. It was located smack dab in the middle of the Green Mountain National Forest and Mad River Valley, and, yes, it had an internet infrastructure.

I searched some on-line rental sites, and within a week I had located the perfect residence, so I took a leap of faith and signed a one-year lease to live in the ground floor apartment of a two-story ski house. The owners were rabid skiers, so they'd be living upstairs most weekends during the winter, but otherwise I would have the place pretty much to myself.

It was a great fit, so I sold off my furniture and drove up to Vermont in late April, 2006, my car stuffed to overflowing with all of my remaining earthly possessions.

It might have been late April, but it snowed the first night I arrived in Vermont.

Nonetheless, after three hot years in Florida a little snow was welcome, so I went outside and threw snowballs at the trees.

They seemed to take it all in stride, and I soon learned that up there everybody seemed to take everything in stride, all the time, so maybe, just maybe, Wes could do so as well.

That night I slept like a baby, dreamless in the pitch-black, perfect silence that one can only experience in the backwoods of the mountains.

≈≈≈

Okay, so here's the thing about being an alcoholic on a run – you stop having choices, you surrender your free will, your decisions are made for you by the bottle and the coke spoon, and you become a prisoner to the darkest forces of human nature, both yours and those of the addicts you chose to run with.

That had been my history for twenty-five years, but now I had become absorbed in my AA recovery by virtue of a spiritual awakening that had crept innocuously into my life. My sobriety impacted all areas of my existence, and it was the one stabilizing element that I could always depend upon. It was the pillar, the touchstone for my freedom, and it allowed me to make the transition from Florida to Vermont living without a hitch.

Everything slowed down up there, and I stopped worrying about the future, lamenting the mistakes of my past, or searching for something "better," because "here and now" was perfection in and of itself.

I thrived in the laid-back atmosphere of the Mad River Valley, found some great AA meetings, and met many wonderful recovering people. For perhaps the first time in my life I experienced a feeling of being at home, at being at one with my surroundings, and with the world at large.

Over the next eighteen months I learned the true meaning of gratitude, as my life rolled quietly along in the pristine hills and forests of Vermont.

I recalled then the humble words of Carl Sagan, astronomer, intellectual and humanitarian, who just before his death had written that Planet Earth was "a mote of dust suspended in a sunbeam" in a vast universe of billions of galaxies.

Well, if that was the case, I wondered, what did that make me?

How about just another Bozo on the bus, and in Vermont I was perfectly content with that.

But I'm a Bozo who loves you, so like my first sponsor, Jack, told me, "and there's absolutely nothing you can do about that."

≈≈≈

And then one day my Higher Power said, "Let it snow," and man, did it ever!

The winter and spring of 2006–2007 almost set a state record for snowfall. More than two hundred inches of the white stuff fell that year, including a fifty-inch classic on Valentine's Day, and we experienced not one, but two mud seasons that turned the dirt roads into axle-deep quagmires for weeks at a time.

I lived on a hill, on a dirt road, so need I say more?

But thanks to the teachings of AA I persevered, and adapted, and made the most of things.

In a word, and as difficult as it was occasionally, I practiced acceptance.

So I made it to my meetings, learned to stock up on a couple of weeks' worth of canned goods, kept plenty of dry firewood on hand, carried a tub of dirt and sand in the trunk of my car, snowshoed nearly every day in the pristine wilderness of the surrounding forests, and made damned sure that I would nevuh, evuh, spend anothuh wintuh in Vermont!

You see, I had learned a simple rule of life that I still adhere to - when the squirrels start nesting on your engine block in late October, you know it's time to slip out of town.

So I became a commutuh, as they say in Vermont, or as they say in Florida, a snow bird.

I was able to spend another perfect summer in the Mad River Valley, however, and then on a whim I decided to head south to St. Augustine Beach just after the first Vermont autumn snows fell.

That became my travel itinerary for the next four years. I commuted between Florida and Vermont every six months, hauled all of my worldly possessions in my car, traded stocks, lived simply, seamlessly and unencumbered in rented condos at each end, and accepted life on life's terms.

That lifestyle might not have been a good fit for everyone, but for me it was perfect, and just what the doctor and my gimpy back and knees ordered for that period of my life.

And, as an added bonus, I was able to hang out with my AA friends at both ends of the east coast.

I was learning, little by slow, that by reaching out to engage life, take chances, open myself up to the wisdom and infinite opportunities of the Universe, take a leap of faith, and venture outside of my self-made boundaries, I was able to navigate the path to a serenity that carried me through the good, the bad and the indifferent.

Life, for me, became simple then, and I finally understood that the only challenge I could fail at was the one that I didn't attempt.

Part Five: Independence Day

"The secret of this kind of climbing is like Zen.
Don't think. Just dance along."

From the novel, "The Dharma Bums"
by Jack Kerouac

I have been blessed to receive the Gifts of the Paradoxes, for today I am capable of shedding tears in the presence of beauty, to understand that there is always something to be grateful for in the face of defeat, that through surrender I find freedom, that life is not a zero-sum game because by "giving it away" I will always receive more back than I have sacrificed, to believe that a broken heart will always be followed by a smile for having tried, that by "keeping it simple" I can accomplish great things, that in one fleeting kind word or good deed I may change a person's life forever, for having received the grace of God when I was at my worst, for understanding that life is but a dream, here today and gone tomorrow, so I must seize the day, the moment, the light, for life is what we make of it, a gift, and we are all on the stage for just one short blink of God's eyes.

≈≈≈

I awoke from a deep, dreamless slumber shortly after dawn on July 4, 2008.

Daylight was just beginning to peek through my bedroom windows in the condo that I had rented for the six warm months, which was located directly on the Village Run trail at the Sugarbush Ski Area in Warren, Vermont.

The rising sun's welcoming glow held the promise of a beautiful summer's day in the Green Mountain National Forest, and I had some big plans afoot - big by my standards, anyway.

But first I hit my knees to say my simple daily prayer:

"Good morning, God,

Please, keep me away from a drink and a drug and a cigarette, just for today. And please, God, help me to remain humble and grateful for my sobriety, that I may accept life exactly as it's presented to me today. Please allow me to stay present, centered and aware, and grounded and mindful, and, if I should have the opportunity, please let me help another alcoholic today.

Thy will, not mine, be done.

Thank you, God."

I don't ask for any of the material stuff when I pray, or to fall in love, or to play for the Boston Bruins. I just request the things that will help me maintain my peace of mind, my emotional balance, that magical state of "being" that I had never known for the first forty-one years of my life. I had been far too busy attempting to kill myself with alcohol and drugs to think about much of anything else during most of those years, but now, with sixteen years of sobriety under my belt, I finally understood that the simplest approach to life was also the most productive.

Somewhere along the way I had been granted the gift of powerlessness, and acceptance of that powerlessness, because there are just so many wars I no longer need to fight these days. And, besides, my Higher Power was taking far better care of me than I ever could have done, so why should I try to complicate things?

So I pray, my Higher Power gives me what I need, and I tell Him, "Thank you for keeping me sober" at the end of the day. And that works just fine for me, because as far as my sobriety is concerned I am a big believer in the KISS formula - keep it simple, stupid, ask for help and be grateful for what I have.

I put the coffee on, splashed some cold water on my face, and then dressed for my climb. I planned to be humping up the Village Run Trail by seven o'clock, so I choked down a couple of granola bars, a half dozen vitamins, and two cups of strong black coffee while I did some stretching exercises.

I was out the door, across the yard, and stepping onto the trail a few minutes before seven.

This had all the makings of another classic Vermont summer morning, sunny and cool, and at this time of year the mountains were exploding into the billion hues of verdant green that make the Mad River Valley so special, so welcoming, so restful for the spirit.

There was an energy in the air up here that made me believe there was nothing I couldn't accomplish in my life, that all of the pain and suffering I had put myself through was just part of a plan that was much larger than myself, and that I been destined to be delivered to this one single perfect moment in time.

And now I was free, unbound from the chains of fear, doubt, and insecurity, and I had found redemption in these mountains, and on a beach in Florida, after a lifetime of struggle.

I had known from the time I was a little kid that I belonged out here, in the hills and forests, out in Nature, out on the edge, out where things always made sense to me. It's where I found logic and order and truth and innocence amongst the chaos of my past life, the place where everything fit together like in a puzzle, the only place I ever felt at peace with myself, or with the world, the only place I ever truly understood.

And now I was home.

≈≈≈

It was a tough ascent from where I entered the trail, which was exceptionally steep and rugged here. The first two or three hundred yards were straight up, and dotted with widely scattered moguls, a few rushing streams still draining off the last of the spring rains, and everywhere I trekked there was a carpet of knee deep grass that concealed numerous expanses of entangling, prickly vines and shallow, nasty potholes.

And then there were the chiggers, those tiny, almost invisible insects from Hell, whose bite you never felt until a couple of hours later, but then you'd be scratching that infuriating welt raw for a week or more.

I was in pretty decent shape for an old fart in his mid-fifties. I'd been slinging the weights around, and hiking the mountain roads every day for the past six weeks, since my return from Florida, but nonetheless I was somewhat dizzy and gasping for breath within fifteen minutes after commencing the climb.

Regardless, it felt good to be pushing myself, and I was grateful that I'd brought along my favorite walking stick that I had rescued out of a deadfall several weeks earlier. Gnarled and crooked, like me, it was nevertheless perfect for my needs, and it was coming in handy on this steep section of the trail.

Five minutes later I struggled up to the big ninety-degree turn that marked the start of the sharpest angle of descent on the Run. This was the spot where the skiers got a good finishing kick onto the last downhill segment that I had just climbed.

There, that hadn't been so tough, I thought, even though my heart was pounding in my chest, and there was a roaring sound reverberating in my ears.

But that was all to be expected when you were hiking up here, especially for an old coot, so I paused to catch my breath while I surveyed my progress.

I could barely discern my condo building through the last of the morning's mist, and from this perspective I realized that it had been a decent slog to make it up here.

Then I breathed a sigh of relief as I glanced up the path ahead of me, because this upcoming section of trail was relatively flat and smooth for the next quarter-mile, which meant that I could relax and take in the scenery without worrying about tripping over hidden obstacles, and perhaps breaking an ankle.

After all, it wasn't good form to be helicoptered off the mountain at this time of year, because a Medevac flight over the Roxbury Hills to the hospital in Barre might be considered somewhat of a badge of honor in ski season, but certainly not in the summer.

And as bad as it would be physically, I'd also be branded with the locals' ultimate insult, a "Flatlanduh," and my buddy Jason, born and bred right here in the Valley, would never let me hear the end of it if I were to take a header up here today.

Jason and I had hit it off right from the moment we met at my first Vermont AA meeting in 2006. We were as alike as two peas in a pod, same age, same temperaments, same drinking and drugging history, same life experiences.

But I figured out early on that the Fates had been with us, because we never met up back in the day. The odds suggested that we would have had one hell of a great time for ourselves, but in all likelihood neither of us would have survived to tell the sordid tale.

That's one of those things that an alkie just knows.

≈≈≈

My breathing returned to normal in a couple of minutes, which meant that my conditioning had paid off, so I concluded that all in all it was a fine start to the day. This first leg had been a good appetizer for the challenging main event that would take me all the way up North Lynx Peak, right to the top of Birch Run, and I was getting stoked.

Just as I was about to move off along the level path, however, I noticed a sign posted in front of an auxiliary trail that branched off to the right. It was a warning in big black letters to keep out because of bears.

I hesitated, considering whether to take a quick detour to see whether I might be able to meet up with Yogi as he foraged for his breakfast somewhere down along that section, but I decided against it because I wanted to stick to my schedule, and I had a busy day ahead of me.

And, besides, now that I knew about this restricted area I figured that I'd be humping back up here soon enough to check it out. I considered the sign to be a friendly challenge, almost an invitation rather than a warning, because most of the time you were safe if you ran across black bears up here. They were more frightened of people than we were of them, and who could blame them?

Unless, of course, it was a Momma with cubs, fresh out of the winter den, because then you'd better beat feet fast.

*****

This next trail segment always reminded me of an arboreal tunnel as it snaked its way through the ancient forest, or the interior of a massive natural cathedral, the trees crowning into a perfect arch far above my head. I took this opportunity to relax and take a swig from my water bottle, then stepped off along the smooth, wooded incline.

The air was warming up nicely, and through the occasional breaks in the trees I was able to observe that the sky was crystal clear, imbued with the deep blue celestial tint that you only notice up here in the northern mountains, where the atmosphere is thinner.

I hadn't seen another living creature since I left the condo, except for some songbirds that were chirping away, keeping me company, serenading me.

All I could think was, "Thank you, God, for delivering me to this perfect place, on this perfect day!"

I found myself thanking my Higher Power frequently during the course of most days. It had become a reflex action – when something good, or beautiful, or enlightening, or just out of the ordinary occurred, the first words to pop into my head were always, "Thank you, God," because these daily nuggets never failed to fire my gratitude for being sober, and alive.

Those three simple words had become my mantra, and oddly enough the more I thanked Him, the more He seemed to bestow His grace upon me - it's funny how that works, eh?

≈≈≈

I soon exited from under the canopy of trees, and found myself in a large open space that always reminded me of a science fiction alien landing zone, just like the ones that I had read about in the hundreds of sci-fi books I had devoured as a shy, lonely little kid.

This area was a hub for several chair lifts and a gondola that serviced this part of the complex, but the machinery looked so out of place amongst the rest of the natural surroundings that it always sent my rather fertile imagination running wild with outer space fantasies.

Fortunately, however, Gort didn't step out of his spaceship on this perfect morning, which meant that the Onion was the sole Earthling on these Plains of Saturn, so I spent a few minutes catching my breath and checking out the views across the Mad River Valley, toward the scenic Roxbury Hills that lay four miles to the east.

I had lived over that way for eighteen months when I first returned to Vermont two years previously, and I had enjoyed hiking those hills that teemed with moose, black bears, deer, foxes and all manner of other wildlife.

I had also experienced many serene afternoons in the heart of winter while snowshoeing through knee-deep powder in that cold, silent forest, alone save for the company of my Higher Power and the occasional hawk or great horned owl circling silently overhead.

It was easy to understand how Thoreau and Emerson must have felt nearly two centuries previously.

The views from the top of the Mountain Gap Road that looked west across the Valley, back toward where I now stood, were spectacular. There had been nothing more exhilarating than to stand at the top of the Gap in the springtime, observing a hawk as it caught a thermal and went spiraling on the updraft thousands of feet into the clouds - would that I could be free to soar like those magnificent creatures!

And then I laughed at the irony of it all, as it struck me that I was already free, and a rush of gratitude and adrenaline coursed through me as I gazed across the quiet valley. I was free from the alcohol, free from the drugs, free from fear, free from the bondage of self. Sixteen years sober and by the grace of God and the fellowship of AA I had my life back. I had choices today, and I never had to feel lost or alone ever again.

And as the price for my liberation all I needed to do was live my life in one simple little time machine that existed for one day at a time, one hour at a time, one minute at a time, one heartbeat at a time, or whatever it took.

In the end it was all so simple, yet it had taken me most of my life to figure it out.

But I had survived, unlike many of my drinking and drugging friends who had passed on, either sober or still using, and who were now memorialized by drops of blood flowing down from a dragon's claw that had been carved into my shoulder in solemn remembrance. Praise be to the noble Dragon, guardian of the gates to Heaven and watchman of my soul, may they rest in peace.

And there, but for the grace of God go I, for I was celebrating this Independence Day on behalf of them as much as for myself.

I glanced at my watch. It was time, so I took a long swallow of water and a deep, cleansing breath, then made my way over to the base of Birch Run.

≈≈≈

It was a beautiful trail, perfect in its symmetry, straight and wide and steep, dissolving into the deep blue northern heavens at the top of the peak.

In the distance I could make out a birch glade about three quarters of the way up the slope that divided the upper part of the trail into equal halves, and that glade was my goal. I knew that the views would be spectacular from that vantage point, so I leaned sharply into the narrow dirt path that bordered the trail and stepped off at an aggressive pace.

It was only a little after eight o'clock, but the sun was already warming the still mountain air, so I soon broke out into a light sweat from my exertions. This was one steep trail, my blood was pumping hard, and I was grateful that I'd been doing the heavy workouts every day.

I stopped after fifteen minutes to catch my breath and take a mouthful of water, then again ten minutes later - I was almost there.

Finally, my breath ragged and coming in rasps, I turned off the path and into the knee-deep grass that blanketed Birch Run.

I moved slowly, reverently, into the center of the glade, then laid down, corpselike, floating gently on a rippling sea of green.

I found myself then in a field of smiling wildflowers waving gently in the breeze. They appeared to number a thousand or more, weaving, undulating, flowing effortlessly along the soft currents of air, each one bowing politely on the zephyrs as they murmured a kindly greeting to me. And everywhere I looked I was surrounded by butterflies floating languorously on the wind, it seemed another thousand or more, and honey bees dancing from flower to flower, lighting on me, kissing my skin, their soft humming sounds lulling me into a dream.

I was home. I didn't move for thirty minutes, nodding in and out, basking in the warmth of the morning sun, my eyes filling with sweet tears of joy. I had nearly died a thousand deaths that I might live for this single sublime moment in time, and then I said a silent prayer of thanksgiving for my deliverance, and for the souls of the departed, for Greg, and the Steve's, and Colleen, Kevin, Frank, Doc, Lorraine, Peter, Craig, Ulysses, and so many more.

Dear God, after all of the pain and sorrow I had finally come home.

≈≈≈

Eventually I stirred and celebrated the wondrous vista that stretched before me in all directions - across the vibrant green swath of the rolling Sugarbush mountain complex, across Lake

Champlain to the sharp, ragged Adirondacks that punctured the western skies over upstate New York and, finally, east to Mount Washington, glistening, and reigning over the White Mountains of New Hampshire with stoic pride.

I thought then of Jack, my first sponsor, and realized once again that I had finally let go of "IT," and my tears began to flow anew.

≈≈≈

I stepped off Village Run one hour later, made a quick pit stop at the condo to grab my wallet and keys, then drove down off the mountain to the outskirts of Warren Village, where I managed to find a parking space about a half-mile from the quaint downtown area.

The Village's year-round population ordinarily numbered in the low hundreds, but on this day the iconic Warren 4th of July Parade was about to begin, and the community's population had swelled by several thousand freewheeling celebrants who had arrived from as much as a hundred miles away to participate in the day's festivities.

The Warren 4th is always a world class event, a parade for the ages, a kaleidoscopic counter-culture supercharged rave, and I knew that things were ramping up quite nicely when Jim Parker went hurtling just above the tree line as he performed a tight series of barrel rolls in that oh so cool cherry red Pitts biplane.

I could swear that I heard his fiendish laughter emanating from the aircraft's open cockpit every time he flipped upside down. His precision flying was a work of art, pure poetry in motion, and his flyover was one of those special touches that I had come to expect from the Warren 4th.

Moments later I crossed the narrow bridge over the Mad River, elbowed my way through the mobbed downtown area where the world-famous Warren Store was located, and then maneuvered toward the post office.

That was pretty much the extent of Warren's downtown commercial section, except for an inn, a few real estate offices, some art and photography studios, two dozen or so residences, and the combination town hall and library.

≈≈≈

This village, tucked quietly away in the Green Mountains, represented for me the ideal image of small town America, pure and untouched for perhaps a century, picturesque, the textbook setting for a Currier and Ives masterpiece.

And today it was full to overflowing with several thousand joyful celebrants who represented every political, economic, social, religious, spiritual and philosophical persuasion that one could imagine. The crowd encompassed all ages, all walks of life, and was a veritable melting pot of diverse individuals who had each come here today seeking their bliss in the Mad River Valley.

So what more could a recovering alcoholic who still had a taste for the extreme ask for?

≈≈≈

I soon found my friends, who were holding their ground on the packed sidewalk that stood directly across from the Warren Congregational Church, and the fire station.

I exchanged high fives and hugs all around with Mary, and Jason, and Daryl, and Laurel and Kristen and Tony, and we quickly caught up on all of the local news, politics and gossip. I had only known these kind and gracious people for two years, but our souls had been forged in the same fires, so we were as one. We had developed a level of mutual understanding and intimacy born of similar life experiences that allowed us to cut through all the chaff and get right down to the business at hand, whatever that might be on any particular occasion.

We even spoke a special language, our own unique patois, known only to those who had passed through the gates of Hell, and survived to tell about it.

≈≈≈

I had arrived in Warren two years previously, in the early afternoon of the last Sunday in April, 2006. I picked up the keys from the owners of the house I was renting on the back side of

Fuller Hill, and quickly unpacked my car, which held all of my earthly possessions. Then I drove back down Brook Road to the Warren Store, where I picked up a 'Turkey Tumble,' which for my money is one of the most soul-satisfying sandwiches I have ever met.

Then I relaxed on the upper deck of the house, taking my first long views down that pristine valley while I polished off my sub and thanked God for delivering me to that most perfect time and place.

Soon I checked my watch, jumped into my car and drove to a quiet little church that was situated one town up on Route 100.

It was seven o'clock in the evening by then. I had only been in the Valley for five hours, but I already found myself walking into my first meeting of Alcoholics Anonymous, Vermont style.

I had attended a lot of meetings in a lot of places over the years since I got sober, so I wasn't bashful about introducing myself to a new group of people - in fact, I rather enjoyed it.

And so, an hour later, through the magic I knew only in AA, I had made a half dozen new friends for life who I would gladly follow to the ends of the Earth if asked.

And now we were at a parade, and not just any old parade.

≈≈≈

Unless you've experienced it for yourself it's pretty much impossible to adequately describe the Warren Parade. In some ways it's like taking a forty-year leap back in time to a more innocent era, and it starts with the people, because there was a sense of community and fellowship here in the Valley that you felt before your suitcases were unpacked.

The thing I had found most fascinating after my arrival in 2006 was that so many of the people who had built their lives here had come from somewhere else a long time ago, or their parents had, and after a few weeks or months or years they just never found a good reason to leave.

You see, the Valley sneaks up and catches you off guard. It seizes your imagination and seduces you with its beauty, granting you a quality of life, and a liberation of the spirit that you had never known could exist, and then it owns you forever.

You might have come on a lark, just for the uniqueness of the experience, but even if you ultimately move to the other side of the world you will still have a Mad River soul, and you will know in your heart that it is your destiny to come home again someday.

Imagine the late '60's, communes, hippies, a melting pot of free thinkers and intellectuals blown into the Valley like autumn leaves on the four winds, contributing their talents to build an eclectic community in which they could feel safe bringing up their children.

Over the decades more followed, and they became artisans, craftsmen, contractors, businesspeople, medical professionals, writers, musicians, teachers, shopkeepers, each one melding with the hard working native Vermonters, a disparate collection of individuals who had become one.

Every one of those people brought their own unique spirit of independence and entrepreneurship to the mix, each helping to build something that was far greater than the sum of its parts.

And then they built loving, tight-knit families, passing down their life's lessons throughout the generations.

In so many ways they reminded me of how it is with the thousands of courageous people I have met in the community of Alcoholics Anonymous over the years, through whom I have seen displayed lifetime bonds of friendship, and hard-earned trust that was such a terrifying word to me for so long, the unselfish and unconditional love of one human being for another, honesty, humility, the unique generosity of people who have been to Hell and back, and who have survived to pass on their stories of experience, strength and hope to those who are still suffering.

I was probably the same as most who came before me, for in the beginning I didn't plan to live near any particular people, no matter how special, or Nature, no matter how awe-inspiring.

No, rather I came simply to rest my weary soul for a year, and then my Higher Power blessed me with this bounty that I shall be forever grateful for.

≈≈≈

The Warren 4th is a joyous celebration of that spirit, writ large, an annual gathering of a diverse collection of individuals who have found their Muse here in the Valley, and I was ecstatic to be able to participate in their bash once again, and to be with my friends.

The next ninety minutes were a feast for the senses, a blur, a nonstop cavalcade of imaginative, artistic, thought-provoking and hilarious floats, pickups, buses, motorcycles, jeeps, vans, bicycles, stilts, helicopters, jets, clowns, marching bands, drum majorettes, dancers, walkers, uniforms, horses, ponies, dogs, a llama, sheep, and open convertibles full of preening politicians pressing the flesh with the crowds.

Oh, and yes, the Red Baron made a couple more overhead sweeps in his cherry red Pitts.

Meanwhile, the food stalls offered up a smorgasbord of Valley specialties that ranged from tender Vermont lamb kabobs to a cornucopia of home-baked goods, and the first samplings of sweet, fresh Valley produce still damp from the fields, while a hard rock Phish tribute band serenaded the crowds from the balcony of the Warren Store.

I had only consumed those few granola bars that morning, so I proceeded to make a serious dent in the culinary tents, paying special attention to those offering lamb, fresh baked breads and assorted chocolate-based food products, with a heavy emphasis on the latter.

We hung around until the very end of the parade, talking and laughing as the crowd thinned out. I was enjoying the company of my friends, talking AA even here, always slipping into a comfortable, relaxed state of mind whenever I was around them, always feeling secure in the AA cocoon no matter what storms raged around me.

In another time and place I had always sought out solitude, and the intense privacy that was merely an excuse for hiding away from a world I couldn't understand, never sharing anything of myself with a single human being, never comfortable living in my own skin.

I was always looking for an out, an escape, to be that Lone Wolf that I had bragged about to Bill on my last trip to Beech Hill. I had been a control freak for my entire life, micromanaging every aspect of my existence lest some harm come to me should I ever let my guard down, missing out on so many of life's joys by my stubborn reluctance to change, to take chances, to live, desperately hiding out in a bottle or a joint or a cocaine straw for twenty-five years.

For several decades I had always attempted to be somewhere else, rather than committing to the "here and now." But now, through the miracle of recovery, I couldn't imagine being anyplace else except "right here, right now," at home with my friends.

Standing there, as the crowds dispersed, I realized that one day at a time I was becoming present, centered and aware, and grounded and mindful, living only for the moment. My daily prayer was being fulfilled, little by slow, in my Higher Power's time, not my own.

I had finally found the courage to close my eyes, take my hands off the wheel, and just trust.

≈≈≈

I awoke from a brief, revitalizing nap just before two o'clock that afternoon. It took me a few moments to regain my bearings, and then I splashed some water in my face, dressed and drove back down to the Village. I was meeting Jason, Kristen, Laurel, Tony and Daryl for another gastronomic treat – the annual Pig Roast sponsored by the Warren Congregational Church.

I suppose that I might have been pushing things a little by going back to back with the morning's pillaging of the food stalls, but I was a huge fan of that good 'ole downhome Valley cooking, so I immediately latched on to the lame excuse that my morning hike justified the extra calories.

And, besides, I was just planning to sample enough for one decent-sized helping. After all, some very nice people had gone to a lot of trouble to set up this shindig, and there was table after table of home-cooked delicacies that someone had put a lot of heart into preparing, so who was I to hurt their feelings by not doing my fair share?

And, really, what possible harm could a single plate of sweet, tender barbequed pork, homemade potato salad and a helping of baked beans do?

Okay, so who was I kidding? I was going light on the healthy stuff because I was planning an all-out assault on the dessert tables, particularly those of the chocolate variety. And why not, because it's been scientifically proven that chocolate activates our feel-good neurotransmitters, hence our mood, so here's your free psychiatric advice for the day – eat chocolate and have a happy soul!

≈≈≈

I met up with my dining crew over at the barbeque pit, where Jason was leading the cooking effort, and we continued our morning's conversation without missing a beat.

It soon turned into the typical "meeting after the meeting," touching on sobriety, family, sports, valley news, the weather and local politics. For whatever reason, with people in AA, it just seems to work out that whether you saw someone yesterday, or last year, the first time you meet up again you'll be picking up your prior conversation like it had happened ten minutes ago.

I guess that's just the way it is in a program of recovery where unconditional love and gratitude for our friends are the bedrock upon which we build a new life.

It was an idyllic early summer Mad River afternoon, replete with bright sunshine, deep blue skies dotted with white puffies that blew up occasionally over the mountains, and temperatures holding steady in the upper seventies.

So once again, for the nth time that day, I couldn't imagine being anyplace other than right there, right then.

I broke off from the conversation for a few minutes, and walked across the parking lot to a spot where the Warren Library had set up a few tables and was selling used books for a dollar apiece. The books had been donated mostly by local residents, and it was the perfect opportunity for the library to pick up a few hundred dollars to pay for incidentals. It had become an annual event, and the perfect place for me to drop off last year's books and spend ten bucks to take care of the summer's reading material, which consisted primarily of spy thrillers and science fiction stories.

I stowed my new books in the car and returned to the pit area just as my friends were lining up in the chow line. We moved rapidly through the entrees and side dishes, and then I made a stealth detour to reconnoiter the chocolate table before joining the others under the dining tent.

I had been prudent to go light on my entree choices, because as the artillery guys say there was a "target rich environment" in the chocolate section, so I had seven or eight prospects lined up in my sights.

≈≈≈

One of the great things about the Pig Roast is the people you meet. On any given day you might find yourself speaking to a retired couple from New York, vacationers from Montreal, a local writer or painter, or the town of Warren's chairman of selectmen. I've met some of the nicest people at the Roast, had some fascinating conversations, and I have always come away from the affair with a little more hope for humanity than when I arrived.

Today was no exception, so I took the opportunity to speak at length with a successful author who lived in the Valley for the six warm months, similar to what I was doing in those days. I was shameless, prying for every bit of information I could dig out of him about writing, and he graciously provided it.

And, yes, the chocolate table rated three stars in my Michelin guide.

≈≈≈

By four o'clock the festivities were winding down, so I was preparing to head back up onto the mountain for a quick read and another nap.

Fate had other plans for me, however, because I was about to be taken on a really fun adventure.

My friends hooked me in slowly, never disclosing the actual destination, just teasing my imagination by tossing breadcrumbs along the trail.

Jason, always the ringleader, asked, "What are you doing right now, Wes?"

"I was planning to head back to the condo, clean up, nap, maybe walk over to the Lodge for the fireworks display up on the mountain tonight."

"You can't do that yet," said Laurel.

"Oh?"

They all started talking at once, overwhelming me.

Kristen: "We decided to let you in on a discovery we made, so you need to go on a mystery ride with Daryl, because you won't believe what we found!"

Daryl: "You have to do this Wes, it'll blow you away."

Tony: "You're gonna love it Wes, it's like nothing you've ever seen before."

Laurel: "Wes, it is sooooo coooolll!"

"A mystery ride?" I asked, nibbling at the hook.

Jason: "Yes, but you need to keep it a secret, because there's only a few of us who know about it. We discovered it about a month ago. It's our secret, and we don't want the whole world finding out about it, they'd spoil it!"

"Discovered "IT?" Spoiling "IT?" "IT's a secret? What's "IT?"

I thought that I had finally found "IT" a few hours earlier, up on the mountain, yet now "IT" was back once again, so I sent a quick headmail to the Big Guy, "Ok, so what's up, God, what am I being pulled into here?"

Tony chimed in again, "Seriously, we're not saying, you need to be surprised. It's the greatest thing, but you must keep it just between us, all Program people, you, me, Kristen, Laurel, Jason and Daryl. No one else can ever know about it, because that will spoil it!"

"Why me?"

"We talked it over. We trust you, so we figured you'd really, really like it," Jason said, "but remember, you need to make a solemn promise never to tell anyone, so do we have your word on it?"

"Yeah, yeah, of course, but it better be worth it!"

"Oh, it is, you'll thank us."

"Okay, I always like a mystery."

In another time and place I would have been smelling the perfect set-up, a practical joke masterminded by Jason, and I even waited a couple of seconds for the alarm bells to start ringing, but they didn't. It's a funny thing about trust in the Program, but sooner or later you have to walk your talk, step up and leave it in your Higher Power's hands. Open yourself up to change, and to taking chances. Let go, let God, close your eyes, recite a prayer, grab that steering wheel, hold on tight and go along for the ride.

Which I did, and I'm grateful, because I was in for a special treat.

≈≈≈

Ten minutes later Daryl and I were tooling south down Route 100 toward the Granville Gulch, taking the sharp turns hard in his ancient MGB-GT. I won't give out any more directions, or landmarks, because my friends were right. This was one of the coolest things that I've ever experienced, but it needs to remain just our little secret lest its pristine isolation and innocence be spoiled, and that certainly wouldn't be fun for those very special inhabitants.

But I didn't know any of that yet, so I tried one more time to drag the truth out, "C'mon, Daryl, you can tell me. What's this all about?"

He just shook his head and laughed, "No way, Wes, you need to wait. It'll be worth it, guaranteed!"

I surrendered and changed the topic of conversation to music at that point. Daryl is an accomplished guitarist, songwriter and vocalist, so we talked about the blues, and a few minutes later he made a series of turns off the main road that eventually brought us onto a narrow, bumpy dirt track.

I recalled that I had done some hiking down in this general area the year before with Daryl and Mary, so I knew that at the very least we were still somewhere in the Green Mountain National Forest. The terrain looked vaguely familiar, but that was about it.

We continued jolting along for a few hundred yards until the track came to a dead-end, and then Daryl shut down the engine.

"Ok, Wes, be prepared for the best surprise ever. The only thing is, we have a short hike to get there."

Oh, swell! I had worn my Docksiders to the Pig Roast, and they weren't exactly appropriate footwear for a hike into deep forest and mountains.

Well, hopefully there'd be a decent path to follow.

This being Vermont there wasn't, of course, but at first it was easy going as we maneuvered through the sparse vegetation that lay scattered between the trees, and we made good progress for a couple of hundred yards.

But then, after about ten minutes, the undergrowth thickened appreciably, and we began to have some difficulty holding to a straight course. Daryl seemed to know where he was headed, however, so I just followed along and looked for landmarks in case we got separated in the brush. We appeared to be on a southerly bearing, and I tried to orient myself to the sinking afternoon sun that peeked through the trees a few times on it's descent toward the western hills.

Several minutes later we arrived at a rushing stream that was too wide to jump at that location, so we moved upstream for about fifty yards to a spot where we could make the leap.

Daryl made it, easily, and then I did, barely.

By now I was pretty much clueless as to what direction we were headed in, so my thinking reverted to the basics, "Oh well, time to just trust in my Higher Power, because this too shall pass, one moment at a time."

We spent a few more minutes struggling through the dense underbrush, and by now the orienteering skills that I had learned back in my Army days were useless, so I just slogged along. We crossed a second stream, and then a third a few minutes later.

But, ever the optimist, I doubted that it could get much more challenging, and at least I was still reasonably dry.

Wrong, and wrong. It did get more challenging, and I didn't stay dry, and I soon found myself sloshing through a lowland area in ankle deep water and mud that was left over from the spring rains.

I wondered briefly what I could possibly have done that would have motivated my Higher Power to submit me to this fun adventure, but then I recalled all the times that this same Higher Power had kept me on the path, and from my biggest losses had come my greatest victories. So, in retrospect, this was nothing.

Once again it was, "Don't sweat the small stuff, Wes, because it's all small stuff, so just drive on," I thought, as my breath began coming in rasps for the second time that day.

But, on the flip side, at least I wasn't feeling guilty about all of those desserts I had pounded down, because the sugar rush was keeping me energized.

"Okay, God," I muttered to myself, "I know that acceptance is the key to all of my problems today, so please help me to accept the outcome of this little walk on the wild side, whatever that might be. Oh, and thanks for reminding me about humility, again!"

We maneuvered through the marsh area for several more minutes, and then I called up ahead, "Hey, Daryl, are we still on the right course?"

"Sure, we're almost there, no problem," he replied, chuckling at the pathetic Flatlander as he forged ahead through the mud, his own feet no doubt dry as a bone in his hiking boots.

Finally we exited the muck, and the trees opened up into a small clearing that was bordered by a stream. I caught up to him just as he whispered excitedly, pointing at the ground nearby, "Hey, take a look at that, it looks like a moose or a bear slept here last night."

Sure enough, there was a large indentation in the soft, deep grass, the dimensions indicating that some very large denizen of the forest had indeed rested there recently.

"My money's on the moose, that's a hell of a big bed," I said.

"Yeah, I think so too."

My spiritual meeting with Bullwinkle was still a year away, so I asked, "Moose are friendly, right?"

"Sure, Wes, absolutely!" Daryl said, laughing, then added, "Oh, but by the way, do you know how to climb a tree?"

≈≈≈

We moved off across the field, keeping parallel to the stream, but then, just as we were about to enter another wooded area, Daryl stopped in his tracks and pointed excitedly toward the water.

I followed his motion and was dumbfounded by what I saw.

"What the heck?" I began, squinting hard, and then it hit me, "Oh, my God!"

"Do you believe that, Wes?"

At first I didn't. I was staring at a pile of logs that blocked the narrow stream. It was a wall of wood, easily twelve feet across, six feet high and a couple of feet thick. It consisted entirely of long, narrow logs and large, thick branches, birch, maple, oak and pine. They had been stacked on top of each other with military precision to form a giant barrier.

"Incredible," was all that I could whisper, astonished by the strength, persistence and engineering skills of the creatures that had constructed the marvel which now stood before us.

We were staring at a giant beaver dam.

"And guess what, Wes, you haven't seen anything yet, there's more," and with that Daryl began to pick his way carefully along the stream.

We headed south for the next five minutes, keeping close to the water, where the vegetation was sparse and our progress was unimpeded.

I was getting ramped up, because it was now clear what our ultimate goal was, and I had never seen a beaver lodge out in the wild before.

Soon we rounded a bend in the stream and there, towering in front of us, was the second dam, easily as large and brilliantly engineered as its twin.

"Wes, is this incredible, or what?" Daryl asked in a hushed, reverent tone.

I must admit that it was difficult for me to conceptualize the intelligence that must have gone into the construction of those dams.

How had they taken down all of those trees? How did they have the strength to carve them up, drag them to the sites of these dams, and stack each piece so meticulously? It must have taken a dozen of them months, working together as one, to create such intricate engineering marvels.

It almost defied imagination, because I was viewing miracles of Nature before my very eyes.

These were things that my logical mind told me should never have been possible for denizens of the forest to accomplish, but which my eyes now confirmed were evidently an everyday occurrence if I merely took the trouble to seek them out.

And then it came to me. These incredible creatures were a lot like me, and all the courageous people who I knew in Alcoholics Anonymous.

There's a saying that we hear a lot around the halls, about unity, about the need to have a singleness of purpose, and it's expressed as, "WE did what I couldn't do alone."

And now I saw that same principle being applied in Nature, and I laughed as I realized once again that I wasn't so special after all, that there is a Power at work in the Universe that makes people and beavers and ants and elephants and bees and all of the other creatures that share this planet so similar, so beautiful, so perfect.

And once again I recalled my old friend Lois's saying, "We all think we're so damned important!"

Well, as of that moment, Lois, I felt pretty damned humble, to tell you the truth.

Five minutes later Daryl and I came across the third and final of the 'Great Walls of the Beavers.' It was almost an anticlimax by then, because I was champing at the bit to get a look at the 'Big Hacienda.'

Then Daryl told me that we were nearly there, and once again the request came to please keep this location our secret.

He needn't have bothered, because wild horses couldn't have dragged it out of me.

≈≈≈

Suddenly we stepped out of the forest and found ourselves in a large, shallow, open bowl that had been carved out between several small hills and mountains many eons ago.

In the middle of the bowl was a pond that encompassed perhaps a dozen acres. It was surrounded by a fifty-yard wide expanse of low brush, an ankle-deep mat of thick grass, and hundreds of tree trunks that had been cut close to the ground. The trunks appeared to have been cut by a giant lawn mower, but I realized that they had been harvested by a community of hardworking beavers.

It might have been due to the encroaching dusk, as the sun sank toward a western mountain, but the lake and the bowl had a dreamlike quality about them, for there was an extraterrestrial, almost alien aura surrounding the area.

In a way I felt like I had stepped through Alice's looking glass and straight into a parallel universe where Daryl and I were the visitors coming to pay homage to the occupants.

I sensed a certain structure and orderliness in this quiet valley, a perception of intelligence and community and family that was not unlike the world I had discovered in Alcoholics Anonymous, and in the Mad River Valley.

Then I scanned the pond, and quickly detected it down at the far end, near the eastern shoreline – the lodge, their home, rising eight or ten feet out of the water, perhaps the size of a small one room cabin, and with even more living space situated below the water line.

Even from this distance I could see that the massive structure had been built with the same military precision as the three dams had been.

It was impossible to determine how many beavers the lodge housed, but even from where I was standing I imagined it could be a dozen or more.

It was also impossible to determine how old the dams and the lodge were – they could be several years old, or a decade, or even a century.

Nor was there any way of determining how many generations of beavers had created and maintained this, and perhaps prior structures.

What was certain, however, was that this beautiful little secret valley had been claimed by them as home for a very long time, and that their lodge had been built slowly, lovingly, and that these creatures had persevered through harsh weather, attacks by predators, and no doubt by all manner of pestilence, fire, and other obstacles.

They had built their world and nurtured their young one log, one branch, one stick and one heartbeat at a time, just as I had built my sobriety.

Strange as it might seem, it would appear that the beavers and I were soulmates.

I laughed to myself then, as I wondered whether they might have their own Twelve Step program, or a Higher Power, or a spiritual basis for living.

And why wouldn't they, for how could I assume that Wes was unique in that regard? Here they were, out in Nature, free, blissful, accepting whatever life dealt them one day at a time, working, growing families, and living in harmony with the rest of the creatures of the forest.

So what made me think that I was so different, or special, or privileged?

Nothing, so I stood and stared in wonderment and gratitude for several moments, and then recited a silent prayer of thanks.

≈≈≈

Daryl broke into my thoughts then, and asked whether we should try to get a little closer to the lodge, but before I could reply we heard a sharp slapping sound nearby, about thirty feet out in the water.

Startled, we both turned at once to see what was happening out there.

And there it was, one lone guardian of the gates, a solitary beaver floating languidly on its back, slapping its large, flat tail on the surface of the water, politely informing us that we had come as close to their home as his family would like us to be.

We stared, laughing, as the beaver repeated its actions for a few more minutes, the claps echoing throughout the valley, and then I mentioned that dusk was almost upon us, and that we still had a pretty long trek ahead of us. I was beat from the day's activities, and I had no desire to intrude further into the beavers' world at this time - there was always another day to return for a visit.

Daryl agreed, so with reluctance we bade good-evening to Mr. Beaver, and slogged back up the stream toward the car.

≈≈≈

I remained silent for the duration of the hike, and the ride back to Warren, as I reminisced on all of the day's events. I didn't even notice the mud and the muck, the mosquito bites, the streams, or the scratches from the thorny underbrush that I'd experienced coming in to Beaver Valley.

So I guess it just came down once again to, "Don't sweat the small stuff, Wes, because it's *all* small stuff."

Nonetheless, I'd been going straight out since dawn, and now I was exhausted.

But it was a good feeling, the kind that kicks in after a hard workout in the gym, or running a ten miler, when the body's natural painkillers flood the system with a sense of relaxation, accomplishment and serenity. It was a natural high that left me in a state of physical, mental and spiritual equilibrium, rested, confident, at peace with the world.

And, miracle of miracles, at peace with Wes.

≈≈≈

I shook hands with Daryl when we arrived at the church, and thanked him for the trust and honor that he and the others had bestowed upon me by their gracious invitation to visit with the beavers.

We agreed to meet at the Tuesday night AA meeting up the road, then went our separate ways.

It was almost pitch dark when I drove back up the Lincoln Peak Road. I had initially been planning to crash back at the condo, but now the cool, crisp mountain air was giving me a second wind, or was it my third?

Whatever, I decided that I'd drop off the car, splash some cold water on my face, choke down a couple of granola bars, and then walk over to the ski lodge to watch the fireworks that were scheduled to be set off at nine o'clock on the top of one of the ski trails.

Traffic was already heavy up by the lodge, but I managed to make it back to the condo before they shut down access to the road and parking areas.

I cleaned up, ate my granola bars and the remaining pieces of homemade fudge that I had squirreled away after the Pig Roast, then walked over to the lodge.

≈≈≈

It was a perfect Vermont midsummer's evening up on the mountain, clear and cool, and the spine of the Milky Way filled the skies with a billion sparkling stars.

There were several hundred people staking out their claims to the best spots for viewing, so I jumped up onto a low retaining wall and squeezed into a space next to a family vacationing from upstate New York.

We introduced ourselves and spoke briefly, but by then I was on the verge of exhaustion, so I politely dropped out of the conversation after a few minutes.

The fireworks were spectacular, lighting the entire mountain complex, their concussions echoing throughout the surrounding hills.

I briefly wondered how the wildlife up on the Birch Run Trail was tolerating the spectacle, because it was certainly nothing most of them had ever experienced.

Hopefully they were patriotic enough to understand our need to celebrate our independence, although I doubted it.

As for me, well, I was celebrating independence of a different type on that perfect evening.

I was free, mercifully released from a life of pain, fear and despair by a Power greater than myself, a Power that loved me unconditionally, and had delivered me from hopelessness, self-hate, and from the bondage of self. It was a feeling and a gift unlike any I had ever known before, a liberation of the spirit that granted me hope for a better life, one day at a time.

So while most of the people on that mountain that evening were celebrating America's independence, I was celebrating my own freedom from alcoholism and addiction.

And, more than anything, I was celebrating my freedom from fear, for I knew that I would never have to be alone again.

I meandered back to the condo, exhausted and overwhelmed by the events of the day.

I quickly undressed, hit my knees, then recited my prayer of thanks to my Higher Power for getting me through another day sober, and for blessing me with the love and support of my friends in the fellowship of Alcoholics Anonymous.

The last thought I had before slipping off into the Sleep of the Dead was that this had been, once again, just another perfect twenty-four hours in my time machine.

Heartbeats

Epilogue

God rang me up the other day, and said unto me, "Greetings, my son, I need to keep this short, but I have some sad news that I want to talk to you about."

"Uh-oh, are you feeling alright, God?" I asked, alarmed.

I mean, the guy's pushing 14 billion years old, and that has to be hard on the spine, even for a tough old buzzard like Him. I never asked, but I got the impression that He hardly ever slept during those eons.

And God said, "Yes, thanks for asking, and I just wanted to let you know that I love you, my child," and then He hesitated for a moment before adding, "but I'm afraid that we need to cut back on the calls."

I felt a painful twinge, although I had known that it was bound to happen sooner or later, but then I smiled and said, "I understand, and I love you also, God, for you have saved this broken man, and made me whole."

And God said, "Okay, enough with the flattery already, we both have work to do. I need to map out the next billion years of the Universe's expansion, and you have a book to finish."

I said, "Cool, I'll race you to see who gets done first."

God chuckled, then said "Yeah, good luck with that, Skippy," and then poof, He was gone, off no doubt to save another lost soul in need.

He does send me a postcard every once in a while, however, and it's usually delivered by a newcomer to the Halls, lost, lonely, shaking and terrified, wondering how his or her life had ever gotten so crazy that they'd ended up here.

So I always make it a point to walk up to the poor soul, hold out my hand, and say:

"Welcome, my name is Wes H., and I'm an alcoholic. You're among friends here, you're right where you're supposed to be, and if nobody told you today that they love you, well, I do."

Acknowledgments

The list would be long, in the thousands, if I were to mention the names of all the kind, courageous and loving individuals who I've met and learned from over the years, who have taught me so many of life's lessons with patience and unconditional love. But I'll keep things short, and mention those who have had an exceptionally big impact on my life, and on my sobriety.

First, all of my AA friends from the Massachusetts meetings, where everything started - Tony, Andy, Christine, Paula, Holly, both Lynn's, both Patrick R's, Dave W., Eileen, Eddie and a hundred more, and those who have passed on: Walter, Betty, Jack, Mary, and Roger, and the entire group from my Vermont days, whose names I won't mention because it's a small world up there, but you treated me like family from the moment I walked into my first meeting, so y'all know who I mean, and, finally, Running Water from my Florida meetings, a man of logic and humor.

I also want to give a big shout out to my proofreaders, who kept me on message, and who encouraged and supported this rookie writer - Tammy Kubiak, Linda Lewis, Brian Preston, Zack Weston, and my cousin Donna Migdal, and to my graphics designer, Jason Barton, who jumped through so many hoops for me and my constant change requests.

And finally, but certainly not least, my love and gratitude goes out to all of my family and friends who never gave up on me, even when I was at my worst - Harry, Mo, Kelley, Michaela, Scott and Nancy (who each did double duty as proofers), Brad, Warren, and so many more. You loved me, no matter how hard I tried to push you away, and I will be forever in your debt.

Made in the USA
Middletown, DE
08 May 2019